LIBRARY IN A BOOK

RIGHTS OF
THE ELDERLY

Fred C. Pampel

Facts On File
An imprint of Infobase Publishing

Rights of the Elderly

Facts On File, Inc.
An imprint of Infobase Publishing
132 West 31st Street
New York NY 10001

Library of Congress Cataloging-in-Publication Data

Pampel, Fred C.
 Rights of the elderly / Fred C. Pampel.
  p. cm. — (Library in a book)
 Includes bibliographical references and index.
 ISBN 978-0-8160-7196-8 (alk. paper)
 1. Older people—Legal status, laws, etc.—United States—Popular works.
 2. Older people—Medical care—Law and legislation—United States—Popular works. 3. Older people—Civil rights—United States—Popular works. 4. Older people—Legal status, laws, etc.—United States—Bibliography. I. Title.

 KF390.A4P36 2008
 342.7308'774—dc22   2007037434

Facts On File books are available at special discounts when purchased in bulk quantities for businesses, associations, institutions, or sales promotions. Please call our Special Sales Department in New York at (212) 967-8800 or (800) 322-8755.

You can find Facts On File on the World Wide Web at http://www.factsonfile.com

Text design by Ron Monteleone

Printed in the United States of America

MP Hermitage 10 9 8 7 6 5 4 3 2 1

This book is printed on acid-free paper and contains 30 percent postconsumer recycled content.

CONTENTS

PART I
OVERVIEW OF THE TOPIC

Chapter 1
Introduction to Rights of the Elderly **3**

Chapter 2
The Law and Rights of the Elderly **71**

Chapter 3
Chronology **105**

Chapter 4
Biographical Listing **120**

Chapter 5
Glossary **128**

PART II
GUIDE TO FURTHER RESEARCH

Chapter 6
How to Research Elderly Rights **135**

Chapter 7
Annotated Bibliography **146**

Chapter 8
Organizations and Agencies **203**

PART III
APPENDICES

Appendix A
The Age Discrimination in Employment Act of 1967   **217**

Appendix B
Model Statement of ERISA Rights, 2004   **236**

Appendix C
Your Medicare Rights and Protections, 2006   **239**

Appendix D
What You Need to Know When You Get Retirement or Survivors
Benefits, 2007   **249**

Appendix E
Nursing Home Residents' Rights, 2007   **263**

Index   **266**

PART I

OVERVIEW OF THE TOPIC

CHAPTER 1

INTRODUCTION TO
RIGHTS OF THE ELDERLY

Older persons want the same rights as most everyone: to work if they choose, enjoy a decent income, receive quality medical care, participate in social life, and have some choice in how they live their life. Like other age groups, they expect protection from discrimination, poverty, and mistreatment.

Few would dispute the fairness of such rights, especially for the elderly. These rights have both a legal and moral basis. The legal basis comes from laws that forbid age discrimination in hiring and firing of workers, the denial of medical treatment to elderly Medicare recipients, and the abuse, neglect, and exploitation of elders. The moral basis comes from beliefs that the elderly, given their past contributions to society, deserve adequate income and good medical care.

But despite such popular support, do the elderly actually get these rights? Sometimes the elderly face forced retirement and bias in hiring. Sometimes they must survive on inadequate Social Security benefits. Sometimes they receive poorer medical care than younger persons do. And sometimes they are subject to neglect or abuse from caregivers. Misleading stereotypes about the looks, competence, and mental abilities of the elderly are sometimes used to justify violations of their rights. Advocacy groups fighting to protect the rights of the elderly believe that more needs to be done. New laws, stronger enforcement of existing laws, generous public policies, and special protection of the most vulnerable elderly will do much to guarantee equal treatment.

These rights come with costs, however. Those born during the high-fertility years between 1945 and 1965—the baby boomers—soon will begin to enter old age. In the next several decades, their huge numbers will swell the retired population, raising the costs of Social Security and Medicare and the taxes to support the programs. Unless the programs undergo drastic change, young and middle-aged groups will pay these costs. For example, most workers now pay 7.65 percent of their wages in taxes for Social

3

Security and Medicare (and employers match that amount). Despite the low-paying jobs of many young people, they are taxed to pay the Social Security and Medicare benefits of often affluent older persons. These costs to workers will only increase in the future and make the topic of elderly rights one of concern to all generations.

What are the rights of the elderly? How are they enforced and how have they influenced the well-being of the elderly? What gaps exists in protection of the elderly? The following sections consider these questions and the controversies they generate. The chapter begins with a discussion of the demographic and social changes that have led to concern about elderly rights, and then examines rights to work, retirement income, quality health-care, and protection from abuse.

CHANGES IN THE ELDERLY POPULATION

The elderly are a diverse group. They include the very poor and very rich, the vigorous and the disabled, the healthy and decrepit, the attractive and the unattractive, the young old and the oldest old, and the powerful and the weak. Among the elderly are billionaire investor Warren Buffett, singer Barbra Streisand, and Senator John McCain as well as nameless persons too poor to eat, too sick to walk, and too lonely to care about living. The group includes whites and blacks, Latinos and non-Latinos, immigrants and natives, and men and women. It is hard to generalize about a group with such diversity.

Even defining old age and the elderly presents difficulty. Age 65 has come to indicate the start of old age, largely because workers traditionally became eligible then for full Social Security retirement benefits. Yet, one could say that old age begins both earlier and later. On one hand, retirement often occurs before age 65 and the country's largest organization of older persons, AARP (formerly the American Association of Retired Persons), accepts members at age 50. On the other hand, with people living so much longer than in the past, old age and associated problems of health do not really begin until well after age 65. As one expert states, the boundaries of old age "begin at 65, give or take 15 years either way."[1] Far from an exact category, old age depends more on physical and mental fitness rather than years since birth.

Underneath this diversity, however, lie forces that link the elderly. Changes occur in the mind and the body that distinguish older persons from children and younger adults. Aging increases the risks of disease and death, and even the healthiest older persons generally have weaker muscle strength, slower reflexes and movement, less energy and stamina, and poorer vision and hearing than younger persons. Aging also produces positive traits of greater experience, better concentration, and less aggression. That age-based changes occur at different rates among people does not make age differences meaningless. Some people seem young even given their old age and others seem to age quickly. Even so, old age generally involves changes that make the stage different from other life stages. Despite notable exceptions, older people on average differ physically and mentally from young people and middle-aged adults.

Aging also involves more than physical changes—it has a social component as well. People tend to view the elderly as having special needs, interests, and accomplishments. Advocates of the elderly minimize the importance of physical and mental changes in old age relative to social treatment. They say that negative stereotypes about decline among the aged create inaccurate perceptions of the elderly. These perceptions in turn lead people—including the elderly themselves—to exaggerate the special problems and limitations of old age.

Whether due to differences in physical capacity or socially based beliefs, the elderly have common membership in an age group. Government programs, lobbying organizations, and a field of study called gerontology all distinguish individuals based on their age. Indeed, defining rights of the elderly has little meaning without shared group membership. If the elderly do not make up a meaningful group, they would neither differ from other age groups nor require special efforts to protect their rights.

To help understand the problems shared by the elderly today and the sources of concern over their rights, it helps to understand the social changes that have led to their current circumstances. Even given diversity of the elderly and difficulties in defining old age, these changes have brought special problems and opportunities to the elderly in the 21st century.

PREINDUSTRIAL SOCIETIES

The lack of rights of the elderly seldom has importance in preindustrial or agricultural societies. To the contrary, the lack of rights of young people and children seem a greater concern. Wealth and power come from ownership of land and small businesses in these societies. Until they die, older men typically own farms, stores, and shops, and this ownership upholds their rights. They give their property to children after death, but while alive can use their position to protect their interests. They typically decide how long to work, how to support themselves, and what to do with their assets. Even as grown adults, children might have little freedom or independence while working for a parent and waiting until they inherit the family business.

Such relationships characterized colonial America and the decades just after the American Revolution. In *Growing Old in America*, historian David

Rights of the Elderly

Hackett Fischer argues that the elderly had more than economic resources back then—they also had respect and reverence.[2] He calls the time from 1607 to 1820 a period of the exaltation of old age in America. The exaltation came from several sources.

During these centuries, the average length of life was only about 40 years. High mortality killed most newborns before they reached childhood, and teens, young adults, and middle-aged adults died at shockingly high rates by today's standards. Under these conditions, anyone who lived to old age, say to age 60, had done something remarkable. For example, a study of England from 1591 to 1791 found that only eight out of 100 persons survived epidemics, harsh living conditions, and poor medical care to reach that milestone.[3] The ones who did seemed blessed by God. They were special, deserving of admiration and awe.

If the accomplishment of living long were not enough, the elderly had other assets. The experience, wisdom, and knowledge they accumulated in a slow-changing society gave them a natural sense of authority and position of leadership. Churches reserved their front pews for the elderly and gave them key roles in guidance (the term elder still today refers to church leaders). Ministers, schoolteachers, business owners, and landowners seldom retired to let younger persons take over—they kept their position and power as long as they wanted, most often until they died.

Fischer refers to some fascinating examples of the exaltation of age. Census figures around 1800 indicated that people exaggerated their age, claiming to be older than they were, rather than lying to appear younger. Fashion likewise reflected the prestige of the elderly. Imitating styles popular in Europe during the 18th century, American men dressed in ways that made them look older rather than younger. Wigs with powder made the hair of even young men appear white; long coats with narrow shoulders and wide waists fit the pear-shaped figure of older men rather than the broad-shoulder and narrow-waist figures of young men; and using a cane, necessary for older persons who had trouble walking, became popular among the young as well. Among women, styles included dresses that ballooned out to hide less youthful hips and legs. Even if hair color, clothing, and accessories could not hide one's age, the styles indicated the respect given to elders.

Fitting with their power and influence, the elderly acted distant and reserved. As sources of knowledge, wisdom, and authority, they gave orders to family and community members rather than worried about mistreatment. They expected, even demanded respect and veneration from younger persons. Rather than warm, lovable, and easygoing, the elderly more likely came across as arrogant and powerful. Younger people did not always appreciate being subject to this power but nonetheless accepted the rights of the aged.

Introduction to Rights of the Elderly

Even with power and respect, the life of the elderly in colonial America was far from ideal. For one, they suffered more than their share of health problems. In such harsh circumstances, long-term survivors carried injuries and faced daily pain. At age 83, Benjamin Franklin once wrote to George Washington, "For my own personal ease I should have died two years ago . . . those years have been spent in excruciating pain."[4] However, the elderly could rely on other family members to help them when sick, disabled, or unable to work. When adult children lived in the same house or nearby in small villages, they were expected to help care for older parents.

Some historians of old age object that Fischer's depiction of life in colonial America may be too positive. The young may have respected the economic power of their elders but often had little respect for old age itself. Rather than harmony between the young and old, the differences in power led to resentment below the surface and occasionally to open power struggles. According to some historical reports, the elderly were depicted as touchy, peevish, angry, forward, hard to please, and full of complaints.[5]

The most positive images of the elderly may in fact have applied to a minority of the richest and most powerful. The poor suffered terribly in agricultural societies, whether young, middle age, or old. Older slaves, once thought to have become ineffective workers, received little in the way of respect or power from plantation owners. Widowed women with few family ties often had little in the way of support and faced poverty in old age. Most elderly were not immune from disease, hard work, and financial insecurity.

Even if less than ideal, the life of the elderly in preindustrial societies had some advantages. Whether community members once exalted old age or not, historians generally agree on the relatively high status of the elderly in preindustrial societies. And they agree that changes occurring during industrialization led to a loss of that status and today's concerns about elderly rights.

AGING IN THE 20TH AND 21ST CENTURIES

Historians can identify no exact date when the elderly lost the position of dominance and respect they enjoyed in colonial society. Perhaps it came in the early 1800s from new ideals of equality brought by the French and American revolutions. Perhaps it came from the drop in mortality at young ages and the growing association between old age with death in the late 1800s. Or perhaps it came from new stereotypes fostered by doctors, social workers, and business leaders who came to see the elderly as a uniquely needy group in the early 1900s. In any case, changes occurred in age relationships that have continued into the 21st century.

Three major social trends involving longevity, retirement, and family relations affected the elderly. On the plus side, people began to live longer than ever before, enjoying an active life well into old age. Governments and businesses started offering retirement programs that created a period of leisure and affluence for older persons. And the elderly began to be able to live independently for most of their older years, maintaining close contact with children and grandchildren but without having to share housing. At the same time, however, the changes brought new problems. The elderly today face a longer period of dependency on public programs for retirement and health, sometimes are forced out of work before they are ready, and must deal with negative stereotypes and discrimination about growing old. These changes have in turn created pressures and demands for elderly rights.

Longevity and Population Aging

For more than a century, Americans have enjoyed remarkable progress in reducing sickness and death. The reductions in mortality began in the late 1800s with cleaner living and better food. Cities did more to keep the water supply pure, properly dispose of garbage and human waste, and limit the spread of disease through densely settled areas. With better technology, farmers grew more and better crops, ranchers raised more food animals, and sellers learned to ship food quickly and safely to buyers. People of all ages benefited from cheaper, more varied, more nutritious, and more plentiful food. These changes increased resistance to diseases that once killed often and early in life.

In the early 20th century, advances in medical care, vaccines, and antibiotics helped even more in prevention and curing infectious diseases. Pandemics such as an outbreak in 1918–19 of the Spanish flu, which killed 50 million people worldwide, have largely ended. In recent decades, amazing advances in medications, drugs, technology, and prevention have pushed down mortality rates from causes such as heart disease. Appreciation of the benefits of exercise and a further understanding of healthy diet has also helped. There is no end in sight yet to the progress against disease.

As a result, life expectancy has steadily improved in the United States. It grew from 47.3 years in 1900 to 77.6 years in 2005. Projections from the U.S. Census Bureau suggest that by 2050, life expectancy of males will rise to 81.2 and of females to 86.7. In just over 100 years, life expectancy grew by 30 years.

With lower mortality and longer life expectancy, nearly everyone could expect to live to old age. No longer was reaching old age something special—it became a routine part of living. Early death instead became shocking. At the same time more people lived to old age, dropping fertility decreased the number of children and young adults. The size of the elderly population relative to the size of the rest of the population grew enormously. In 1900, those over age 65, about 3.1 million in total, made up about 4 percent of the population or one of every 25 Americans. In 2005, persons age 65 and over reached 35 million in number, about 12.4 percent of the population or one out of every eight Americans. By 2050, they are estimated to reach 87 million and 20.7 percent of the population, about one out of every five Americans.

These figures hide diversity among the growing aging population. For example, an increasing percentage of the population has reached the oldest ages. Those over age 85 as a percent of all aged persons reached 14.6 in 2005 and may reach 24.1 percent in 2050. For another example, longevity among women has increased faster than among men. In 2004, the female life expectancy of 80.4 exceeded the male life expectancy of 75.2 by 5.2 years. As a result, 58.1 percent of persons over age 65 and 68.5 percent of persons over 85 are female.

Extending life has been one of the greatest accomplishments of modern societies. Yet it comes with some costs. The aging of the population has created new responsibilities for support and health care of the elderly. Infectious diseases, once the major cause of death, killed victims relatively quickly. Today, deaths come most often from chronic diseases such as heart disease, lung problems, and cancers. With older persons living longer and needing more health care, the costs of supporting the elderly population have risen. This has changed relationships between generations and made many elderly dependent on care by others. It also has increased the potential for mistreatment of the elderly and concerns over their rights.

Retirement

As people live longer, they might expect to work longer. In fact, the opposite has occurred. Retirement has become the norm for persons age 65 and over and even common at ages 55 to 64. The trend comes in large part from the nature of work in an industrial, urban society. With jobs in agriculture replaced by jobs in industry, older workers had less choice about how long they stayed on the job.

During the late 1800s, large companies in modern societies increasingly viewed older persons as unsuited for the strenuous and fast-paced life of a factory worker and reserved their jobs for younger workers. As a result, older persons often had to start working at menial jobs to survive. Historian Pat Thane describes some older workers during the 19th century: "Old factory hands presented with a broom, shovel, and wheelbarrow, old farm workers employed at stone-breaking and roadwork, old artisans in repair work, old miners working at odd jobs at the pithead, old dressmakers on rough sewing work, and old servants at daily work."[6] Those too infirm to work or without a family to provide support ended up begging or in the poorhouse.

Rights of the Elderly

By the early 20th century, images of the overworked and destitute elderly led to calls for a period of retirement before death. Old age was increasingly seen as a time when people deserved rest from their labors and some support from society. It seemed unfair, even cruel, to make older persons do backbreaking work, beg on the streets, or live in a poorhouse during the last years of their lives. Perceptions of mistreatment of the aged thus helped create retirement as a new stage of life. However, little in the way of financial support came with the new stage. Several European nations had already responded to the problem with public pensions to support retired workers, but the United States lagged behind in such programs.

Later in the 20th century, another justification for retirement emerged, one that came with more money. Rather than a respite before death, retirement was increasingly seen as a reward for decades of work. Positive images of retirement as a time of earned leisure replaced negative images of retirement as a time to rest before death. Older workers earned their reward of retirement through hard work and loyalty to the company. Based on this view, both private and public retirement programs expanded during the mid-20th century. Those who spent many years with their companies and contributed part of their wages to a special fund received private retirement benefits. Those who contributed to Social Security for a specified period received public retirement benefits. They became eligible for benefits at a fixed retirement age—65 in normal circumstances and sometimes earlier—but also faced mandatory retirement at age 65.

Although private and public pensions prevented the destitution common earlier in the century, they hardly made for a comfortable life. In 1959, more than one of three persons age 65 and over had income below the poverty level. They could not afford a minimally nutritious diet and adequate shelter and clothing, much less money for entertainment, travel, or a few luxuries. In his 1962 survey of poverty in America, Michael Harrington reported that an elderly retired couple received only $804 a year from Social Security.[7]

Since then, a third justification for retirement has replaced those based on rest and reward. Today, scholar Sarah Harper suggests that retirement has come to be seen more as a right than an earned reward.[8] A period of funded leisure later in life was not only earned through work but also a right deserved by all. Indeed, retirement came at increasingly younger ages, when persons were healthy and active. It involved travel, housing in retirement or resort areas, and enjoyment of hobbies, sports, and other activities. After years of responsibility for working, saving, and raising a family, persons in their late 50s, 60s, and early 70s could have the freedom to enjoy personally fulfilling activities before they faced major health problems and death. Books and web pages on partial or semiretirement encourage older workers to leave the stress and pressure of full-time jobs for a lifestyle that gives more freedom.

Introduction to Rights of the Elderly

Figures for 2004 show that 19 percent of men and 11 percent of women age 65 and over are in the labor force (that is, either working or looking for work). Not all retirement comes from older workers enjoying a period of freedom and affluence, however. Many who preferred to continue working had to cope with pressures from their employers to retire. Companies sometimes responded to competitive markets by cutting their older and higher-paid workers. To do so, they might use firings and layoffs or early retirement incentives. If out of full-time work by necessity, many older persons have trouble finding jobs that fit their skills and experience. Age discrimination in hiring and firing affects millions of older workers.

Family and Care

A third trend in family relations and care has affected elderly rights. In agricultural societies, adult children usually lived near parents, if not in the same household, and helped during times of sickness and poor health. Cousins, aunts, uncles, and other relatives likely lived nearby as well. Three-generation families under the same roof remained rare for the simple reason that grandparents seldom lived long enough to share housing with their children and grandchildren. While living, however, proximity made for close ties between parents and adult children.

Today's families differ from those of several centuries ago. The decline in mortality meant more people survived to old age and, once having reached old age, more lived to ages when they needed care for problems of health and disability. At the same time, the shift to an industrial wage economy changed family relations. Young adults moving to other towns and away from parents to attend college, take jobs, or find new opportunities meant that children lived farther away from older relatives. Reduced fertility meant older parents had fewer adult children, either nearby or distant, to help them. And greater income meant that older persons who wanted to live independently could afford to do so. Economist Robert Samuelson cites some statistics to illustrate the change: "In 1880, almost half of retired men lived with children or relatives. Even in 1940, about a fifth (22 percent) did. Now, only about 5 percent do."[9]

In recent decades, new types of families have created more complexity in the relationships across generations. The rise in divorce rates have left many older persons, most often women, living alone rather than with a spouse. With smaller families, older adults have fewer siblings and cousins to help care for one another. Further, increases in remarriage, cohabitation without marriage, single-parenthood, blended families, and childlessness have made family relations more tangled than in the past. Children still feel obligations and responsibilities toward their parents and provide help when needed, but the way to do so is less clearly defined than it once was.

These changes have not weakened ties across generations so much as changed their nature. Except when parents need constant monitoring or children need financial help, older persons and adult children prefer to live independently. Yet, as two historians of the family suggest, living separately does not equal abandonment: "Contemporary investigations of the elderly's family life have found intergenerational exchange to be vibrant, instrumental, and essential to the elderly's well-being. . . . Children continue to provide assistance to older people in amounts far greater than any government-sponsored programs."[10]

The assistance comes from giving personal support, helping with finances, and arranging for care. Combined with support from government programs, such assistance allows most older persons to maintain their independence. Adult children help their older parents when needed but not always by living nearby or in the same house. As one gerontologist comments, "Families supply 60 to 80 percent of the initial care for dependent elders before turning to institutional facilities when the elders' decline becomes too physically and emotionally draining to handle."[11]

For older family members who need constant care, assisted living and nursing homes offer alternatives to family living. Sometimes assisted living or home health care provides monitoring and independent living, and sometimes moving older parents closer to their children can do the same. However, few families can care for those with Alzheimer's disease, severe physical disabilities, or diseases that need treatment by trained medical personnel. For these cases, nursing homes become the choice of last resort. According to a 1997 survey, only 4.3 percent of persons age 65 and over live in nursing homes and the average length of stay is 2.5 years.[12] However, the likelihood becomes more common at the very oldest ages.

At the oldest ages, when persons most often face severe problems of poor health, mental decline, and physical disability, they become vulnerable to mistreatment by family members and care facilities. Family members who care for older relatives often have reached their 50s and 60s and face their own problems of raising children, working, and paying bills. The stress increases the potential for abuse. Nursing homes likewise face pressures to keep down costs and deal with difficult patients that increase the potential for abuse. When the elderly cannot protect themselves, their rights are easily violated.

GOVERNMENT POLICIES FOR THE ELDERLY

Along with changes in health, work, and family relationships came changes in social policies for the elderly. These policies have created legal entitlements or rights to income, medical treatment, and long-term care that have improved the lives of the elderly. However, the expanding rights and benefits have raised the costs to support the elderly. According to some, the high costs to the federal budget will lead to a crisis in government funding.

Old-age policies emerged slowly in the United States. After the American Revolution, soldiers injured during war and unable to work were eligible for modest pensions. After the Civil War, injured veterans from the northern states (but not the Confederacy) were eligible for pensions. By the early 20th century, the eligibility rules had relaxed enough that veterans reaching old age, even if not suffering from war injuries, could receive benefits. Still, the benefits remained modest and went only to former soldiers. In contrast, Germany had in 1889 set up a more extensive pension program for retired workers, and many other European nations followed suit. Not until 1935 did Congress pass legislation for a broad-based program for support of the elderly in the United States.

Social Security and Medicare

The passage of the Social Security Act of 1935 occurred in the midst of the Great Depression, a time of severe financial hardship for the elderly. With jobs scarce, unemployment high, and private pensions rare, the demand for government action grew. Responding to the vigorous support of President Franklin Roosevelt, Congress passed legislation that linked eligibility for public retirement or Social Security benefits to work experience. After contributing to the Social Security system through payroll taxes, workers could receive modest retirement benefits at age 65 (or, since 1961, reduced early retirement benefits at age 62). By contributing while young, workers earned the right to benefits while old.

Social Security determined benefits based on both contributions and need. On one hand, the program highlighted the link between what a person paid in and took out; the greater the contributions, the higher the benefits were. On the other hand, to help those most in need, low-income workers received more benefits relative to their contributions than did high-income workers. However, benefits did not come directly from a worker's own contributions. Rather, current workers paid the benefits of current retirees in the expectation that new workers would pay the benefits when current workers retired. This pay-as-you-go system rested on the assumption that there would be many workers able to pay small taxes for relatively few retirees.

Social Security was never meant to be the sole source of retirement income. The program aimed to supplement retirement income from private pensions, savings, and family assistance. As part of the broader strategy of old age support, large companies increasingly offered private retirement benefits to their workers. Private pension plans generally worked like Social Security. They required workers to contribute to the pension fund and stay with a company for a set period, now a maximum of seven years, to qualify fully for the benefits. Alternatively, employers contribute into an individual fund controlled by the worker and used later to pay for retirement benefits.

In 1965, 30 years after establishing Social Security, another major entitlement program for the elderly began. The Medicare Act amended the Social Security Act to provide insurance for hospital stays, doctor bills, and other medical costs to those elderly eligible for Social Security. Like Social Security, Medicare was funded by a payroll tax and provided benefits at age 65. Unlike Social Security, recipients did not get cash benefits, but hospitals and physicians submitted charges to Medicare rather than to the elderly patient. A companion program set up by the Medicare Act, Medicaid, offered benefits to the poor of any age through programs run by the states.

Many changes in Medicare since 1965 have attempted to balance the competing goals of providing better service and care to the elderly while limiting the cost. Initially, physicians could bill elderly patients for any costs that exceeded what Medicare would reimburse. Beginning in 1975, however, the Medicare program and Congress attempted to limit the cost of charges to Medicare patients. They also set up fee schedules that put a cap on what hospitals and doctors received for Medicare patients. Even so, new and more expensive procedures combined with demands of the elderly for high-quality care kept Medicare costs rising.

Of major note, legislation passed in 2003 added prescription drugs to the insurance program, an expense not covered for the previous 38 years. Two factors increasing the out-of-pocket expenses of the elderly for prescription drugs led to the new entitlement. First, the development and widespread use of prescription drugs to treat high cholesterol, heart disease, insomnia, arthritis, and other chronic diseases made drug use a growing part of health care. Second, the high costs for the drugs made their use a major part of the budget of the elderly. The Medicare Prescription Drug Plan allows those eligible for Medicare benefits to sign up for a drug insurance plan. The plans require monthly premiums and co-payments but save money for most older persons.

Graying of the Federal Budget

The growth of public programs for the elderly has created new entitlements. Not all elderly persons qualify for Social Security and Medicare, but most do. Others can qualify for programs targeted for the poor such as Supplemental Security Income and Medicaid. Since all these programs come with guarantees of certain levels of benefits and services, the escalating costs have limited benefits and compromised services.

For Social Security, rising costs will accelerate with the retirement of baby boomers in the next several decades. Payments for Old Age and Survivors

Insurance in 2005 reached $441.9 billion—4.2 percent of gross domestic product. Social Security has become the federal government's largest program and greatest expense. Taxes paid into Social Security have always exceeded payments of benefits, but based on current trends that will change by 2017. A large reserve in the trust fund will then cover the gap. Yet, the trust fund now lends money to the federal government. To meet Social Security demands, the federal government will have to pay back the loans by raising taxes or cutting expenditures. Even with that, projections of spending and contributions show that Social Security will run out of money in 2041.

The source of the problem is not hard to understand. The growth of the aged population relative to the size of the workforce means the number of workers who receive Social Security has increased relative to the number who contribute. In 1960, more than five workers supported each Social Security beneficiary. Today, only 3.3 workers per beneficiary do so, and by 2040 only 2 workers per beneficiary will do so. Although long-term projections are notoriously inaccurate, an aging population puts clear pressures on Social Security funding. If in the future each worker must pay taxes for half the Social Security income of a retiree, the high costs may threaten popular support for the program.

Even more than for Social Security, costs for Medicare have exploded. According to a 2005 report from the trustees, Medicare received $357 billion in contributions and spent $336 billion. Its assets grew to $310 billion, not enough to cover one year of expenses. Further, Medicare spending is expected to grow by about 7 percent per year for the next 10 years. The report concludes that the program does not have adequate financing. Expenditures will soon exceed income, requiring spending of the reserve. Based on current trends, assets will be exhausted by 2018.

Much like for Social Security, the problem of Medicare comes from too few workers paying the health costs of too many beneficiaries. In addition, the problem comes from rising medical costs. New technologies, diagnostic tests, and surgical procedures make health care increasingly expensive. Recently added coverage of drug benefits adds to that expense.

The growth of Social Security and Medicare contributes most to the graying of the federal budget. About 7 percent of national income now goes to Social Security and Medicare. Social Security makes up about 21 percent of the federal budget and Medicare makes up about 12 percent. By 2030, as aging of the baby boomers further increases the size of the elderly population, spending on Social Security and Medicare could rise to 12 percent of national income and 66 percent of the federal budget. Other programs such as Medicaid that provide long-term care and services for the elderly push costs even higher.

With the graying of the federal budget, elderly interest and lobbying groups have grown in influence. Henry J. Pratt coined the term the gray lobby to describe the age-based interest groups that lobby on behalf of older persons. By some counts, there are more than 1,000 such groups.[13] The largest organization, AARP (formerly the American Association of Retired Persons) has 35 million members and a budget of $800 million. Its leaders take stands on public issues affecting the elderly, testify before Congress, and mobilize elderly members to support or oppose legislation. As one senator said about discussions to put Social Security on a sounder financial basis, "It will be very difficult to do anything without AARP's support."[14]

Another smaller but well-known group, the Gray Panthers, takes a more activist and liberal approach to issues affecting the well-being of the elderly. Founded in 1970 by charismatic 66-year-old Maggie Kuhn, the group adopted its name from the Black Panthers as a way to reflect its sometimes controversial calls for change in the treatment of the elderly. Since Maggie Kuhn's death in 1995, the organization, its executive director, and board of directors have worked on several issues relating to rights of the elderly. They favor a single-payer health system for the United States, oppose any cuts in funding or privatization of Social Security, and call for expanded Medicare payments for prescription drugs.

Other organizations advance the interests of the elderly in different ways. The National Institute on Aging (NIA), one of the 27 institutes and centers of the National Institutes of Health, provides leadership in aging research, training, and dissemination of information toward the goal of improving the health and well-being of older Americans. It does not engage in political activity but with a budget just over $1 billion, its sponsorship of research and training programs involves researchers, educators, physicians, and others in its goals. NIA has thus gained considerable influence on highlighting problems of the elderly and devising solutions to these problems.

Responding to the growth and costs of programs for the elderly, some say that the entitlements to Social Security and Medicare benefits should come from need rather than age. They view it as wasteful for the richest as well as the poorest elderly to get Social Security and Medicare benefits. Others defend the current structure of Social Security and Medicare as both popular and successful. These diverging views on the need to cut benefits differ in the importance they give to maintaining the rights of the elderly.

NEGATIVE IMAGES AND TREATMENT OF THE ELDERLY

Aging today involves more than special concerns of health, work, and government support. It also involves dealing with negative images and stereotypes about the elderly. Robert N. Butler, a physician and first head of the National Institute on Aging, coined the term *ageism* in 1969 to highlight the denigration of the elderly. Aiming to draw parallels with treatment of women and African Americans, he defined ageism as "systematic stereotyping and discrimination against people because they are old, just as racism and sexism accomplish this for skin color and gender."[15]

The use of stereotyping and discrimination tends to place all aged persons in categories. Butler summarizes the common stereotype:

> *An older person thinks and moves slowly. He does not think as he used to or as creatively. He is bound to himself and can no longer change or grow. He can learn neither well nor swiftly. . . . He is a study in decline, the picture of mental and physical failure. He has lost and cannot replace friends, spouse, job, status, power, influence, income. He is often stricken by diseases which, in turn, restrict his movement, his enjoyment of food, the pleasures of well being. He has lost his desire and capacity for sex. His body shrinks, and so too does the flow of blood to the brain.*[16]

Not all stereotypes are so negative. Older persons also are seen as warm, friendly, and wise from experience. However, even these images can do harm by overstating the boundaries between the elderly and other age groups. The positive images can easily shift into less attractive ones of weakness, dullness, and excessive concern with the past.

Although the term is modern, the attitudes and actions behind ageism have existed for some time. Even ancient writings showed distaste for the physical changes that accompany old age—declining strength, more difficulty in moving, and less youthful appearance. According to one classics scholar, Aristotle viewed older people as "overly pessimistic, distrustful, malicious, suspicious and small-minded because they have been humbled by life and so their greatest hopes are raised to nothing more than staying alive. They lack generosity, are cowardly, and always anticipating danger."[17] Such views did not overcome the large degree of respect for the elderly in preindustrial societies but did indicate the tendency to use stereotypes.

Negative images became more common in modern, industrial, and urban societies. Since the 19th century, dozens of new words emerged (or old words changed) to describe the elderly: old fogy, codger, old goat, fuddy-duddy, oldster, geezer, old hag, old biddy, and old coot. People began to speak about being over the hill, past one's prime, and put out to pasture. Used in certain ways, even endearing terms like old-timer, pops, gramps, or granny could show disrespect. Along with derogatory names, humorous birthday cards and jokes about growing old promote stereotypes that older persons are in poor health, rigid in their views, physically unattractive, and lacking in fun, excitement, and sexual interest.

More than in the past, people in modern societies seem to worship youth and beauty. As illustrated by the growing use of cosmetic surgery, many middle-aged persons do all they can to hide their birth age. It is ironic that younger adults who themselves will become old sometimes have such distaste for old age. Those discriminating against the elderly are, in a figurative sense, discriminating against their future selves. Perhaps growing old is an unpleasant reminder of the heightened risk of death that comes with aging. As Robert Butler says, "ageism serves a highly personal objective, protecting younger (usually middle-aged) individuals—often at high emotional cost—from thinking about things they fear (aging, illness and death)."[18]

Women face a special burden in dealing with the consequences of ageism. Men can make up for a less youthful appearance in old age with wealth and power—successful men are often viewed as distinguished rather than old. Women, who traditionally have been judged more for their looks than men, face greater prejudice as they grow older and their appearance becomes less youthful. The discrimination women face in youth and adulthood magnifies the discrimination they face in old age.

Regardless of its source, ageism in modern society has real consequences. Misleading and excessively negative stereotypes about the elderly justify discrimination against them. Exaggerated beliefs about the limitations and incompetence of the elderly can lead to removal from their jobs and age bias in hiring. The beliefs can encourage subtle public slights and pressures for older persons to slow down and stay out of sight. Sometimes adults treat the elderly like children, assuming they cannot understand, need help with simple tasks, and are too frail to act normally. Sometimes physicians see the health problems of the elderly as the untreatable outcome of aging rather than as amenable to diagnosis and cure. Even if motivations come from the urge to help, actions can be disrespectful and demeaning.

When the elderly adopt the ageist views of the larger society, they may accept mistreatment. They may isolate themselves when they feel uncomfortable with younger adults, believe they cannot handle tasks that others do, and assume they cannot overcome the problems they face. Acceptance of negative images can lead to loss of self-esteem and depression. Suicide rates are highest during old age, perhaps in part because of the adoption of negative images of aging.

Ageism also affects public policy. With the growth of social programs for the elderly, some critics of spending have represented older persons as "greedy geezers." They accuse the elderly of demanding public funds for retirement and health, even when younger groups are struggling financially and federal spending is excessive. They note that even the richest elderly get Social Security and Medicare benefits, discounts on public services, tax deductions, and special deals on hotels and travel. Since the elderly are generally prosperous, politically powerful, and well treated, they enjoy much more support from government programs than any other group. These arguments lead to calls for limits on spending for the elderly.

According to advocates of the aged, however, views of the elderly as prosperous and selfish represent a form of ageism. This kind of ageism has the potential to worsen their treatment and reduce their support by the government. Views of the elderly as prosperous and selfish rely as much on stereotypes as views of the elderly as poor and feeble. Both sets of views fail to recognize the diversity of the aged and treat elderly persons as individuals. Both views can encourage violation of the rights of the elderly.

RIGHTS INVOLVING WORK

The elderly have no guarantee to a job, any more than the non-elderly have a guarantee to one. Nor do the elderly have a guarantee to retire when they want. In a market economy, opportunities for work and retirement follow from labor market forces of supply and demand, the preferences and actions of employees and employers, and the characteristics of public and private retirement programs. However, the elderly do have the right to fair treatment in hiring and firing and to freedom from discrimination based on age.

BARRING AGE DISCRIMINATION IN HIRING AND FIRING

Age discrimination refers to unfair treatment of a person in employment decisions because of age. The unfair treatment usually involves bias against older workers and stereotypical beliefs about their abilities. Workers are judged on beliefs about general characteristics of their age group rather than on their qualifications or past job performance. Employment decisions based on the poor performance or lack of qualifications of individual workers do not constitute discrimination, even if the individual worker is old. Like race and gender discrimination, age discrimination involves the use of irrelevant characteristics in hiring, firing, wage levels, or work evaluation. It thus involves a form of ageism. However, courts have ruled that age discrimination can also occur from actions that are not directly motivated by bias. Policies that unintentionally lead to unequal treatment of older workers can also constitute age discrimination.

In principle, age discrimination applies to all age groups. Young people can face discrimination if employers think that all persons under a certain age are too immature to do certain kinds of work. However, the main motivations behind efforts to end age discrimination come from the desire to protect those approaching old age or who are already old. They are most likely to face forced retirement, long periods of unemployment when let go, and misleading ideas about their capabilities as workers. Laws therefore protect persons age 40 and over rather than persons of all ages.

Rights of the Elderly

The Push for Age Discrimination Legislation

Until the 19th century, age discrimination was rare. No formal policies determined when farm and business owners should turn things over to their children, or when judges, ministers, and other employees should retire. The decision was largely voluntary. Some exceptions began to develop in the 1800s. According to one historian, "A few states set maximum ages for judges and justices of the peace and, in 1861, Congress required naval officers below the rank of vice admiral to reside their commission upon reaching age 62."[19]

The real change came with the growth of large companies and corporations in the late 1800s and early 1900s that set mandatory retirement rules. The rules rested on beliefs that the physical stamina needed to work in factories and the speed needed to keep pace with new machinery made older workers poorly suited for continued employment. Even in nonmanual jobs, the demand for innovation and new skills put older workers who received training many decades ago at a disadvantage. Businesses also had economic reasons for mandatory retirement. It allowed them to use less expensive younger workers to replace more highly paid older workers. Setting a formal policy to have all workers retire at age 65 replaced the task of evaluating each older worker on a case-by-case basis.

Although many welcomed relief from work during old age, others expressed concern about forced retirement. It seemed unfair to prevent qualified older workers from continuing on the job. With most older persons having little or nothing in the way of retirement benefits before Social Security, forced retirement threatened many with poverty. In 1938, for example, a report from the New York State legislature described the harm of age discrimination. The report noted that many older persons forced to retire or let go before retirement wanted to work but could not find jobs.

Some states already had acted against age discrimination, but their laws were largely ineffective. Colorado passed the first law prohibiting age discrimination in the workplace in 1903, but it benefited only a small part of the nation's population. Massachusetts passed a bill prohibiting age discrimination in employment in 1937, but it placed no penalties on violators. Responding to its report on age discrimination, the New York State legislature proposed a bill to combat age discrimination in employment, but it failed to pass.

During World War II, concern about age discrimination subsided as businesses replaced younger workers now in the military with older workers. Yet the problems became more serious after the war. Even during the good economic times of the 1950s, older workers complained about being laid off or forced to retire. In 1951, one gerontologist wrote, "Most older people work as long as they can and retire only because they are forced to do so."[20] Scholars expressed concern in the 1950s that forcing healthy and active workers to retire made them feel unwanted, speeded physical and mental decline, and even led to early death.

By the 1960s, calls for the end of forced retirement grew. The calls recognized the unfairness of forcing competent workers to retire and the flaws in using age alone to determine the ability to work. Indeed, critics argued that such discrimination hurt the economy. Forcing retirement of productive older workers with experience, knowledge, and low rates of absenteeism lowered productivity of businesses. Yet, in a 1967 speech, President Lyndon Johnson said, "approximately half of all private job openings were barred to applicants over 55."[21] Old-age pressure groups founded in the 1940s and 1950s such as the National Retired Teachers Association (NRTA) and the American Association of Retired Persons (now the AARP) joined in calls to ban age discrimination.

The Age Discrimination in Employment Act (ADEA)

The first federal law against age discrimination came in 1967 with the Age Discrimination in Employment Act (ADEA). It prohibited employment discrimination based on age against persons 40 to 65 years old. The ban on age discrimination specifically applied to use of age in hiring, firing, layoffs, promotions, training, and compensation; in job advertisements listing age preferences or limitations; and in denial of health, retirement, unemployment, or other benefits to older workers. Employers with 20 or more employees and involved in interstate commerce were subject to the law.

However, the 1967 law remained incomplete—it did not include persons over age 65. Congress believed that, because older persons generally had access to pensions, they suffered less than workers ages 40 to 65 from age discrimination. The law thus allowed companies to continue mandatory retirement polices. Congress later rejected that reasoning. In 1978, an amendment to the ADEA increased the covered ages to 70. In 1986, another amendment removed this age limitation. That meant companies must abolish mandatory retirement policies at any set age. The 1986 legislation allowed institutions of higher education to continue to set mandatory retirement ages for tenured faculty, but this exemption ended in 1993.

The ADEA did make a few exceptions. High-level policy-making executives with access to generous pensions can be forced to retire (presumably to make room for new leaders). It also allowed exceptions where age is a legitimate requirement (actors playing grandparents) or where public safety is at stake. Airplane pilots have since 1959 faced mandatory retirement from flying at age 60. However, many former pilots wanting to keep flying past that age consider this policy discriminatory. In response, President Bush signed a bill on December 13, 2007, to raise the retirement age for commercial pilots from 60 to 65.

Rights of the Elderly

All states now have age discrimination laws to supplement the federal law. By 1965, 23 states had passed laws making it illegal to use age as a criterion in hiring and firing workers between the ages of 40 and 60.[22] Since passage of the ADEA in 1967, all other states have followed (Alabama became the 50th state in 1997 to outlaw age discrimination). Most state laws now follow the lead of the ADEA by prohibiting discrimination among employees age 40 and over for companies that do business within their state. These laws took on special importance in 2000 when the Supreme Court ruled in *Kimel v. Florida Board of Regents* that state employees could not sue state governments under the federal ADEA. They must instead use state laws.

The federal and state laws are needed because the Constitution does not protect citizens from age discrimination (as it does for race and religious discrimination).[23] In 1976, the Supreme Court ruled in *Massachusetts Board of Retirement v. Murgia* on use of mandatory retirement at age 50 of Massachusetts state police officers. It concluded that constitutional protection against age-based job discrimination would inappropriately give older workers a constitutional right to employment. The ruling further noted that old age differs from race because everyone who lives out a normal life span will become old but race does not change. The protection instead must come from age discrimination laws.

A second federal law came with the Age Discrimination Act of 1975. It prohibited "discrimination on the basis of age in programs or activities receiving Federal financial assistance." This excluded programs for which age defined eligibility, such as Social Security and Medicare for the elderly and Head Start and school programs for children. It did affect medical and graduate schools, which could not receive assistance if they prohibited older applicants or favored applicants based on age alone.[24]

Effects of the Legislation

Age discrimination laws have largely eliminated one concern in the past—mandatory retirement policies. With few exceptions, formal policies that require retirement at a specified age have disappeared, and suits based on forced retirement occur rarely (though are successful when brought). The laws have also eliminated certain forms of discrimination in hiring. Companies advertising for jobs cannot mention age limits, and job interviewers must avoid using age as a job qualification.

The ADEA has also eliminated some job requirements that on the surface appear to be age neutral. Even without referring to age, job ads and hiring criteria that indirectly affect older employees more than younger employees may show age bias. For example, one court case ruled that a school district could not have a policy of hiring only teachers with less than six years experience. The policy referred to job experience rather than age, but the association of age with experience made it discriminatory. Even stating a preference for recent college graduates is suspect; job requirements must instead refer to needed skills and qualifications for the job.

Other blatant forms of discrimination have ended. Airlines once hired only young women as flight attendants and allowed them to stay on the job only through age 32. American Airlines once justified the policy by stating that women over age 32 lacked physical agility and endurance and were "subject to changes in metabolism and in the endocrine, circulatory, digestive, nervous and cutaneous system, symptoms of which would interfere with the desirable performance."[25] Such discrimination against older women (and all men) by airlines has ended.

Although laws prevent the most obvious forms of age discrimination such as in written policies for mandatory retirement, less obvious forms of discrimination persist. An expert writing on age discrimination says, "Nearly all middle-aged and older workers, at some time during their work careers, will suffer the consequences of age-biased employment-related actions. Although the law bars age discrimination in the workplace, middle-aged and older workers are nevertheless subjected to adverse employment decisions."[26] As stated by John Rotter, Director of Policy and Strategy at AARP, "Resources to enforce age discrimination legislation will never be sufficient to monitor every hiring, termination, or compensation decision."[27]

Other evidence suggests that problems remain. In fiscal year 2006, the Equal Employment Opportunity Commission (EEOC), the agency of the federal government that investigates charges of age discrimination, received 13,569 complaints.[28] At the peak in 2002, the EEOC received 19,921 complaints. Although the charges allege rather than prove age discrimination, they indicate the perception of a problem by tens of thousands of workers.

A 2003 survey done of 278 senior executives similarly reveals concern with age discrimination.[29] Of those surveyed, 72.3 percent believed that age discrimination had increased in the past five years. Half thought age discrimination began before age 50, and 95 percent thought it began before age 61. Nearly three-quarters feared being victimized by age discrimination, 40 percent thought they would be forced into early retirement because of their age, and 36 percent thought they were too old to find another job.

Indeed, there are good reasons to worry about age discrimination. Persons who lose jobs in their 50s and 60s have the most trouble finding other jobs. By some estimates, 3.5 million people between the ages of 40 and 58 left the labor force from 2001 to 2004. Many of those had high-paying jobs, were successful in their careers, and wanted to continue working, but could not find jobs. For example, when 55-year-old Bob Miller lost a banking job, he expected that with his previous success in finding jobs, proven record of accomplishment, and hundreds of contacts, he would soon find another job.[30] After two years of failed job hunting, however, he has become a forced early retiree. According to the Bureau of Labor Statistics, the mean length of unemployment is 17.7 weeks for ages 25–34, 20.0 weeks for persons 35–44, 23.8 weeks for persons ages 45–64, and 25.2 weeks for persons age 65 and over. Middle-aged and older workers who lose their jobs typically will not find other jobs quickly. Those who do often must accept jobs well below their skills and qualifications.

Sometimes the effects of age discrimination stay hidden. For example, employers may remove older workers by using early retirement incentives to get around restrictions on mandatory retirement. Companies that are downsizing offer older workers special early retirement benefits if they leave their jobs right away. Employers reason that, even with the incentives, early retirement of older workers saves them money by reducing salaries and wages. Although acceptance of the offer is voluntary and many workers are pleased to take it, the subtle pressures lead some workers to leave the labor force before they are ready. Those who prefer to wait to retire must balance that preference with the loss of extra benefits.

Sometimes inducements for voluntary retirement come with the threat of dismissal. For example, on reaching age 65, Olga Cazzola told her company that she changed her mind and decided not to retire. The company in turn reduced her job responsibilities and gave her poor performance ratings that contrasted with those before she reached age 65. She was told she would be demoted to a low-level clerical position or fired if her performance did not improve. She sued on grounds of age discrimination and won her case.[31]

At one time, companies attempted to get around the ADEA by having older employees waive any age discrimination claims in order to get severance pay or early retirement benefits. However, the 1990 Older Workers Benefit Protection Act put limits on this practice. It requires that a valid ADEA waiver meet several conditions:

- It must be in writing and be understandable.
- It must specifically refer to ADEA rights or claims.
- It may not waive rights or claims that may arise in the future.
- It must be in exchange for valuable consideration.
- It must advise the individual in writing to consult an attorney before signing the waiver.
- It must provide the individual at least 21 days to consider the agreement and at least seven days to revoke the agreement after signing it.[32]

Under any other conditions, a waiver eliminates the rights of older workers and creates a form of age discrimination.

Introduction to Rights of the Elderly

Persistent Beliefs about Older Workers

Why would age discrimination in employment continue despite laws against it? One answer is that negative beliefs about the skills and productivity of older workers persist. According to lawyer Raymond Gregory, "Despite the fact that many thousands of these victims of age discrimination have obtained some measure of relief under the provisions of the ADEA, the law's primary goal, namely, the elimination of commonly held attitudes that falsely depict the capabilities of older workers, have not been realized."[33] He believes that the ADEA has failed dismally in changing beliefs.

Consider some of the beliefs of employers about older workers that might be used to justify discrimination:

- Older persons will have a shorter future career with a company than a younger person, giving less return to the costs of training.
- Older workers will bring in fewer new ideas and be more resistant to major changes.
- Older workers will be less satisfied than younger workers with a low rate of pay.
- Older workers with much experience will be overqualified for jobs.
- Older workers will run up costs of company health insurance plans.
- Older workers will face greater health problems and sick leave.
- Older workers will less successfully present a youthful, hip image of the company.
- Older workers will have less energy, stamina, and drive to prove themselves.

Some older workers may fit these generalizations, and employers may disqualify them from jobs based on their merit and suitability. However, when the beliefs are applied to all older persons, it constitutes age discrimination.

Few employers will state these beliefs outwardly, but many still rely on them in making hiring decisions. According to a survey done by the Society for Human Resource Management, 53 percent of 428 human resource managers interviewed said older workers "didn't keep up with technology," and 28 percent characterized older workers as "less flexible."[34] These attitudes sometimes show up in questions asked during interviews. Older applicants can expect to be asked whether they can work with young people, adapt to new situations, and stay current with innovations.

Negative beliefs about older workers prevail most clearly in the high-tech industry. Although employers have complained about a lack of qualified programmers, many experienced but older programmers say they cannot get hired. In San Jose, California, programmer James Wick, 62, "had

25

left the profession, demoralized by his failure to convince a series of young job interviewers that a 30-year career with Control Data and General Electric, among others, had taught him anything of value."[35] The image of geeks spending day and night to finish a program penalizes older workers who are believed to lack the energy and endurance to keep up the pace. The image of the young as technological innovators also penalizes older workers. Critics claim that such images are misleading and ignore the value of experience and thoughtfulness.

Negative beliefs about older workers may most penalize women. Those who stopped working for family reasons but want to reenter the labor force after raising their children or experiencing divorce often have trouble finding a job. Compared to older men, they have fewer contacts, less recent experience, and can apply to a smaller pool of suitable jobs. Because of the difficulties they face in finding work, women have become an increasing part of age discrimination suits.

Negative beliefs about older workers may have an underlying economic source. Companies wanting to cut labor costs look first to higher-paid employees. Since salaries tend to rise with experience, seniority, and age, the most savings come from cutting older workers in middle- and upper-level management. Once let go during cutbacks, older workers then find that their previous success and high salary prices them out of the market. Such employment problems have become particularly serious during recent decades as the large numbers of baby boomers have worked their way up to senior positions. Their jobs are costly to companies, and in the view of young people, block promotion opportunities.

Although employment decisions based on cost may sound like smart business strategy, critics say they are really a way to hide bias against older workers. As an example, they point to a 2001 suit involving Capital One Financial. The corporation cut payroll through firing what it claimed were its worst performers. However, a class action suit brought by 60 former employees alleged that the corporation systematically let go its oldest workers and changed performance ratings to justify the firings. The employees said that the performance rankings did little more than hide discrimination against older workers. Settling the lawsuit out of court in 2003, Capital One Financial promised to improve its evaluation processes and its awareness of age diversity needs.[36]

PROVING AGE DISCRIMINATION

Older persons can file a charge of age discrimination under the ADEA simply by submitting a complaint to the Equal Employment Opportunity Commission (EEOC) within 180 days of the alleged violation. Whether submitted by mail or in person, the charge must include the name and address of the complaining party, information about the employer alleged to have committed the violation, a short description of the violation or the event believed to have caused a violation, and the date or dates of the violation or violations. Victims may also file charges with a state or local agency that deals with fair employment policies.

The EEOC then investigates the charges. If an initial review shows they fit under the ADEA, the EEOC notifies the employer of the charge. Based on information from the charging party and the response of the employer, the EEOC investigation first determines if there is reasonable cause to believe a violation of the ADEA has occurred. If so, the EEOC recommends that the parties try to resolve the problem through mediation. A neutral mediator can help resolve disputes by negotiating a voluntary agreement. If that fails, the EEOC can choose to sue the employer for discriminatory practices. Individuals also have the right to bring their own private suits, if they do so before the EEOC sues.

According to figures from the EEOC, few age discrimination charges end up in court. In fiscal year 2006, 61.8 percent of investigations found no reasonable evidence of age discrimination.[37] For 18.7 percent of the charges, the EEOC closed the case because the charging party failed to respond to further inquiries, withdrew the charge, or rejected an offer of full relief. For another 15.4 percent of the cases, the parties settled their dispute without involvement of the EEOC. That left about 4.1 percent of the charges where the EEOC found reasonable cause of age discrimination. With some of the remaining cases undergoing successful mediation, the EEOC ended up litigating only a tiny fraction of the filed charges.

Of those cases that go to litigation, few end up victorious. Judge Richard Posner examined the decisions of 381 court cases brought under the ADEA from January 1, 1993, to June 30, 1994. He found that only 11.4 percent of the suits were successful, and almost all of those involved a loss of a job. Cases involving discrimination in hiring made up only 10.5 percent of the total, and only 4.4 percent of these—two out of 43—won.[38]

The EEOC takes a more positive view of the result of age discrimination cases. Focusing on monetary damages, it notes that those charging age discrimination in 2006 recovered $51.5 million in monetary benefits before going to court. Similarly, those few cases that won in court received high damage awards. According to figures reported by Jury Verdict Research, the median award in age discrimination cases reached $269,000. In contrast, the medians were $121,000 for race discrimination awards and $100,000 for sex discrimination awards.[39] Despite some high payoffs, however, the likelihood of winning damages for age discrimination remain small.

Rights of the Elderly

Evidence of Age Discrimination

Success in winning age discrimination suits depends on the evidence of wrongdoing. Direct evidence of age bias makes it easier to prove violation of rights. For example, written employment rules that limit the age of workers, require retirement at a specific age, or set aside better benefits or wages for younger workers than older workers clearly demonstrate age discrimination. So do verbal or written statements of employers that applicants or workers are too old for a job. Unless the charged parties can prove that the age requirements are necessary for the job or that they had not really acted on the age limitations, such evidence makes a strong case for victims of age discrimination.

In one case brought against K-Mart for dismissal of older managers, the corporation argued that scanners and computerized records made the main task of managers—keeping track of inventory—unnecessary. However, the plaintiffs pointed to statements made in a press conference by Joseph Antonini, the former chief executive officer. He said, "We are blessed with an officer group whose average age is slightly under 50."[40] Indicating the use of age as a way to evaluate the performance of managers, the statement gave evidence of age discrimination. In another case, a 60-year-old Massachusetts employee won a suit for $624,504 because the president of the company told him, "You've been doing a good job, but I want a younger man."[41]

Evidence of age discrimination is seldom so direct, however. Employers avoid statements and written policies that can be used against them in court. One article advising companies on how to avoid age discrimination suits said, "It is important to sensitize all managers to the fact that any type of age reference, even in informal conversations, may have a negative impact on the organization's position [in age discrimination suits]."[42] When companies and employers use this advice, age bias may be hidden rather than obvious.

Instead of presenting direct evidence, age discrimination suits typically must rely on indirect evidence. When layoffs of a company largely affect older workers, when a company has no older employees, or when no older applicants are hired, it may indicate an unstated preference for younger workers. In one case, Carol Gallo, an employee of Prudential Residential Services was let go at age 50 during a cut in the company's workforce.[43] However, the company soon after advertised for a job that sounded similar to what Gallo had done. She applied, but the job went to a younger applicant. In this case, her replacement by a younger, less experienced worker gave evidence of age discrimination. She sued, and after a judge rejected a claim to have the suit dismissed, the company agreed to a settlement.

Other types of indirect evidence may prove age discrimination. Consider the case of 61-year-old Ann Hertz.[44] After she applied to the Gap for a sales or office position, she was asked to come in for an interview. Since the application did not ask about age, the manager and associate manager were visibly surprised to meet Hertz, who was obviously much older than the typical employee. After only two perfunctory questions, the associate manager told Hertz they had no interest in hiring her and abruptly left the interview. Hertz sued for age discrimination, and a judge rejected the defense from the Gap that they wanted someone to work at night. The company agreed to a settlement.

More often, however, suits based on indirect evidence fail. Courts have ruled that age must be the determining factor in an employment decision to prove age discrimination. Companies can argue that, despite appearances of age discrimination, they have legitimate, nondiscriminatory reasons for their employment decisions. They can say that they fired older workers or did not hire older applicants because of poor performance or a lack of relevant qualifications. Contradicting such claims can be difficult. Because employment decisions are in part subjective, judges seldom want to substitute their judgments of the suitability of workers for the judgments of employers. If employers can offer legitimate-sounding reasons for their employment decisions, judges hesitate to overrule them.

Cases of age discrimination in hiring are particularly difficult to prove. Victims know too little about the hiring process, other applicants, and the person hired to recognize age discrimination. If those denied a job ask why, employers can most always find reasons other than age to justify hiring someone younger. In contrast, older workers fired from their jobs know about their performance, their qualifications, and the persons who replaced them. They have information to use in bringing charges that job applicants seldom have.

Disparate Impact

In 2005, the Supreme Court in *Smith v. City of Jackson* ruled that older workers charging age discrimination do not need to prove that employers intentionally discriminated. Instead, they can show that a policy had a discriminatory impact on older workers, even if employers did not intend it to. Not having to show evidence of motivation of employers to mistreat older workers makes it easier to prove age discrimination. Lower courts in the past had rejected many age discrimination claims under the interpretation of the law that the discrimination must be intentional. The ruling changed this interpretation.

The case involved older police officers in Jackson, Mississippi. They opposed a policy to give greater raises to officers with less than five years experience. The police agency claimed it needed the policy to recruit and retain young officers. The Supreme Court accepted the justification of the police agency for the raise policy, agreeing that legitimate reasons existed for the policy. The older police officers did not get the policy overturned. However, the decision allowed other cases alleging unintentional discrimination to go to trial. Those fighting age discrimination gained a new weapon in their efforts to prove mistreatment of older workers.

Again, however, it turned out as hard to prove unintentional discrimination or disparate impact as to prove intentional discrimination. To protect themselves against charges of age discrimination while continuing policies that have disparate impact by age, employers merely had to demonstrate that the policies were based on reasonable factors other than age. For example, the Loral Corporation laid off highly paid workers, hoping to cut costs by replacing them with lower salary workers. However, since older workers earned higher salaries by virtue of their seniority, they suffered most under the policy. In response to a suit brought by older workers, a California court ruled in *Marks v. Loral Corporation* that as long as cost cutting rather than age bias motivated the layoff policy, it did not constitute age discrimination. Employers can similarly claim that physical fitness, close ties to youth culture, or knowledge of new technology, although closely related to age, are legitimate occupational qualifications.

Although promising in theory, the use of disparate impact to prove age discrimination is difficult in practice. Advocates for older workers have criticized courts for making it difficult to prove age discrimination. By unfairly requiring a higher standard of proof for age discrimination than for race and sex discrimination, the courts fail to take age discrimination seriously. The advocates worry that court decisions have done little to eliminate age discrimination in employment and call for vigorous enforcement of the law.

The Case for Age Discrimination

Nearly everyone opposes the worst forms of age discrimination such as arbitrary retirement ages, mistreatment of older workers to get them to quit, or rejecting older applicants without considering their qualifications. However, some critics of the ADEA say that it encourages unwarranted suits and ultimately hurts older workers. In contrast to those calling for courts to treat age more like race and sex in discrimination suits, these critics defend the skeptical examination of age discrimination suits by judges.

Some argue that it is rational to make distinctions based on age. In *Forbes Magazine*, Dan Seligman writes,

> *Employers have solid economic reasons for not wanting to hire and train employees who will soon be retiring. . . . Furthermore, people really do "slip" with age. . . . It is true that not all mental abilities are affected to the same extent, and not all individuals slip at the same rate. An exhaustive study of age-based*

slippage, published last year in an issue of the journal Intelligence, *showed that highly educated people with superior verbal skills retain those skills fairly well. Slippage is substantially greater in mathematical and spatial reasoning than in verbal reasoning. Nevertheless, all reasoning skills decline with age, and the decrement is greatest in what psychologists call "fluid intelligence," i.e., the ability to learn new tasks and see things in new ways. The ancient adage about old dogs and new tricks really has something to it.*[45]

Although some people retain amazing vigor and perform at high levels well into old age, Seligman suggests that these rare exceptions should not define the norm. For most jobs, he believes that a preference for younger workers makes sense.

According to Judge Richard Posner, using age is an efficient and generally effective way to make judgments about job skills.[46] He argues that few employers dislike the elderly so much as to overlook their value. Rather, employers recognize that younger workers often perform better at lower cost. Successful companies act rationally in hiring the best people rather than act irrationally in rejecting qualified older workers. Decisions about the use of age in employment decisions thus should respond to economic competition rather than to the government and courts.

Posner similarly defends use of a mandatory retirement age to promote economic efficiency. He argues that obtaining information on individual performance—measuring physical fitness, mental skills, and job effectiveness—is expensive, arbitrary, and subjective. It forces employers to evaluate older workers negatively rather than letting them retire gracefully at the selected age (as most prefer to do anyway). Simple retirement policies based on age make for orderly transitions of older workers out of a company and for movement of younger workers into better jobs. Posner agrees that mistakes will come with a mandatory retirement age. Some workers may have to retire before they are ready, while other workers may continue past the time when they should retire. Even so, treating individuals as a member of a group makes for simplicity and efficiency.

Seligman and Posner believe that, by obstructing the workings of the labor market in employment decisions, the ADEA has had unwanted consequences. It in fact may increase rather than reduce age discrimination. Despite the effort of the Supreme Court to clarify the issue with its 2005 decision, the standards used to prove age discrimination remain confused. Although few age discrimination suits win, the confusion in standards makes employers vulnerable. The costs of fighting age discrimination suits and paying damages for the occasional successful suit become expensive. This situation gives employers less reason to hire older workers. They worry that if an older worker performs poorly, warrants lower pay, or deserves firing, the company will end up fighting a lawsuit.

In the end, these critics deny that age discrimination is comparable to sex and race discrimination. African Americans, Hispanics, and women are permanent members of disadvantaged groups, but people change age groups as they grow older. Do young people discriminate against older workers when they themselves will become old? Do older employers discriminate against the interests of their own age group when they fire older workers? Critics say no. Neither young nor old employers have economic incentives to act in this way. Who wins from age discrimination suits? Unlike sex and race discrimination suits, the ones who win age discrimination suits are usually part of a select group of people that rarely need protection: highly paid white male executives and managers. Because this group already has many advantages, the ADEA does little to foster equality.

RECOMMENDATIONS FOR CHANGE

Advocates of tough age discrimination laws suggest that the critics miss a crucial point when focusing on efficiency and planning. Banning age discrimination is a matter of justice and civil rights rather than economics and profit. People should be judged on their individual merit rather than group membership. Older workers should have the right to prove they do not fit stereotypes about their age groups. They do not differ from women and minority groups in this regard.

Rather than to weaken the ADEA, many want stronger enforcement of the law. Raymond Gregory, a lawyer who has worked on many age discrimination cases, recommends that employers be required to keep records of the age of job applicants, hires, company employees, and firings. Allowing the EEOC to scrutinize age records and statistics would help prove age discrimination cases. Even without lawsuits, keeping records would alert employers to possible age discrimination. Gregory also recommends extending the ADEA to cover all employers rather than employers of 20 or more workers. Millions of workers in small firms may suffer from age discrimination but lack protection under federal law. Similarly, many part-time, temporary, and contract workers lack the protection of permanent employees.

Some suggest the need for something more radical—a kind of affirmative action policy for hiring older persons. Affirmative action programs set goals and take special action to hire members of a class of people facing discrimination, and they give preferences among equally qualified persons to underrepresented groups. To correct an imbalance in the ages of workers and counter negative images of the aged, affirmative action programs would favor older workers in hiring. However, many oppose such a proposal as discriminatory toward younger workers.

In decades to come, economic pressures more than changes in the law or affirmative action may do the most to help older workers. As the size of the aged population grows, the need to keep them in the labor force will increase. Without sufficient numbers of younger workers to replace older baby boomers leaving the labor force, employers may need incentives to keep older workers or hire new ones. Older workers today are well prepared to respond to this need. By one report, "68 percent of workers between the ages of 50 and 70 say that they plan to work in some capacity during retirement or never retire at all."[47] They are healthier, more educated, more experienced, and likely to live longer than ever before. With many years of productive work left, use of their talent makes both economic and ethical sense.

RIGHTS INVOLVING PENSIONS AND INCOME

According to a study from the AARP Public Policy Institute, the elderly depend greatly on private and public retirement income.[48] Just under one-third of persons age 65 and over receive private pension benefits, which on average make up 21.5 percent of their total income (the percentage is lower for older women than men). In addition, nearly 90 percent of those age 65 and over receive retirement income from Social Security. This source makes up 40.8 percent of their total income, although the percentage is higher for the poor than the well off. A small portion of income comes from another public source, a means-tested program for the elderly poor called Supplemental Security Income. Both the private and public sources of income in old age entitle recipients to certain rights.

PRIVATE PENSIONS

Although based on agreements between workers and employers, private pensions come with protections guaranteed by the government. Several laws passed since the 1950s, including an important one in 2006, aim to protect these private pension rights of workers and retirees, though not always successfully.

Pension plans come in two basic types. One called a defined-benefit plan offers fixed monthly retirement income based on years of service and earnings prior to retirement. The employer offers the plan as part of a worker's compensation and maintains a fund to pay the current and future retirement benefits it has promised to its workers. Defined-benefit plans offer several advantages to workers. They set a specified benefit amount at retirement that will last until death of the retiree and then, at a lower benefit amount, until the death of a surviving spouse. The benefit amount usually is based on a percentage of the salary paid to an employee during his or her last years of work.

Such plans also have weaknesses. Federal rules require that employers set aside enough money to cover its pension obligations, responsibly manage the fund, and live up to the promises made to retirees. However, companies sometimes fail to meet these requirements. Companies having financial troubles, going bankrupt, or shrinking in size often cannot pay what they owe to retirees. A federal government insurance agency, the Pension Benefit Guaranty Corporation (PBGC), covers at least a portion of pensions of retirees when companies cannot.

Another weakness of defined-benefit plans is that workers must stay with a company long enough to qualify for the benefits. Vesting refers to the period of time it takes a worker to gain the right to retirement benefits from a company. Once vested, an employee becomes entitled to retirement benefits even if they leave their job. Under some plans, workers receive full vesting after five years but have no rights to pensions for shorter service. Under other plans, workers gain the right to 20 percent of the pension benefits after three years of service for a company, 40 percent after four years, 60 percent after five years, 80 percent after six years, and 100 percent after seven years.

According to legal requirements, defined-benefit pension plans must designate an administrator to provide certain information to workers who participate in the plan. The information comes in the form of a summary plan description that explains how to begin participating in the plan, how service and benefits are calculated, when benefits become vested, when payments will begin, what form the payments will take, and how to file a claim for benefits. The administrator must notify participants if changes occur in the plan and submit an annual financial report. Plan fiduciaries, those with authority over a plan's management, investments, and assets, have duties to ensure the proper operation and financial safety of the plan. The legal requirements allow workers to learn of their pension rights and keep track of the pension-fund performance. Participants have the right to sue for benefits if they believe that the administrator has violated these requirements.

A second type of private pension has become more common in recent decades. Defined-contribution plans put contributions from employers and employees into an investment account that belongs to the worker. The employer promises to contribute a specified amount to a worker's retirement fund during the period of employment rather than pay a specified benefit during the period of retirement. After many years of contributions and building up a reserve with investments, an employee withdraws funds for retirement. Defined-contribution plans do not require vesting; workers keep their contributions when they change jobs or when a company goes bankrupt. However, the plans do not promise a benefit amount at retirement—the amount depends on the size of the accrued investments and decisions of the retiree on how to spend the money.

One popular form of a defined-contribution plan is called a 401(k) (named after a section of the U.S. Internal Revenue Code). Set up by the employer, a 401(k) allows workers to contribute to the retirement account (employees without such an option can contribute on their own to an Individual Retirement Account). The contributions are taken automatically from wages before taxes, and investment growth in the account remains free from taxes until withdrawn. Employers often match employee contributions and, up to a certain threshold, the contributions remain exempt from taxes. Since the 401(k) account belongs to the employee rather than the company, the employee rather than the company directs investment of the funds.

Owners of the 401(k) accounts can withdraw funds starting at age 55 if retired or at age 59 ½ if not retired. However, the funds available at retirement depend on the investment decisions made by the employee. Wise investment of contributions over several decades will create higher retirement income than poor investments. In this way, 401(k)s shift responsibility for the costs and risks of retirement away from employers and onto employees. If employees save too little or manage investments poorly, they cannot retire comfortably. Even large accounts, when paid out in a way to last the full life of a retiree and spouse, may produce only modest income.

Employee Retirement Income Security Act of 1974

Until 1974, workers could do little to protect their pension benefits. They had to rely on the good will and success of their employers. For example, when Studebaker automobile manufacturers went out of business in 1963, some 4,000 workers lost all or part of their promised retirement benefits. Even financially sound plans had long periods required for vesting, up to 10 years. In one case brought before the Supreme Court (*Hazen Paper v. Biggins*), a worker accused his employer of firing him just before he would qualify for the 10-year pension vesting.

In 1974, Congress passed the Employee Retirement Income Security Act (ERISA). The legislation set minimum standards for private pension plans, including requirements for reporting to participants and vesting employees after a specified number of years. It also mandated that plans include some provision for surviving spouses to continue receiving benefits after the death of a pension recipient. However, it did not specify minimum benefit levels or require that a company have a private pension plan. Rather, it set standards for those that chose to provide a plan for employees.

ERISA also created the PBGC to protect the pensions of workers with defined-benefit plans. Companies with such plans pay an insurance premium that goes into a fund supervised by the PBGC. When a company does not have the funds to pay its promised benefits or risks going out of business by paying the benefits, the PBGC covers the pension obligations to workers (while trying to recover funds from the company). Thus protected from default by their company, current retirees can continue receiving benefits and workers can count on benefits when they retire. According to the PBGC, "It currently protects the pensions of nearly 44 million American workers and retirees in 30,330 private single-employer and multiemployer defined benefit pension plans."[49]

In spite of ERISA requirements, private plans regularly experience problems. In 1994, Congress attempted to stiffen requirements with the Retirement Protection Act. At the time, private pension plans in aggregate had shortages—the difference between their assets and obligations—of $71 billion. The 1994 law forced companies with more than 100 employees and less than 90 percent of assets needed to pay its promised benefits to send letters to its employees warning of the shortfall. Northwest Airlines and Westinghouse, for example, had to send such letters. More important, the law also forced companies with underfunded plans to increase their contributions.

Despite ERISA and the 1994 legislation, problems in private pension funding have continued. According to a report from the Public Broadcast Service (PBS), "A 2003 study by Watson Wyatt of pension plans in the United States covering 1,000 or more active participants found that the percentage of underfunded plans increased from 15% in 1992 to 52% in 2002. A late 2002 Merrill Lynch survey found that the pension liability of 348 S&P 500 companies lies somewhere between $184 and $342 billion—a drop from a reported $2 billion surplus in 2001."[50]

Some examples from the PBS report and other sources illustrate the risks to retired workers. When U.S. Airways went bankrupt in 2004, it had $2.5 billion in unfunded pension liabilities. Because of limits on the maximum amount it can pay per month to retirees, the PBGC picked up only about $600 million of the liabilities. Some pilots expecting a pension of $75,000 now expect only $25,000. When Bethlehem Steel declared bankruptcy in 2001 and sold off its divisions, the company had pension liabilities of $7.8 billion and owed benefits to 95,000 former workers. Even with $3.5 billion in assets to use and $3.7 billion from the PBGC, the plan ended up $600 million short in promised benefits. When the Enron Corporation of Houston, Texas, filed for bankruptcy on December 2, 2001, it left 17,000 workers without pensions. The bankruptcy proceedings set aside only $321 million from the sale of company assets to devote to pensions. Yet, the collapse of Enron stock wiped out the 401(k) accounts of many employees. When United Airlines went through bankruptcy proceedings in 2002, the PBGC took over its $9.8 billion in pension obligations. Yet former and current United employees worry that they will not receive their full pensions.

Many other intact companies have had problems with their pension plans. In 2002, Ford Motor Company reported that its U.S. pension plan was underfunded by $7.3 billion.[51] The problem at Ford and many other large corporations such as IBM, United Technologies, and General Motors came during the downturn in the economy in the early 2000s. As pension liabilities continued to grow, a stock market slump reduced the return on pension investments. Low profits and pressures to invest in new products further made funding for the pension reserve a low priority. When low equity returns called for more pension contributions, companies could least afford to make them. Those eligible for pensions accused the companies of breaking promises and sacrificing their workers for profits, while the companies said that putting funds into pensions cut earnings and stock values.

In some ways, ERISA and similar laws increase the risk of unfunded pensions for workers. Knowing that the PBGC will cover a shortfall, companies can more easily underfund or renege on pension obligations. Bradley Belt, former Executive Director of the PBGC says, "There may be occasions when companies, and even labor [unions], have incentive to promise higher pension benefits rather than current wages, because they know that [if they fail to meet their promises] they have the backstop provided by the PBGC."[52] He claims that ERISA is filled with loopholes that allow companies to intentionally underfund their pension plans.

Recent Trends in Pension Funding

Problems in funding for defined-benefit plans have led companies to prefer defined-contribution plans. They can make contributions as part of employee fringe benefits but then remain free of future obligations to pay employees when they retire. New businesses can establish a defined-contribution plan at the outset, but older businesses face a more difficult problem in shifting from defined-benefit to defined-contribution pension plans. To do so, companies make cash-balance conversions. These involve giving credits to employees for a portion of their wages or salaries in each year they have worked for the company and then adding an assumed increase from interest and dividends. The worker can use the amount credited to them at retirement, much as they would with a defined-contribution plan. The employer still pays the cash balance for retirement in the form of an annuity or lump-sum payment but, once this is done, no longer pays benefits. The cash-balance plan thus represents a hybrid form of pension.

The attractiveness of cash-balance pensions to employers makes them less desirable to workers. Although the cash-balance plan is intended to give retirees the same benefits they would get under the defined-benefit plan it replaces, it does not always work out this way. Older employees in particular may get less than they would under a defined-benefit plan. A cut may come in part from assumptions made in calculating the cash conversion. It may also come from an essential difference in defined-benefit and defined-contribution plans. Defined-benefit plans usually determine the yearly retirement benefits based on a percentage of wages made during the last few years before retirement—the years when the worker earns the most. The cash-balance conversion uses a portion of wages throughout their career with the company, including low-paying early years as well as high-paying later years. The conversion may work fine for younger workers who have plenty of time to allow the cash balance to grow, but it hurts older workers.

For example, when downsized from his tech job at AT&T in 2001, 55-year-old Larry Cutrone found he was eligible for much lower pension benefits than he expected.[53] He says that, in converting its defined-benefit plan to a cash-balance plan in 1998, AT&T slashed his pension from the $47,000 a year he had expected to just $23,000. When IBM moved to a cash-balance pension in 1999, older employees sued, claiming that the conversion penalized them. Under the plan, a 35-year-old worker would retire at age 65 with a normal retirement benefit of $1,259.22 per month, but a 50-year-old employee would retire with a benefit of only $1,099.10 per month.[54] The district court ruled that the plan violated age discrimination laws, but the appeals court later overturned the decision and the Supreme Court upheld the appeals court. The ruling noted that IBM contributed the same amount to younger and older workers, though younger workers had more time to allow the benefits to accrue.

While cash-balance conversions caused controversy, so did the continuing problems in funding defined-benefit plans. The PBGC, the agency set up to safeguard the pensions for employees of companies that go bankrupt, itself faced financial problems. Given the costs it faced over the years in covering the pension programs of bankrupt steel and airline companies, the PBGC ran up huge deficits. It paid out $22.8 billion more than it took in 2005 and $18.1 billion more in 2006.[55] The agency funds the pensions of 1.3 million workers and retirees but not always to the satisfaction of beneficiaries. Its cap on benefits means that highly paid workers and early retirees receive lower benefits than they would have from their companies.

Given disputes over cash-balance conversion and difficulties with private pension funding, Congress passed the Pension Protection Act of 2006. In signing the legislation, President George W. Bush called it "the most sweeping reform of America's pension laws in over 30 years."[56] The law requires companies to shore up the finances of their pensions, which means that 30,000 underfunded plans will need to invest $450 billion. As President Bush said, "If you offer a private pension plan to your employees, you have a duty to set aside enough money now so your workers will get what they've been promised when they retire."[57] It also increases premiums paid to the PBGC and shores up the agency's poor finances.

Along with changes in funding for defined-benefit plans, the 2006 Pension Protection Act aimed to improve defined-contribution pension plans. It allows companies to enroll employees in 401(k) plans automatically rather than doing so only after the employee makes a request. The law ideally will encourage workers to set aside more of their own money for retirement. The act also set up a legal test to ensure that cash-balance conversion plans do not discriminate against older workers. The change should make this hybrid pension more attractive to those approaching retirement.

However, some worry that the law will have unintended consequences. Financial writer Jane Bryant Quinn predicts that the new reforms will lead more companies to eliminate defined-benefit plans. When forced to pay more to bring underfunded plans up to standard, many companies will instead move to defined-contribution and 401(k) plans. Reinforcing concerns about the change, Quinn says, "Pension plans also earn more on their investments than a typical 401(k) due to better management and lower expenses."[58] Despite the new law, the shift from defined benefits to defined contributions may hurt the retired elderly.

Private Pension Rights

Although older workers can do little about pension laws and economic trends, they can learn about their pension rights. The complexities of the plans, accounting terms, and income needs for retirement make it hard to master even the basics. Yet dependence on pension income makes such knowledge critical for a comfortable retirement. The Pension Rights Center sponsors the National Pension Assistance Resource Center to help people with pension problems or questions. Other local and state agencies offer help as well.

Short of becoming an expert, plan participants can follow recommendations of the Department of Labor by checking for 10 signs of abuse of a pension fund:

1. Your 401(k) or individual account statement is consistently late or comes at irregular intervals
2. Your account balance does not appear to be accurate
3. Your employer failed to transmit your contribution to the plan on a timely basis
4. A significant drop in account balance that cannot be explained by normal market ups and downs
5. 401(k) or individual account statement shows your contribution from your paycheck was not made
6. Investments listed on your statement are not what you authorized
7. Former employees are having trouble getting their benefits paid on time or in the correct amounts
8. Unusual transactions, such as a loan to the employer, a corporate officer, or one of the plan trustees

9. Frequent and unexplained changes in investment managers or consultants
10. Your employer has recently experienced severe financial difficulty.[59]

With any of these signs of abuse, first contact the employer or plan administrator. If problems remain, workers covered by ERISA can sue to clarify rights to future benefits, recover due benefits, or stop illegal practices. They can also bring charges to the Department of Labor, which enforces pension laws.

Even if all existing pension plans worked well and participants could count on receiving the full benefits, a more serious problem would remain: Most workers are not eligible for or choose not to participate in a private pension plan. According to a report from the Employee Benefit Research Institution, "About 58 percent of all working-age (21–64) wage and salary employees work for an employer or union that sponsors a retirement plan. Of these working-age employees, slightly less than half (47 percent) participate in a retirement plan."[60] Participation is higher at the older than younger ages (56.5 percent at ages 55–64 versus 18.4 percent at ages 21–24). It is also higher among male than female workers, whites than blacks and Hispanics, and residents of the Northeast and Midwest than the South and West. Even so, the low participation in employer-sponsored pension plans will lead to income problems in old age among all groups.

Women face special problems in old age because they work less and accrue private benefits less often than men. Nearly nine out of 10 older married women depend on their spouse's pension income while both are alive. Plans must provide benefits to surviving spouses when the pension beneficiary dies, but couples often receive lower benefits while both are alive to ensure that a surviving spouse gets benefits later. The Pension Protection Act of 2006 gives more flexibility on how to distribute benefits to a surviving spouse, but some loopholes remain. For example, when a husband who leaves a job cashes out his 401(k) plan and rolls it into an Individual Retirement Account (IRA), the wife then loses her right to a share of the money in the 401(k) plan.

Divorced spouses similarly can lose their share of a spouse's pension. According to the Pension Rights Center, a public interest organization that helps pension recipients, "Private retirement plans are required to pay private retirement plan benefits to former spouses only if the former spouses submit a special kind of court order to the plan specifying the amount, form, and timing of payments."[61] The Pension Protection Act of 2006 now makes it easier for a spouse who did not receive the right kind of court order at the time of the divorce to go back to court to get one. Still, divorced spouses remain vulnerable.

For both men and women, the lack of coverage by a private pension can make the difference between retiring and working. Many approaching old age want to continue working because they find it fulfilling. At the same time, those without a private pension may have little choice in the matter. Even those with a private pension may not get what they expect and need to plan carefully for a secure retirement.

SOCIAL SECURITY INCOME

Government income programs for the elderly such as Social Security and Supplemental Security Income (SSI) have done well to maintain minimum income levels. Only 9.8 percent of the elderly today have income below the poverty line; by comparison, the poverty rate for children, those under 18 years old, is 17.8 percent. But how well do these programs meet the need for a normal lifestyle? And how secure are the benefits for retirees in the future? These questions relate directly to concerns about economic rights of the elderly.

Benefit Entitlements and Restrictions

Benefits from Social Security or Old Age and Survivors Insurance are far from generous. The average monthly payment to a retired worker in 2006 was $1,002—only $12,024 a year. The average monthly payment to a single retired worker was somewhat lower, $967 a month or $11,604 a year, while the average for couples both receiving benefits was somewhat higher, $1,648 a month or $19,776 per year. These amounts just exceed the poverty level in 2006 of $9,800 for one person and $13,200 for two persons. Social Security lifts many elderly above the poverty line but does not guarantee much more.

With about 53 million people receiving Social Security benefits, the figures on average benefits hide much diversity. In general, those contributing more taxes to social security earn more benefits. The formula to determine benefit levels is complex but first depends on an index of average monthly earnings for up to 35 years (and adjusted for increases over time in general wage levels). Second, the formula makes adjustments to give extra to those most in need. In 2007, benefits are paid for 90 percent of the first $680 of average monthly earnings, 32 percent for average monthly earnings between $680 and $4,100, and 15 percent of averaged monthly earnings over $4,100. Given limits on their benefits, high-wage workers have a limit on their contributions (currently at $97,500). Even so, benefits replace a larger percentage of those with lower preretirement earnings than those with high preretirement earnings. This makes Social Security a program of income redistribution as well as an insurance program.

Rights of the Elderly

Early retirees receive lower benefits than those retiring at the normal age. Early retirement can begin at age 62, while normal retirement, once set at age 65, is slowly rising. For example, those born in 1940 can retire with full benefits at age 65 and 6 months, those born from 1943 to 1954 can do so at age 66, and those born in 1960 and after can do so at age 67. Early retirees get lower monthly benefits because they will receive them for longer than normal retirees. A person retiring at exactly age 62 in 2007 receives a benefit that is lower by 25 percent than a comparable person retiring at the normal retirement age. Assuming that early and normal retirees live to normal life expectancy, their lifetime benefits will average out.

Those who have not worked may qualify for additional retirement benefits based on the contributions of a working spouse. At the normal retirement age, these benefits equal 50 percent of the benefits of the working spouse at the normal retirement age. When both spouses have worked and qualified for retirement benefits, they can select whichever formula gives them higher income—that based on their own earnings or that on the earnings of one and the spouse benefits of the other. If their marriage lasted 10 years, divorced spouses who have not remarried can get benefits based on the earnings of the former spouse. Widows or widowers can receive benefits at early or normal retirement based on the eligibility of the deceased spouse; divorced spouses can also receive survivor benefits based on the eligibility of the deceased former spouse.

The benefit levels determined at the time of retirement increase according to annual cost-of-living allowances (COLAs). The percentage increase in benefits equals the percentage increase in inflation as measured by the consumer price index. During periods of high inflation, the allowance can increase benefits substantially—benefits jumped in 1980 by 14.3 percent, for instance. The increase is normally much smaller. The 3.3 percent increase in 2007 translates into $33 more per month for the average beneficiary. The COLAs aim to maintain purchasing power of the benefits in the face of inflation rather than to increase real income.

To limit costs, Social Security will not fully support early retirees who have adequate outside earnings. Early retirees who continue to work and receive earnings above a limit get lower Social Security benefits. Thus, those earning more than $12,960 during early retirement face a cut of $1 in benefits for each $2 in earnings. The threshold goes up and the cut in benefits goes down just before normal retirement age and ends altogether after normal retirement age. At one time, this earnings test applied as well to retirees ages 65–70. It forced those who would like to continue working to retire fully to get all their Social Security benefits. In response, the Senior Citizens Freedom to Work Act of 2000 eliminated the earnings test after the normal retirement age. The act increased the opportunity of older retirees to continue working while getting Social Security benefits.

About one-third of Social Security beneficiaries pay taxes on their benefits. For example, a retired couple with combined income over $44,000 pays taxes on 85 percent of their benefits. This requirement began in 1984 as a means to reduce government costs for Social Security. It also helped target benefits for those most in need. By providing benefits to high-income retirees who have other sources of support, but taking some back with taxes, the government gives a higher proportion of its funds to low-income retirees.

Social Security also is given to persons with disabilities, including but not limited to the elderly. Social Security disability benefits are available to persons who recently worked, have contributed to Social Security for a certain period, and are currently unable to work because of a disability. However, the disability must be severe enough to prevent work and limit activities such as walking, sitting, and remembering; it also must be expected to last at least one year. Benefits for those who qualify under the Social Security definition of disability can start six months after the disability begins. Family members may also receive benefits based on the disability. Benefits last as long as the condition does, but end when the condition or the ability to work improves.

Besides Social Security, older persons receive help from SSI. This means-tested program goes to the poor elderly, those who are not eligible for Social Security or receive low benefits. Recipients must be citizens or qualified aliens who have assets (such as money in a bank account, stocks, land, vehicles, or personal property) of no more than $2,000 for an individual or $3,000 for a couple. In 2007, they also must have income no higher than $1,331 a month in wages or $643 from other sources. In most states, eligibility for SSI benefits also makes elderly persons eligible for Medicaid and food stamps.

SSI benefits are $623 per month for an individual or $934 for a couple. Most states raise the income of recipients by adding to federal benefits; Arkansas, Georgia, Kansas, Tennessee, and West Virginia are exceptions. To apply for benefits, individuals must document their citizenship, income, and assets but can receive help from the Social Security Administration in obtaining the documents they need. Applicants also have the right to see their file, to appeal a decision, and to receive notice of any change in benefits. However, participation of the elderly poor in the program has declined, in part because rising Social Security benefits make it harder to qualify and in part because many eligible elderly persons do not know about the program.

Long-Term Solvency

Current rights to Social Security benefits will likely change in coming decades to meet the demands of a growing elderly population. Such changes will almost certainly involve cuts in benefits levels or added restrictions on eligibility. Raising the age of normal retirement to past 65 has reduced the obligations of Social Security to future retirees. Similarly, taxing Social Security benefits, implemented in 1984 to improve the solvency of the system, represents a cut in benefits for higher-income retirees. Greater change likely will come in the next decades.

The potential future deficit in Social Security spending has generated much political debate on needed changes (but so far no action). On one side, Republicans and supporters of free-market economics suggest that Social Security cannot meet the needs of future retirees without substantial cuts in benefits or increases in taxes. They suggest instead that reforms allow workers to divert at least part of Social Security payroll taxes to individual retirement accounts (IRAs) that can grow with the stock market. Such proposals represent a radical change: Instead of current workers paying for retirement benefits of current retirees, workers would contribute taxes to their own retirement accounts. In this way, the proposed change is analogous to the switch from defined-benefit to defined-contribution pension plans. Advocates suggest that workers will get a better return on their contributions. Since inflation-adjusted stock market returns have averaged, by some estimates, about 7–8 percent per year over the long run, privatized Social Security accounts will enjoy strong growth rates.

Democrats and advocates of stronger government protection of the disadvantaged strenuously oppose privatization of Social Security. They say that critics exaggerate the financial threats to Social Security in the coming decades. The system has worked well for more than 70 years and remains one of the government's most popular programs. Defenders of Social Security say that a mix of modest cuts for high-income retirees, an increase in the cap on earning subject to the Social Security taxes, and penalizing early retirement can protect the system from projected deficits and a growing elderly population. They worry instead that privatization will weaken the current program and ultimately cost taxpayers and retirees. Diverting funds to private accounts, which need time to grow, would cause a short-term crisis in paying current benefits.

Despite making privatization a major goal of his administration after his 2004 election, President George W. Bush has had little success in convincing Congress of the value of his proposals. The current system is likely to remain in place. Even in the absence of new legislation, however, current trends may foster a two-tier retirement system. Lower-income workers and the poor elderly will increasingly depend on Social Security and SSI. In contrast, higher-income workers will depend less on Social Security and more on private pensions and IRAs. Rights to Social Security will take the form of a guaranteed minimum income rather than the form of access to a full-fledged public pension.

RIGHTS INVOLVING MEDICAL CARE

Unlike Canada and countries of western Europe, the United States does not guarantee access to health care as a right of citizenship. However, nearly all elderly persons receive government-funded health care through either Medicare or Medicaid. They enjoy health care rights not granted to other age groups.

Both Medicare and Medicaid have requirements for eligibility. Those age 65 and over are eligible for Medicare if they are eligible for Social Security benefits or belong to a Medicare-covered plan for government employees. Those persons without sufficient income and assets to pay for health care are eligible for Medicaid, which helps older persons not covered by Medicare. In addition, many older persons needing long-term care, which Medicare does not cover, rely on Medicaid payments. Despite eligibility requirements, a health care safety net in one form or another remains in place for the elderly.

Yet many have concerns about the ability of this safety net to protect the health care rights of elderly patients. Critics say that Medicare and Medicaid programs do much less than they should to help the elderly. Regardless of the health care guarantees they give, the programs do not always live up to promises. Rising medical costs combined with a growing elderly population will only worsen problems of health care quality. In short, elderly rights to health care come with difficulties in delivering them.

MEDICARE RIGHTS

The rights of the elderly who qualify for Medicare depend on the program they select. The original Medicare plan provides for coverage of hospital costs (Part A) and optional coverage of medical costs for doctors and related services (Part B). Part B requires those eligible to enroll and pay a monthly premium. In these fee-for-service plans, Medicare reimburses hospitals and physicians for costs of treating Medicare patients. Those using the original Medicare plan usually purchase Medicare Supplemental Insurance (or Medigap) policies to pay for health care costs that Medicare does not cover.

An alternative to original Medicare called Medicare Advantage (or Part C) involves enrolling in a Medicare-approved plan run by a private company. These plans combine hospital and medical coverage by making enrollees part of a Health Maintenance Network (HMO) or Preferred Provider Organization (PPO). Their services differ depending on the HMO or PPO, but Part C plans have lower costs and more benefits than the original plan. Along with the advantages, however, HMOs and PPOs have restrictions: They require members to go to certain hospitals, get referrals to see specialists, and see doctors who belong to the network.

Rights of the Elderly

Participants in Medicare programs can obtain prescription drug coverage. Those enrolled in original Medicare join plans run by private companies. The Medicare Prescription Drug benefit (called Part D) began in 2006 in response to the high cost of prescriptions for the elderly. The plans require a monthly premium but can save much on the costs of prescription medications. Those enrolled in Medicare Advantage usually get prescription coverage as part of their HMO or PPO.

Medicare otherwise covers basic healthcare costs but does not pay for all the needs of elderly patients. Included are medically necessary items and services for diagnosis and treatment, many preventive services, and short-term care in hospitals, rehabilitation centers, and nursing homes. Also included are skilled home-care services such as nursing, physical therapy, and speech therapy for Medicare patients unable to leave home. Excluded are coverage for cosmetic surgery, custodial care, chiropractic services, dental care, eye care, hearing aids, many lab tests, and most routine physical exams. Of great cost to those in need, long-term care in nursing homes is excluded. In addition, since Medicare requires payments for deductibles, coinsurance, and premiums for Part B and Part D, these costs must come out-of-pocket.

The Centers for Medicare and Medicaid Services, the government organization that runs the programs, guarantees participants the rights to:

- Be treated with dignity and respect at all times.
- Be protected from discrimination. Such protection covers age discrimination as well as discrimination by race, color, national origin, disability, religion, and (under certain conditions) sex; those treated unfairly can contact the U.S. Office for Civil Rights in their state.
- Obtain understandable information from Medicare that can guide healthcare decisions. The information includes answering questions about what Medicare will pay for and what patients will have to pay for; counselors will provide free help in answering questions.
- Culturally competent services. These services include communicating in languages other than English and being sensitive to minority cultures.
- Receive emergency care where needed. This type of care should come immediately—without bureaucratic restrictions and obstacles.
- Learn about treatment choices in clear and understandable language. This allows individuals to participate fully in their health care decisions and requires doctors to tell patients what they need to know about their treatment choices.
- File a complaint. Patients can file a grievance when they believe they are not getting the quality of care and services they deserve.
- Appeal decisions relating to claims. A formal appeals process has been set up to consider disputes over payments.

- Have health information that Medicare collects kept private. Medicare needs confidential information on health conditions and problems but cannot make it public.[62]

These rights apply to Original Medicare and Medicare Advantage but can take different forms under the two plans.

Many disputes over the rights of Medicare patients follow from claims for items or services for which Medicare will not pay. When a claim for a Medicare payment or continued treatment is denied and the patient must pay for the item or service, an appeal can be filed. For example, healthcare providers may say that Medicare does not cover a desired treatment or end payment for skilled nursing care before desired. Procedures are in place to have the appeal considered quickly by an independent evaluator. As the AARP recommends, "Don't take 'no' for a final answer. Many appeals are successful."[63]

For general complaints about Medicare treatment, patients can file a grievance rather than an appeal. Concerns about the quality of care received under Medicare might include poor treatment by staff, difficulty calling or getting an appointment with the healthcare provider, or receiving a referral to a specialist. Problems with the Medicare Drug plan such as waiting too long to get a prescription or having trouble getting through to customer service might also justify a grievance. Grievances for those belonging to Original Medicare go to the Quality Improvement Organization in the state. Those belonging to Medicare Advantage should check their membership plan materials or call their plan's customer service to find out how to file a grievance.

MEDICAID AND THE ELDERLY

Established alongside Medicare in 1965, Medicaid has served the health care needs of the poor. Although intended as a supplement for those unable to obtain coverage from private and other public programs, Medicaid has become a key component of the national health care system. According to a report from the Kaiser Family Foundation, about one of six dollars spent on personal medical care and about half of every dollar spent on long-term care comes from Medicaid.[64] It covers a broad population of low-income Americans, including many elderly.

Medicaid consists of separate programs for each of the 50 states and the District of Columbia. Financing comes from both the federal government and the states, and states administer the programs with oversight from the federal government. Like the Original Medicare plan, Medicaid takes the form of fee-for-service. States pay healthcare providers for the services they give to Medicaid patients. Eligibility for Medicaid is based on having income and assets below a limit set by the states, but federal matching to the states requires that they cover certain mandatory populations: Pregnant women and children under six qualify with higher income than older children and other parents. In all, Medicaid covers about 39 million low-income children and parents. It also covers many persons who cannot work or who do not have health insurance.

Medicaid also covers medical services of many elderly. Seven million low-income Medicare beneficiaries, about one in five, are enrolled in Medicaid. Medicaid provides some services (such as vision, dental, and home health care) that Medicare does not provide, and it helps pay for Medicare premiums. It also has less stringent rules to qualify for home-care services. Most important, however, Medicaid covers long-term care. According to the Kaiser Family Foundation, "In 2003, Medicaid financed 40 percent of the $151 billion spent nationally on long-term care."[65]

Most recipients of these long-term care benefits are old, which makes Medicaid a crucial source of funding for the elderly. Statistics for 2000 demonstrate the expense of nursing home care: It costs about $40,000 a year in Atlanta and $107,000 in New York City. Only 8 percent of these costs come from Medicare (for short-term stays), and 23 percent come from private payment. The rest of the payments, 69 percent, come from Medicaid.

To obtain benefits for long-term care, however, older persons must have income below the limits. In general, this means they must spend down all but $2,000 of their assets. Until 1988, couples had to spend down nearly all their assets to qualify for Medicaid coverage, even if only one spouse needed nursing home care. However, Congress passed a law that year to prevent spousal impoverishment. The house, automobile, and household goods are not counted when a couple applies to receive Medicaid coverage for nursing home care of one spouse. The healthy spouse can keep one-half of the remaining assets without it counting toward the limit for Medicaid eligibility. The spouse's income also does not count against the income limit for the spouse in the nursing home facility. These rules allow those needing nursing home care to get help from Medicaid while allowing the spouse to avoid poverty.

Many view even this revised requirement as unfair and degrading—it forces sick and elderly persons into poverty before they get the care they need. Those familiar enough with the system can often get around these restrictions. According to one expert, "Virtually anyone, regardless of income or assets can qualify for Medicaid's long-term care benefits quickly by sheltering or divesting assets."[66] Moving funds to help older persons qualify for Medicaid benefits requires the help of a lawyer to create trusts, change titles to property, and transfer assets to children. Yet using legal advice on how to protect assets puts the elderly in a position of hiding or giving away what they have accumulated.

Funding Problems of Medicare and Medicaid

In general, Medicare patients seem satisfied with the program. According to a 1997 survey sponsored by the Kaiser/Commonwealth Fund, 57 percent of Medicare beneficiaries said they were very satisfied and 27 percent said they were satisfied.[67] Those with the worst health problems and the lowest income face special problems, but most recognize the value of government-supported health care. More recent polls indicate satisfaction with the new prescription drug benefit (Plan D). A survey of persons age 65 and over that was sponsored by the U.S. Chamber of Commerce found that "A large majority of seniors (84 percent) enrolled in the Medicare prescription drug program are satisfied with their drug coverage and a majority (52 percent) say they are enjoying a significant cost savings."[68]

The problems of Medicare and the threats to the rights of elderly beneficiaries come from efforts to control costs. Like Social Security, Medicare faces rising costs from a growing aging population. In addition, Medicare faces special costs from rising medical expenses. With a rate of spending growth that exceeds the rate for Social Security, Medicare will face a funding crisis sooner.

Possible Solutions to Control Medicare Costs

Neither Congress nor the president has addressed the problem of rising costs with comprehensive reform, but they have made some modest changes to slow rising costs. Many options for change remain, but most generate controversy over the ability to meet the health care rights of the elderly. Six possible solutions are discussed at length below.

First, Congress has over the years attempted to control costs by cutting payments made to doctors, hospitals, and other providers who treat Medicare patients. The proposed 2007 budget continues this strategy. As summarized in a story from the *Washington Post*, President George W. Bush proposed some major cuts in Medicare:

> *Some of the institutions affected most would be hospitals, nursing homes, home health agencies and other providers, whose Medicare payments would be more than $61 billion lower than anticipated over five years (although still higher overall). Bush also proposes automatic across-the-board cuts in provider payments if Medicare spending reaches certain levels for two consecutive years. His budget would not forestall a planned 10 percent cut in Medicare payments to doctors next year.[69]*

Democratic opponents of the president, however, said such cuts will impair the quality of Medicare service, and Congress rejected the proposal.

Physicians and hospital administrators also express opposition to the cuts. Many have complained for years that the fee schedules for Medicare reimbursements fall short of physician and hospital costs. The low reimbursements also entail extensive paperwork and administrative costs, leading one physician to say that there is now "such a complex maze of Medicare rules and regulations that compliance is practically impossible."[70] Some doctors worry that the rules on what Medicare will and will not pay for prevent them from fully meeting the needs of their patients.

As a result, some physicians have opted out of Medicare, agreeing to see older patients only through a special private contract to receive personal payments. The American Medical Association (AMA) reported on results of an online poll in 2006 that showed 29 percent of physicians planned to reduce the number of Medicare beneficiaries they take on in response to cuts in reimbursements.[71] Continued cuts in payments to hospitals and doctors might reduce the choices for care available to Medicare patients and their right to quality treatment.

As a second proposed solution, changes might include increasing the premiums, copayments, and deductible payments that Medicare requires for many services. As of January 1, 2008, high-income elderly (those receiving more than $82,000 for an individual, $164,000 for a couple) began to pay higher premiums than others for Medicare Part B. Since the wealthy can afford to make higher payments, it seems wasteful to provide benefits to the rich. However, critics believe that such a plan sets up a two-tier system. If the wealthy pay more, they will lose interest in Medicare and no longer will give political support to the program. Medicare could end up resembling a welfare program rather than an insurance program.

Experience has shown much resistance to raising costs for the elderly. The Catastrophic Health Care Act of 1988 aimed to protect elderly patients from having to spend all their income and assets for long-term care by having Medicare cover much of the cost. However, rather than tax workers (as Medicare and Social Security do), the new program was funded by a tax paid largely by high-income Medicare beneficiaries. Seniors having to pay the extra amount objected so strongly that Congress repealed the legislation in 1989. Raising premiums for the well off may produce similar problems now.

Third, Medicare has attempted in recent years to control costs by encouraging more market competition among providers. The Medicare Advantage plans, which allow Medicare patients to receive treatment by HMOs and PPOs, reflect this strategy; so does the Part D coverage of prescription drugs. Original Medicare relies on a fee-for-service system in which the government reimburses hospitals and physicians chosen by Medicare patients for the services the patients receive. In contrast, Medicare Advantage plans rely on private companies that compete for patients and, ideally, provide quality care while also keeping costs low and using resources efficiently.

However, managed plans have not yet realized the cost-saving goals. The government initially offered incentives for beneficiaries to enroll in managed plans, but the incentives made the cost for an HMO plan higher than for a traditional plan. As Jane Bryant Quinn says, "In fact, private HMOs can't even compete with Medicare unless they get large government subsidies."[72] Critics say that competition has backfired in another way. Managed plans compete for the healthiest Medicare beneficiaries who cost the least to treat. By some accounts, the plans require more out-of-pocket expenses for sicker beneficiaries and discourage them from enrolling.

Fourth, Medicare could restrict the treatments made available to patients. Some high-tech tests, innovative treatments, and new drugs are expensive but may have less value than other tests, treatments, and drugs that clearly save lives. Medicare covers treatments that are reasonable and necessary but it has not stringently defined these terms. If it did, the restrictions could reduce costs. However, elderly patients would likely view these changes as violations of their rights to quality medical care. A backlash could result from denying patients care that the elderly and their doctors believe are needed. Once stories of mistreatment get the public's attention, Congress would be unlikely to keep treatment restrictions in place.

In fact, pressures to expand rather than contract Medicare remain strong. The recently implemented and expensive Medicare Prescription Drug plan illustrates the government responsiveness to demands for more services. Other demands for expanded coverage may also lead to new legislation. For example, many have called for Congress to eliminate the need for the elderly to rely on Medicaid rather than Medicare for the costs of long-term care. Given the expense of funding long-term care and the failure of the Catastrophic Coverage Act in 1988, Congress has been unwilling to consider such a change. However, pressures remain to find ways to deal with this problem.

Still other pressures exist to have Medicare pay for more home care services. Many disabled elderly persons can live at home with daily nursing help, home care visitors, or assisted living, but Medicaid and Medicare cover such costs only for a short time period. Local services such as Meals on Wheels, adult day care, and special housing can help but are fragmented and difficult to obtain. Without Medicare or Medicaid coverage of home care, many elderly persons must move to institutions to get the help they need. Gerontologist Erdman Palmore estimates that "up to one third of the residents of institutions could be cared for at home as well as, or better than, they are in institutions if there were someone willing to do so and if there were proper community support services available."[73] Critics say health care for the elderly has become too oriented toward nursing home care and, given the high costs of nursing home care, expanded coverage for assisted living or home care ultimately might save money. In the short run, however, it would increase costs.

Fifth, Congress could pass legislation that raises the age of eligibility for Medicare. Although the normal age of retirement is rising for Social Security (up to age 67 for those born in 1960 and after), Medicare eligibility remains at age 65. Extending the age to match that for Social Security would save money but also reduce needed coverage. Many early retirees approaching age 65 lack health care coverage. Advocates call for extending Medicare coverage to those ages 55–64 rather than raising the age of eligibility.

Sixth, the government could raise taxes for Medicare. The hospital insurance program (Part A) is funded primarily by payroll taxes, while the Supplemental Medical Insurance program (Part B) and the Prescription Drug Program (Part D) are funded in part from premiums (25 percent) and part from general revenues (75 percent). Part C, the Medicare Advantage Plan receives funds from both the Part A and Part B trust funds. Raising payroll and income taxes would help pay for rising Medicare costs. Yet, the public has rarely shown support for higher taxes of either type. Such changes are likely to occur only when the funding problems become even more serious.

The Debate over Rationing

One other option to deal with funding problems of Medicare has raised complex philosophical and medical questions about the rights of the elderly. This option involves rationing health care by age, or restricting the services, treatments, and expenditures for elderly persons. Given that resources for medical care cannot meet the needs of all patients, rationing in some form already exists. Insurance companies will not pay for some experimental treatments, physicians balance cost and return for the treatments they approve, and hospitals use triage to care first for those in most urgent need. However, age-based rationing would involve something more: It would devote more resources to younger people who have many years of potential life remaining rather than to older persons who, even with treatment, can expect to die sooner. Although still a debated possibility rather than a formal policy, age-based rationing has the potential to affect the health care rights of the elderly.

Those favoring age-based rationing do not have animus against the elderly. Rather, they believe that, when forced to choose, the young deserve more health care resources. Seniors have lived a long life, and young people deserve the same—to enjoy what their elders have already enjoyed. Rationing then becomes a matter of fairness and sharing. Treatments of young people with life-threatening diseases will help them live many more decades and reach old age. In contrast, older people have a high probability of dying anyway, so treatments for the same disease will not let them live as long as young people. This does not devalue the elderly but simply considers the expected benefits of expensive medical procedures.

Introduction to Rights of the Elderly

Professor Eric Rakowski makes the following analogy: If there is only one cornea available for a transplant, should it be given to someone who has sight in one eye or to a blind person who has sight in neither eye? Both would benefit from the transplant, but the blind person would clearly benefit more. As reasonable people would choose to help the blind person, they should also choose to help those with the greater potential years yet to live. If a 90 year old and a 20 year old would benefit similarly from a scarce drug, the 20 year old should then have priority.[74]

Former Colorado governor Richard Lamm makes the case for rationing from a policy perspective. He says that the country cannot sustain the system of offering nearly free health care to the elderly. As modern medical treatments, problems, and drugs have become expensive, policies should set reasonable and fair limits on health care spending. Since most such spending goes toward the elderly, they would face the most rationing. Lamm famously and controversially said in 1984 that terminally ill elderly people have "a duty to die and get out of the way."[75] More recently, Lamm and coauthor Robert Blank have made the case in less inflammatory language: "The battle against death should not be permitted to hijack a disproportionate share of finite public resources needed elsewhere in society to raise or protect people's quality of life."[76]

Philosopher Daniel Callahan also makes more specific—and controversial recommendations—concerning the aged. In his 1987 book, *Setting Limits*, he suggested that the government not pay for expensive life-extending treatments past age 70 or 80.[77] Health care at these old ages should involve routine care and easing of pain, but not much more. Otherwise, the elderly will use resources that could go to those who have yet to live out a normal life span. Callahan further suggests that rationing health care will lead to a better quality of life and more noble purpose at the oldest ages.

Opponents to rationing reject the use of age as a criterion for medical care, much as they reject it as a criterion for employment. They say that age by itself has little relationship with value to society, future accomplishment, or need for treatment. Claiming that a young person's life deserves saving more than an older person's life is ageist. The claim relies on negative stereotypes about the elderly—they are slow to benefit from treatment, generally sick and likely to die anyway, and able to contribute little to society. True, the country spends more health care resources on the elderly, but this simply results from their needs. The country also pays more for education of the young, again simply because they need it more. It is a matter of justice that older persons get the health care they need.

If rationing becomes necessary, opponents say it should be done in an age-neutral manner. Experts could rank a list of treatments in order of effectiveness, regardless of age. Physicians could then use the highest ranked first and avoid a treatment expected to extend life for only a few months or years. Extraordinary efforts for comatose patients on life support systems or terminally ill patients in severe pain would have lowest priority. Decisions would be based on the ability of patients to benefit from the treatments but not on age alone.

RIGHT TO EQUAL TREATMENT

Whether or not rationing by age is justified, it already may occur. It informally takes the form of discrimination against the elderly in health care. Those concerned about ageism in health care say that providers tend to make assumptions about health based on a patient's age rather than medical needs. For instance, they may view complaints of older patients about pain or lack of energy as a normal part of aging rather than a condition to treat. Older patients sent away with more medication or advice to rest receive less treatment than younger patients receive. The elderly receive 35-45 percent of all prescription drugs, leading some to say they are overmedicated.

Mistreatment shows in other ways. According to the Alliance for Aging Research, elderly persons get less aggressive treatment for heart disease and cancer—even though 80 percent of all fatal heart attacks and 60 percent of all cancer deaths occur to persons age 65 and older.[78] Other studies report that older persons are less likely than younger persons to get aspirin, beta-blockers, and clot dissolving drugs that prevent heart attacks; patients age 75 and over receive less aggressive chemotherapy or radiation cancer treatment. Older women face even greater discrimination than men do. For example, older women are less likely to receive heart bypass surgery, kidney dialysis, and transplants than older men and receive less adequate care for breast cancer than younger women. Physicians say in defense that studies offer little guidance on the effectiveness of many new heart disease and cancer treatments for older people. Yet that gap in evidence indicates the importance of including older persons in trials of treatment effectiveness.

Studies also find that the elderly receive inadequate attention for disease prevention. According to a 2003 report from the Centers for Disease Control (CDC), 90 percent of older persons go without appropriate screenings for hearing loss, heart problems, bone loss, and colorectal, prostate, and breast cancers.[79] Health care providers also do too little to identify and treat dependence on alcohol and prescription drugs among the elderly. Although many elderly persons have addiction problems, physicians often do not expect or look for them. The elderly can further benefit from more counseling to stop smoking, start exercising, and eat right, but they may not get it.

As part of the problem, too few physicians, nurses, pharmacists, medical social workers, and physician's assistants specialize in geriatrics. They consequently have little understanding of the special circumstances of elderly patients. By one account, "There are presently only 9,000 geriatricians in the United States compared to 42,000 pediatricians."[80] Another statistic further illustrates the problem: "Only about 10 percent of U.S. medical schools require course work or rotations in geriatric medicine."[81] Without specialized training, providers cannot fully understand the medical needs and problems of elderly patients. Indeed, given the low rates of reimbursement for Medicare plus the difficult medical conditions of some elderly patients, many health care providers prefer not to deal with elderly patients.

Although they do not always get it, the elderly deserve the right to appropriate treatment for the health problems. The Alliance for Aging Research makes several recommendations to handle this problem:

- More training and education for health care professionals in the field of geriatrics.
- Greater inclusion of older Americans in clinical trials.
- Utilization of appropriate screening and preventive measures for older Americans.
- Empowerment and education of older Americans. [82]

The last recommendation focuses on older persons themselves. They can do more to report their problems to health care providers rather than assume they are a normal part of aging. They need to know that many ailments can be treated and that they deserve first-rate medical care.

THE RIGHT TO REFUSE TREATMENT

Along with the right to obtain treatment, the elderly have the right to refuse treatment. The law requires informed consent from patients, which means that health care providers must explain proposed treatments and get patient permission. The doctrine of informed consent includes the right to refuse treatment. Like others, elderly persons should decide what others can do to their bodies. Hospitals thus ask patients to sign release forms giving health care providers the right to treat them in certain ways.

When unconscious, brain damaged, or severely sick, patients cannot give informed consent for treatment and something more is needed. The Patient Self-Determination Act of 1990 therefore requires hospitals, nursing homes, and other health care organizations receiving Medicare or Medicaid payments to inform patients about their rights in making treatment choices. These rights include directing ahead of time how they want to be treated if incapacitated (in a coma, for example) and typically involve signing an advance directive. Advance directives may include the choice to refuse treatment and to reject extraordinary measures or artificial life supports. For example, they can include an order not to resuscitate when a patient's heart or breathing stops. They can take the form of a living will that states their treatment preferences or a power of attorney that gives a guardian the right to make treatment decisions. They can also take the form of a simple statement of preferences kept on file by health care providers.

These rights have limits, however. While the dying process should not be unduly prolonged, the right to refuse treatment in most states cannot take the form of suicide. Under certain conditions, terminally ill patients can refuse treatment. Those not terminally ill, however, do not have the right to refuse treatment if it would lead to death. Complex legal and ethical issues surround debates over euthanasia, but laws aim to protect depressed patients from harming themselves and unscrupulous healthcare providers from harming patients through lack of treatment. Even without a clear right to die, however, older persons can still make reasoned judgments about the kinds of treatment or nontreatment they would like when near death.

RIGHTS INVOLVING ELDER CARE

At the oldest ages, persons often need more than medical care. They also need custodial care—help with daily activities of bathing, eating, cleaning, moving about, and taking medicine. Sometimes such care comes from a spouse, nearby family members, or community assistance programs. When they need still more care, older persons may move to an assisted-living residence or nursing home. Assisted living allows residents to have their own house or apartment but also receive services for food preparation, housekeeping, bathing, and dressing. On-call services available 24 hours a day also offer emergency help.

Custodial nursing homes provide more intensive care and monitoring than assisted living but differ from hospitals in not providing continuous skilled medical care. They best suit the severely disabled or mentally impaired elderly and accordingly offer less independence. Only 4–5 percent of persons age 65 and over live in nursing homes, making it far from common (and disproving stereotypes about the elderly). When viewed from a different perspective, however, usage appears higher. By some estimates, about 40 percent of older persons will spend some time in a nursing home during their life, most likely in the last years before death.

Elderly who depend on care by others are vulnerable to mistreatment. The mistreatment may come from family members or nursing home staff and in some cases becomes serious enough to be labeled as abuse. Sick, disabled, and mentally impaired elderly have little defense against this mistreatment. They sometimes can do little on their own, remain isolated from the community, and have trouble communicating with those who could protect them. Protection against such elder abuse has become a legal right of the elderly.

Introduction to Rights of the Elderly

WHAT IS ELDER ABUSE?

The American Psychological Association (APA) defines elder abuse as "the infliction of physical, emotional, or psychological harm on an older adult."[83] It can take several forms:

- Physical abuse such as slapping, beating, overmedicating, restraining with ropes, or depriving of food or medication.
- Emotional or psychological abuse such as yelling, threatening, ignoring, treating as a child, belittling, or causing emotional distress.
- Caregiver neglect such as failing to help with daily needs, cleanliness, paying bills, or withholding attention.
- Abandonment or desertion by a caregiver in a hospital, nursing home, or shopping mall.
- Financial exploitation such as stealing money, making inappropriate purchases, or selling unneeded products.

Physical abuse such as hitting, slapping, and using physical restraints occur less often; neglect, verbal and emotional abuse, and financial exploitation are more common. In addition, elderly persons may sometimes neglect themselves to the point that it threatens their health and safety. Filthy homes, dehydration, inadequate clothing, and untreated medical conditions that follow from self-neglect indicate the need for assistance.

Stories of abuse dramatically illustrate the problem. Senator Christopher Bond of Missouri tells of an elderly Kansas City woman whose husband has been charged with abuse. Police discovered the woman, who weighed only 65 pounds, could barely speak, and was covered with bedsores, left lying on the floor and unable to move. She said her husband left her there when he went to work. The APA gives other examples of physical and financial abuse: A 55-year-old woman, Emily, cared for her 85-year-old widowed mother as well as her husband and college-age daughter. When things got tense, Emily found herself yelling at her mother and once even slapped her. In another example, while taking care of her 90-year-old father, Lorraine wrote checks from her father's account and transferred a good part of his assets into her account. Having given his daughter control over his finances, the father knew nothing of the checks and transfers.[84]

How do these kinds of abuse relate to the rights of the elderly? A variety of state laws and two federal laws offer protection. First, all 50 states have laws to prevent and punish various forms of elder abuse. Some forms of elder abuse such as hitting and stealing fall under long-standing laws against assault, battery, and theft. Other forms of emotional abuse and neglect require separate laws, however. States have responded by improving laws on reporting. The state of Missouri, for example, passed the Senior Care and

Protection Act of 2003, which made it a felony to conceal abuse or neglect. With information on abuse, state and local social service and police agencies can respond. States have another weapon against abuse in nursing homes. Along with U.S. attorneys, they can prosecute cases of elder abuse under laws against Medicare and Medicaid fraud. Since abuse of Medicare and Medicaid patients violates allowable uses of government funds for health care, nursing home operators that mistreat patients can face fraud charges and penalties.

Second, the 1987 Nursing Home Reform Act responded to complaints that some nursing homes abused, neglected, and gave inadequate care to their patients. The law required that, in order to receive Medicare and Medicaid patients, nursing homes must get state certification of compliance with minimum standards of care. The standards include regularly assessing the well-being and needs of each patient, setting up a comprehensive care plan for each patient based on their needs, and providing access to nursing, rehabilitation, good nutrition, and pharmaceutical services. Nursing homes with more than 120 beds also must have a social worker. The law prevents "warehousing" of patients, or providing little more than a room, a bed, and food.

The law also established a bill of rights for nursing home residents. A report from the AARP lists these rights:

- The right to freedom from abuse, mistreatment, and neglect;
- The right to freedom from physical restraints;
- The right to privacy;
- The right to accommodation of medical, physical, psychological, and social needs;
- The right to participate in resident and family groups;
- The right to be treated with dignity;
- The right to exercise self-determination;
- The right to communicate freely;
- The right to participate in the review of one's care plan, and to be fully informed in advance about any changes in care, treatment, or change of status in the facility; and
- The right to voice grievances without discrimination or reprisal.[85]

Since the rights mean little without enforcement, the certification includes monitoring whether nursing homes provide these rights.

States have responsibility for certification and follow several steps to ensure compliance. State agents are expected to visit nursing homes at least once every 15 months and evaluate the quality of care, services provided to patients, and well-being of the residents. The agents also use visits to investigate complaints. Nursing homes found to be out of compliance face several sanctions. They might have to set up a plan of correction, send their staff through training and education, pay fines, lose payments for Medicare and Medicaid patients, or replace the management. In one case, the U.S. attorney prosecuted a nursing home chain for fraud under the False Claims Act. Since the nursing home corporation submitted claims to Medicare and Medicaid for services it had not provided, it had committed fraud. To settle the suit, the company ended up paying a $250,000 fine and submitting to ongoing monitoring.

Third, the reauthorization of the Older Americans Act in 1992 created a new provision for protecting the elderly from abuse. The law strengthened the Long-Term Care Ombudsman Program to investigate complaints and advocate on behalf of the elderly. It also gave funds to states for preventing elder abuse. A 2000 amendment to the act added more funds for the goal of fostering coordination across state courts and law enforcement agencies.

THE EXTENT OF ABUSE

Statistics have shown that elder abuse is a serious problem. According to Senator Christopher Bond, "There are studies that report that 4 to 6 percent of America's seniors may at some time become victims of some form of abuse or neglect. Others estimate that there are anywhere from 500,000 to 5 million victims each year."[86] Many settle on an annual figure of 2.1 million victims. Worse, the problem appears to be increasing. From 2000 to 2004, elder abuse reports rose by 19.7 percent, and substantiated cases rose by 15.6 percent.[87] Likely the problem is even more serious than the statistics imply: Only a small proportion of elder abuse is reported—just 16 percent according to one study.

Most elder abuse, about two-thirds of the total, comes from family members such as a spouse or adult child. Family violence may have existed for many years, with elder abuse continuing the pattern; abusive parents or spouses may themselves become victims of abuse when old. However, pressures brought about by problems of old age may create new abuse. The difficulty of caring for a disabled family member may trigger anger. Children taking parents into their home, spouses seeing a loved one change from independence to helplessness, and family members facing burdens of constant care bear difficult and frustrating challenges. Personal problems such as alcohol abuse, financial difficulties, and job demands worsen the pressures leading to abusive relationships.

Other factors heighten the potential for elder abuse. Complete dependence of older persons on caregivers makes it difficult for victims to defend themselves. The isolation of older persons from people outside the family makes it hard to get help. Perhaps ageism leads younger caregivers to devalue the emotional and physical needs of the elderly, to treat them as helpless, defenseless, and unworthy of respect. Those who are sick, dependent, and needing care may seem less than human in a youth-oriented society that values independence and vigor. Motives for financial exploitation are more straightforward: Guardians often want the extra money they can obtain from older persons and may feel they deserve it.

Even one-time powerful people face abuse during old age. Take the example of Brooke Astor, a famous leader of New York high society and patron of the arts. According to a 2006 story reported in the *New York Daily News*, "Astor, now 104, is allegedly being kept inside her dilapidated Park Ave. duplex by her only child, Anthony Marshall—who controls her $45 million fortune, yet refuses to spend money for her care."[88] Diagnosed with Alzheimer's disease, Astor suffered from memory loss, heart problems, anemia, and other ailments. Citing abuse, her grandson, Philip Marshall, sued to have his father, Anthony Marshall, removed as the guardian. A judge approved moving Astor to a hospital for treatment and later to her estate in Briarcliff Manor, New York. Still later, Anthony Marshall, who received $2.3 million a year for caring for his mother, faced accusations of diverting $1 million of Astor's money into theatrical productions. A ruling from the New York State Supreme Court later concluded that claims of elder abuse had not been substantiated. Astor died in August 2007 at age 105.

The Brooke Astor story illustrates the special vulnerability of older women, who are more often abused than men. They typically live longer than men, face greater disability during the oldest ages, and are more likely to be in a position of dependence. Women also are perceived to be less able to defend themselves. Indeed, elder abuse may continue spousal abuse that occurred against wives at younger ages, making discrimination and violence against women a problem that occurs at all ages.

Abuse also occurs in nursing homes, but less often than in family homes because a smaller proportion of the elderly live in institutions and the government makes greater efforts to inspect them. However, the problem of abuse remains. According to government figures, one of four nursing homes is cited each year for causing death or serious injury to a resident.[89] A report from the General Accounting Office on nursing homes in California found similar problems: "Between 1995 and 1998, state surveyors cited 30 percent of nursing homes in California for violations that put residents in immediate jeopardy or caused actual harm to residents. Another 33 percent of facilities were cited with substandard conditions that caused less serious harm, and another 35 percent had more than minimal deficiencies. Only 2 percent of California facilities were found to have minimal or no deficiencies."[90]

In one case reported by CBS News, the children of one nursing home resident, Helen Love, found their mother with bruises on her neck, chin, and legs.[91] Although the nursing home denied any injuries, the children brought their mother to an emergency room where doctors discovered a dislocated neck and broken ribs. An angry nurse's assistant at the nursing home later admitted hitting Love when she soiled her clothes. In another case described at a government hearing, the nursing home caring for Thelma Magruder would not permit her granddaughter, Katie Misuraca, to visit.[92] After hiring a lawyer and obtaining a court order to allow visitation, Misuraca found her grandmother to have some unexplained and serious injuries. Diagnosed with four broken ribs, three crushed vertebrae, and a shoe-shaped bruise on her back, Magruder ultimately died from the injuries. Known cases of such physical attacks are rare but illustrate the potential for violence.

Mistreatment in nursing homes more commonly involves neglect and emotional abuse by staff that comes from stressful working conditions. A shortage of workers makes it difficult to care adequately for patients. Low pay and the demanding tasks of caring for uncooperative patients may lead to frustration among the staff. According to a 2002 survey conducted by the American Health Care Association, turnover of certified nurse assistant positions had reached 71 percent and turnover of other staff had reached 50 percent.[93] A high quit rate in turn leads to vacancies: The survey also reported a nursing home shortage of 96,000 full-time-equivalent health care professionals.

Another problem relates to the use of physical and chemical restraints. When patients risk a serious fall from walking, physical restraints keep them in their chair or bed. When patients risk slipping accidentally from a chair or falling from a bed, physical restrains can prevent injury. However, caregivers should use straps on chairs and beds for arms and legs only as a last resort, when needed to protect the physical safety of the resident. Chemical restraints refer to drugs used to control patient behavior. When prescribed to ease delusions, severe mood swings, and behaviors that threaten self and others, drugs serve a valuable purpose. When used for the convenience of staff, they may lead to abuse. Drugs keeping patients inactive, drowsy, and compliant, perhaps even to get them to accept physical restraints, lead to a form of neglect. Like physical restraints, these chemical restraints should be used only as a last resort.

PREVENTION

The extent of elder abuse highlights the need for effective enforcement. Laws exist to improve nursing home quality and prevent elder abuse, but enforcing the laws is difficult. Most abuse stays hidden inside homes or behind closed doors in nursing homes. Abusers may threaten their victims with reprisals if they tell anyone. Along with fear, the embarrassment of admitting to being abused and the desire to protect abusive family members also keep victims quiet. Sometimes mentally impaired victims have trouble speaking coherently about their abuse.

More frequent and thorough inspections of nursing homes, stronger penalties, and a sustained commitment to correcting the problems would help prevent some forms of abuse. Yet it is expensive to hire more inspectors and prosecute violators. To improve detection, prevention, and prosecution of elder abuse, Congress has introduced, although not yet passed, the Elder Justice Act of 2007. The act will create a new office in the Department of Health and Human Services to collect and disseminate data on the problem and make grants to state Adult Protective Services agencies. Even with more inspections and investigations, however, prosecutors have difficulty proving elder abuse. Victims may hesitate to testify or do poorly as witnesses. Enforcement agencies must gather evidence from a variety of sources, including medical documentation and eyewitness accounts, to prosecute elder abuse successfully.

Adult protective services agencies in each state have hotlines for reporting elder abuse. They respond to legitimate complaints by assigning a caseworker to investigate (within 24 hours for emergencies) and intervening to help move older persons to a place of safety. The agencies also report violations of nursing home laws to enforcement agencies. Other resources for reporting elder abuse include local long-term care ombudsmen or state representatives of the National Citizen's Coalition for Nursing Home Reform.

Given the private nature of elder abuse, prevention must also depend on education. Older persons should know that they can talk to doctors, members of the clergy, and friends about mistreatment or abuse. Neighbors, friends, and others should learn about elder abuse so they can report suspected incidents to authorities. Family members can help by carefully selecting nursing homes for older relatives. They should know that a Medicare- and Medicaid-certified nursing home meets certain health and safety requirements; that nursing homes with care for special health, medical, and psychological needs limit the potential for abuse; and that staff should include a full-time registered nurse on duty at all times, a social worker, and a doctor who can be reached when needed. Of course, the staff should also show respect and kindness to patients.

Caregivers can also benefit from education. Those who feel the urge to abuse someone in their care need some relief from the demands of care or counseling to help deal with their anger. Nursing home aids need training and monitoring to prevent abuse, and those caring for loved ones at home likewise can benefit from training and monitoring.

Education efforts need to address a problem related to elder abuse—consumer fraud. Unethical telemarketing firms appeal to older persons by promising valuable prizes, special promotions, cheap prices, help for charities, or large returns on an investment. The callers often use high-pressure or scare tactics to get naïve customers to pay money. Sometimes phone calls can lead older persons to give out Social Security numbers, credit card numbers, and bank information that then are used for identify theft. Door-to-door salespeople sometimes use similar tactics.

Unfortunately, the elderly appear particularly prone to deceptive offers. By some accounts, nearly one-third of all telemarketing fraud victims are age 60 or older. According to the Justice Department, fraud operators target their scams at the elderly for several reasons. Older persons are more trusting of what people promise, are more apt to be at home to take calls, and are more often alone and willing to talk to telemarketers. Financial fears also motivate older persons. By making false promises of profit, telemarketers appeal to fears of the elderly that they will outlive their savings and to desires to leave something for children and grandchildren. One convicted telemarketer said he became a millionaire by appealing to the loneliness, financial insecurities, and pride of elderly persons. After gaining their confidence, he would keep trying to get them to invest money. If victims eventually stopped paying, he would threaten to shame them by telling family members and neighbors about the lost money.

Experts make several recommendations for older consumers: Never accept prizes over the phone, never respond immediately to a sales pitch over the phone, and never give out private information to phone solicitors. The same recommendations apply to Internet solicitations. If unsure of the legitimacy of a solicitation, call the National Fraud Information Center, the Better Business Bureau, or the National Do Not Call Registry. Perhaps most important, recognize that some telemarketers and Internet contacts are hardened criminals rather than friendly sales people.

THE FUTURE OF RIGHTS OF THE ELDERLY

Pressures to expand or at least better enforce rights of the elderly likely will continue in the next decades. Concerns about violations of the rights of the elderly are reinforced by concerns about violations of the rights of other groups—women, racial and ethnic minorities, gays and lesbians, immigrants, children, the poor, and the disabled. Modern societies tend to strengthen individual and group rights, including those of the elderly.

In addition, demographic forces give the elderly some advantages in protecting and expanding their rights. The size of the aged population will expand as the baby-boom generation continues to grow older. This generation will live longer than any previous ones and take advantage of new medical treatments and healthy lifestyles known to increase longevity. Healthier and more active than previous generations, boomers can create new roles for old age. In so doing, they can do much to improve their rights.

First, the elderly will add to their political power in the future. Compared to young people, older people vote at higher rates, take more interest in politics and elections, and effectively represent their interests. They further belong to large and influential organizations such as AARP that represent the elderly in Washington, D.C., and state and local governments. Combining activism with growing size will strengthen the political influence of the elderly. With size comes diversity, and the elderly have varied political beliefs, splitting their votes between Republicans and Democrats much as younger groups do. However, in dealing with issues affecting their rights—issues that join rather than divide interests—the elderly can do much to shape legislation. Since the 1960s, the baby boomers have transformed the politics and culture of the nation; they can do much the same in the 21st century as they reach old age.

Second, the elderly will increase their economic power. They will bring more wealth into old age than previous generations. Along with Social Security, future retirees can rely on private pensions, 401(k) accounts, IRAs, and stock investments. Many will have retirement income earned by both spouses. Spending income for travel, leisure, hobbies, and lifestyle will make the elderly a lucrative market for goods and services. Not all the elderly fit this picture of affluence—large numbers with debt, little personal savings, and inadequate private pensions face poverty in old age and dependence on Social Security. With great wealth comes great inequality. Even so, the economic power of the elderly gives weight to demands for expansion and enforcement of their rights.

Third, the elderly will change retirement into a stage of life that involves more activity than in the past. The traditional division of life into three stages—education, work, and retirement—no longer fits. Many retire from their jobs well before the normal retirement age, but keep active with part-time work, consulting, volunteering, and traveling. People tend to have multiple careers, some of which begin near old age, especially now that the length of life gives people time to try new work and activities. The trend toward more flexible patterns of work and retirement suggests the need for more flexible hiring practices. Employers need to do more to take advantage of the skills and interests of the elderly, particularly those vigorous and motivated during the early parts of old age. The desires for continued work will translate into greater demands of the elderly for protection against discrimination.

An aging population that is politically organized, economically powerful, and active in work and community life will gain authority in pressing for its rights. Involvement in politics, consumer markets, and social life will further increase ties with younger generations. Such involvement can help combat stereotypes that lead to age discrimination. All these changes give grounds for optimism about the future well-being of the elderly.

Introduction to Rights of the Elderly

To balance pressures for expanded rights, however, concerns about the economic cost of supporting the elderly will also strengthen. Funding for Social Security, Supplemental Security Income, Medicare, Medicaid, and other public programs will certainly rise, if for no other reason than the elderly will make up a larger part of the population. With rising costs to support the elderly, many worry about the need to tax workers to pay for retirement and medical care of the elderly. Younger workers may come to resent paying higher taxes for affluent older persons. If so, some restrictions on the rights of the elderly may follow. Rights concerning access to work, protection of private pensions, and prevention of elder abuse will remain strong, but rights to public benefits may weaken.

Some make an even stronger case that government spending in general, and support for the elderly through Medicare and Social Security in particular, is unsustainable. Comptroller General David Walker of the Government Accountability Office, the nation's head accountant, says, "If the United States government conducts business as usual over the next few decades, a national debt that is already $8.5 trillion could reach $46 trillion or more, adjusted for inflation. That's almost as much as the total net worth of every person in America."[94] He believes that current excess spending and promises for future spending will gradually erode or even suddenly damage the economy, standard of living, and national security. Dealing with the problem requires changes in entitlements (especially Social Security and Medicare), cuts in spending, and tax reform. If fiscal problems are as serious as Walker suggests, economic rights of the elderly may contract rather than expand.

Such a scenario is less than certain, however. Others say that economic growth and changing patterns of work during old age may make it easier to absorb the extra cost of supporting a larger aged population. Indeed, they claim that doomsayers exaggerate the seriousness of the problem and instead call for strengthening Social Security and Medicare rather than restructuring the programs. Younger people should not view the potential costs and higher taxes as a burden but should see rights of the elderly as in their own interest. With better government support for elderly persons, the less family members must pay directly for living expenses, health care, and long-term care of elderly relatives. In this sense, strengthening the rights of the elderly can help all members of society.

---

[1] W. Andrew Achenbaum, Steven Weiland, and Carole Haber, *Key Words in Sociocultural Gerontology*. New York: Springer Publishing, 1996, p. 61.

[2] David Hackett Fischer, *Growing Old in America. Expanded Edition.* Oxford: Oxford University Press, 1978, pp. 26–76.

[3] Sarah Harper, *Aging Societies*. New York: Oxford University Press, 2006, p. 39.

[4] Quoted in Fischer, *Growing Old in America*, p. 67.

[5] Carole Haber and Brian Gratton, *Old Age and the Search for Security: An American Social History*. Bloomington: Indiana University Press, 1994, p. 6.

[6] Pat Thane, *Old Age in English History: Past Experiences, Present Issues*. Oxford: Oxford University Press, 2000, p. 279.

[7] Michael Harrington, *The Other America*. New York: Macmillan, 1962, p. 105.

[8] Harper, *Aging Societies*, p. 122.

[9] Robert J. Samuelson, "Off Golden Pond: The Aging of America and the Reinvention of Retirement," in Olivia J. Smith, ed., *Aging in America*. New York: H.W. Wilson, 2000, p. 16.

[10] Haber and Gratton, *Old Age and the Search for Security*, p. 45.

[11] W. Andrew Achenbaum, *Older Americans, Vital Communities*. Baltimore, Md.: Johns Hopkins University Press, 2005, p. 151.

[12] "Nursing Homes," AARP: Policy and Research for Professionals in Aging. Available online. URL: http://www.aarp.org/research/longtermcare/nursinghomes/aresearch-import-669-FS10R.html. Posted in February 2001.

[13] Achenbaum, Weiland, and Haber, *Key Words in Sociocultural Gerontology*, p. 74.

[14] Quoted in Jeffrey H. Birnbaum, "AARP Leads with Wallet in Fight over Social Security," *Washington Post*, March 30, 2005, p. A1. Also available online. URL: http://www.washingtonpost.com/wp-dyn/articles/A11076-2005Mar29.html. Posted on March 30, 2005.

[15] Robert N. Butler, "Ageism: Another Form of Bigotry," *Gerontologist*, vol. 9, no. 4, 1969, pp. 243–246.

[16] Robert N. Butler, *Why Survive: Being Old in America*. New York: Harper and Row, 1975, p. 6.

[17] Tim Parkin, "The Ancient Greek and Roman Worlds," in Pat Thane, ed., *A History of Old Age*. Los Angeles: J. Paul Getty Museum, 2005, p. 57.

[18] Robert N. Butler, "Ageism," in George L. Maddox, ed., *The Encyclopedia of Aging*. New York: Springer, 1995, p. 35.

[19] Achenbaum, Weiland, and Haber, *Key Words in Sociocultural Gerontology*, p. 17.

[20] Margaret L. Stecker, "Beneficiaries Prefer to Work," *Social Security Bulletin*, vol. 14, no. 1, 1951, p. 17.

[21] Lyndon B. Johnson, "Special Message to the Congress: Proposed Programs for Older Americans," The American Presidency Project. Available online. URL: http://www.presidency.ucsb.edu/ws/index.php?pid=28139. Accessed in February 2007.

[22] Achenbaum, Weiland, and Haber, *Key Words in Sociocultural Gerontology*, p. 19.

[23] Lawrence M. Friedman, "Age Discrimination Law: Some Remarks on the American Experience," in Sandra Fredman and Sarah Spencer, eds., *Age as an Equality Issue*. Portland, Ore.: Hart Publishing, 2003, p. 178.

[24] Friedman, "Age Discrimination Law," p. 177.

[25] Quoted in Friedman, "Age Discrimination Law," p. 189.

[26] Raymond F. Gregory, *Age Discrimination in the American Workplace: Old at a Young Age*. New Brunswick, N.J.: Rutgers University Press, 2001, p. 1.

[27] John Rotter, "Demographic Change and the Labor Market: What Are the Challenges We Are Facing?" AARP. Available online. URL: http://www.aarp.org/research/international/speeches/a2002-09-10-international_unece.html. Posted in September 2002.

[28] "Age Discrimination in Employment Act (ADEA) Charges FY 1997—FY 2006," Equal Employment Opportunity Commission. Available online. URL: http://www.eeoc.gov/stats/adea.html. Updated on January 31, 2007.

[29] "Age Discrimination in the Executive Job Market," ExecuNet. Available online. URL: http://www.clew.us/presspubs/AgeDiscrimination.pdf. Posted in 2003.

[30] John Helyar, "50 and Fired," *Fortune*, vol. 151, no. 10, May 16, 2005, pp. 78–90.

[31] Gregory, *Age Discrimination in the American Workplace*, p. 55.

[32] "Facts about Age Discrimination," U.S. Equal Employment Opportunity Commission. Available online. URL: http://www.eeoc.gov/facts/age.html. Updated on January 15, 1997.

[33] Gregory, *Age Discrimination in the American Workplace*, p. 75.

[34] Helyar, "50 and Fired," pp. 78–90.

[35] James Lardner, "Too Old to Write Code," *U.S. News & World Report*, vol. 124, March 16, 1998, pp. 39–40.

[36] "Age Discrimination in the Executive Job Market," ExecuNet.

[37] "Age Discrimination in Employment Act (ADEA) Charges FY 1997—FY 2006," U.S. Equal Employment Opportunity Commission.

[38] Richard A. Posner, *Aging and Old Age*. Chicago: University of Chicago Press, 1995, p. 331.

[39] Ira Carnahan, "Removing the Scarlet A: Age-Discrimination Laws Can Harm Older Job Hunters," *Forbes*, vol. 170, no. 3, August 12, 2002, p. 78.

[40] Marianne Lavelle, "On the Edge of Discrimination," *New York Times Magazine*, March 9, 1997, p. 69.

[41] John Macnicol, *Age Discrimination: An Historical and Contemporary Analysis*. Cambridge: Cambridge University Press, 2006, p. 242.

[42] Quoted in Posner, *Aging and Old Age*, p. 335.

[43] Gregory, *Age Discrimination in the American Workplace*, pp. 46–47.

[44] Gregory, *Age Discrimination in the American Workplace*, p. 84.

[45] Dan Seligman, "The Case for Age Discrimination," *Forbes*, vol. 164, no. 14, December 13, 1999, pp. 116–120.

[46] Posner, *Aging and Old Age*, p. 324.

[47] Kenneth Terrell, "When Experience Counts," *U.S. New & World Report*, vol. 140, no. 10, March 20, 2006, pp. 48–50.

[48] Ke Bin Wu, "Sources of Income for Older Persons in 2004," AARP Public Policy Institute. Available online. URL: http://assets.aarp.org/rgcenter/econ/dd148_income.pdf. Posted in November 2006.

[49] "Welcome to the PBGC," Pension Benefit Guaranty Corporation. Available online. URL: http://www.pbgc.gov. Accessed in February 2007.

[50] "Pension Pain," NOW with Bill Moyers, PBS Online. Available online. URL: http://www.pbs.org/now/politics/pensions.html. Posted on June 27, 2003.

[51] Larry Dignan, "Pension Gaps Drag Down Earnings," Wall Street Week with Fortune, PBS Online. Available online. URL: http://www.pbs.org/wsw/news/featurestory_20030422.html. Posted on August 22, 2003.

[52] "Interview: Bradley Belt," Frontline: Can You Afford to Retire?, PBS Online. Available online. URL: http://www.pbs.org/wgbh/pages/frontline/retirement/interviews/belt.html#1. Posted on May 16, 2006.

[53] Janice Revell, "Bye-Bye Pension: Soon Hundreds of Corporations May Slash Pensions by as Much as Half," CNNMoney.com. Available online. URL: http://money.cnn.com/magazines/fortune/fortune_archive/2003/03/17/339233/index.htm. Posted on March 17, 2003.

[54] Deloitte, "IBM's Cash Balance and Pension Equity Formulas Violate ERISA, District Court Rules," Benefits Link. Available online. URL: http://benefitslink.com/articles/washbull030804.html. Posted on August 4, 2003.

[55] "Pension Agency Reports Deficit of $18.1 Billion," MSNBC. Available online. URL: http://www.msnbc.msn.com/id/15730546. Posted on November 15, 2006.

[56] Quoted in "Bush Signs Massive Pension Overhaul," MSNBC. Available online. URL: http://www.msnbc.msn.com/id/14391251. Posted on August 22, 2006.

[57] Quoted in "Bush Signs Massive Pension Overhaul," MSNBC.

[58] Jane Bryant Quinn, "A Requiem for Pensions," *Newsweek*, vol. 148, no. 1/2, July 3–10, 2006, p. 53.

[59] "Signs of Pension Abuse," Know Your Pension. Available online. URL: http://www.knowyourpension.org/warningsigns.aspx. Accessed in February 2007.

[60] "Employment-Based Retirement Plan Participation: Geographic Differences and Trends, 2005," Employee Benefit Research Institute. Available online. URL: http://www.ebri.org/publications/ib/index.cfm?fa=ibDisp&content_id=3761. Posted in November 2006.

[61] "Women's Private Pension Reforms," Pension Rights Center Pension Policy. Available online. URL: http://www.pensionrights.org/policy/legislation/company_and_union_plans.html. Accessed in February 2007.

[62] "Your Medicare Rights and Protections," Centers for Medicare and Medicaid Services. Available online. URL: http://www.medicare.gov/Publications/Pubs/pdf/10112.pdf. Accessed in February 2007.

[63] "Your Medicare Rights," AARP. Available online. URL: http://www.aarp.org/health/medicare/traditional/a2003-04-28-medicarerights.html. Accessed in February 2007.

[64] "Medicaid: A Primer," Kaiser Commission on Medicaid and the Uninsured. Available online. URL: http://www.kff.org/medicaid/upload/7334%20Medicaid%20Primer_Final%20for%20posting3.pdf. Posted in July 2005, p. 1.

[65] "Medicaid: A Primer," Kaiser Commission, p. 7.

[66] Quoted in Ken Dychtwald, *Age Power*. New York: Taucher/Putnam, 1999, p. 150.

[67] Cathy Schoen, Patricia Neuman, Michelle Kitchman, Karen Davis, and Diane Rowland, "Kaiser/Commonwealth Fund 1997 Survey of Medicare Beneficiaries," Kaiser/Commonwealth Fund. Available online. URL: http://www.cmwf.org/usr_doc/medicare_survey97_308.pdf. Posted in December 1998.

[68] "Nationwide Poll of Seniors Shows High Level of Satisfaction with Medicare Prescription Drug Plan," U.S. Chamber of Commerce. Available online. URL: http://www.uschamber.com/press/releases/2006/april/06-71.htm. Posted on April 26, 2006.

[69] Christopher Lee and Lori Montgomery, "Bush's Proposed Health-Care Cuts Get Mixed Reviews; Some See Salvation, Others See Doom for Medicare and Medicaid," *Washington Post*, February 11, 2007, p. A3.

[70] Quoted in "Why Doctors Opted Out of Medicare," Medicare Opt Out. Available online. URL: http://www.beliefresources.homestead.com/medicareoptout.html. Accessed in February 2007.

[71] "AMA Warns About Access Problems If Medicare Payment Rates Are Not Addressed," Medical News Today. Available online. URL: http://www.medicalnewstoday.com/medicalnews.php?newsid=39878. Posted on March 21, 2006.

[72] Jane Bryant Quinn, "Medicare's in Good Health," *Newsweek*, vol. 143, no. 21, May 24, 2004, p. 41.

[73] Erdman B. Palmore, *Ageism: Negative and Positive*. 2nd Edition. New York: Springer Publishing, 1999, p. 145.

[74] Erik Rakowski, "Should Health Care Be Rationed by Age: Yes," in Andrew E. Scharlach and Lenard W. Kaye, eds., *Controversial Issues in Aging*. Boston: Allyn Bacon, 1997, p. 106.

[75] Quoted in "Dust-to-Dust Fuss," *New York Times*, April 1, 1984, p. A1. Also available online. URL: http://query.nytimes.com/gst/fullpage.html?res=9C0DE6DC1 F39F932A35757C0A962948260. Posted on April 1, 1984.

[76] Richard D. Lamm and Robert H. Blank, "The Challenge of an Aging Society," *The Futurist*, vol. 39, no. 4, July/August 2005, pp. 23–27.

[77] Daniel Callahan, *Setting Limits: Medical Goals for an Aging Society*. New York: Simon and Schuster, 1987.

[78] "Ageism: How Healthcare Fails the Elderly," Alliance for Aging Research. Available online. URL: http://www.agingresearch.org/brochures/ageism/ageism_booklet_final.pdf. Downloaded in February 2007.

[79] "Healthy Aging: Preventing Disease and Improving Quality of Life among Older Americans," Centers for Disease Control and Protection. Available online. URL: http://www.cdc.gov/nccdphp/publications/aag/aging.htm. Updated on July 10, 2006.

[80] Achenbaum, *Older Americans, Vital Communities*, p. 81.

[81] "Ageism: How Healthcare Fails the Elderly," Alliance for Aging Research.

[82] "Ageism: How Healthcare Fails the Elderly," Alliance for Aging Research.

[83] "Elder Abuse and Neglect: In Search of Solutions," American Psychological Association Online. Available online. URL: http://www.apa.org/pi/aging/eldabuse. html. Downloaded in February 2007.

[84] "Elder Abuse and Neglect: In Search of Solutions," American Psychological Association Online.

[85] Martin Klauber and Bernadette Wright, "Legislation: 1987 Nursing Home Reform Act," AARP: Policy and Research Information for Professionals in Aging. Available online. URL: http://www.aarp.org/research/legis-polit/legislation/aresearch-import-687-FS84.html. Posted in February 2001.

[86] U.S. Senate. *Elder Justice and Protection: Stopping the Abuse*. Hearing before the Subcommittee on Aging of the Committee on Health, Education, Labor, and Pensions, United States Senate One Hundred Eighth Congress First Session. Washington, D.C.: U.S. Government Printing Office, 2005, pp. 1–2.

[87] "Elder Rights and Resources: Elder Abuse," Administration on Aging. Available online. URL: http://www.aoa.gov/eldfam/Elder_Rights/Elder_Abuse/Elder_Abuse.asp. Updated on June 6, 2006.

[88] Helen Peterson, "Battle of N.Y. Blue Bloods," *New York Daily News*, July 25, 2006, p. 1.

[89] Vince Gonzales, "Tracking Abuse in Nursing Homes," CBS News Healthwatch. Available online. URL: http://www.cbsnews.com/stories/2002/01/31/health/main327525.shtml. Posted on December 27, 2000.

[90] Quoted in Bernadette Wright, "Nursing Homes: Federal and State Enforcement of the 1987 Nursing Home Reform Act," AARP: Policy and Research Information for Professionals in Aging. Available online. URL: http://www.aarp.org/research/longtermcare/nursinghomes/aresearch-import-686-FS83.html. Posted in February 2001.

[91] Vince Gonzales, "Tracking Abuse in Nursing Homes," CBS News Healthwatch.

[92] U.S. Senate. *Elder Justice and Protection: Stopping the Abuse*, pp. 6–7.

[93] "Results of the 2000 AHCA Survey of Nursing Staff Vacancy and Turnover in Nursing Homes," Health Services Research and Evaluation, American Health Care Association. Available online. URL: http://www.ahca.org/research/rpt_vts2002_final.pdf. Posted on February 12, 2003.

[94] Quoted in Mick McNesby, "Government Spending: What Does the Comptroller General Say," Ezine Articles. Available online. URL: http://ezinearticles.com/?Government-Spending:-What-Does-The-Comptroller-General-Say?&id=463542. Downloaded in February 2007.

CHAPTER 2

THE LAW AND RIGHTS
OF THE ELDERLY

Laws guaranteeing the rights of the elderly cover diverse areas of social life. Of importance to the largest number of elderly persons are federal laws for Social Security and Medicare benefits. Other noteworthy federal laws cover age discrimination, private pensions, and elder abuse. With each of the 50 states also having laws in these areas, legal rights of the elderly encompass a virtual library of regulations, codes, and restrictions. A brief overview of the laws and related court cases follows.

LAWS AND REGULATIONS

FEDERAL LEGISLATION

In the early decades of the United States, the government seldom provided support for the elderly based on age alone. Rather, support came indirectly. For example, soldiers or widows of soldiers wounded in battles of the Revolutionary War and pleading dire poverty could receive public benefits. In the first half of the 19th century, laws extended pensions to all veterans, making soldiers' pensions a crude way to protect some older and disabled persons from poverty. Still the numbers eligible for these pensions remained tiny.

Economic protection of older veterans expanded with the Civil War.[1] An 1862 statute that was intended to help attract men into the military during the war ended up paying pensions to millions of war veterans in the late 19th century. Soldiers whose later disability or disease was caused by or could be traced back to a combat injury could collect a pension when older. The veteran's military rank and seriousness of disability determined the size of the pension, which could go to widows and orphans of deceased veterans. Since huge numbers of young men from the North joined the armed forces, the law created a broad-based population of pension beneficiaries. The law excluded Confederate soldiers from eligibility for the pension, but some state governments in the South helped their soldiers in old age.

In 1890, the Dependent Pension Act further expanded the benefits. The law allowed all disabled veterans to receive benefits, not just those disabled by a war injury. It still placed some limits on the benefits: The veteran's disability must prevent manual labor and earning income. Even so, the disability could emerge in old age rather than stem from combat. Widows could receive benefits as well. According to the 1890 act, widows could claim a soldier's benefits if married to the soldier before the date of the act and able to prove that the soldier died, served in the military for at least 90 days during the Civil War, and received an honorable discharge. However, the widow must also lack means of support other than her daily labor.

Over the next decades, the conditions for eligibility loosened more. A 1907 act changed the rules so that old age alone, even without disability, became sufficient justification to receive a veteran's pension: "That any person who served ninety days or more in the military or naval service of the United States during the late Civil War, or sixty days in the war with Mexico, and who has been honorably discharged therefrom, and who has reached the age of sixty-two years or over, shall, upon making proof of such facts, according to such rules and regulations as the Secretary of the Interior may provide, be placed upon the pension roll, and be entitled to receive a monthly pension."[2] Southern states also passed laws to furnish modest pensions for Confederate veterans.

Although these programs helped many, they neglected nonveterans. Older persons without pension rights managed to support themselves in old age through continued work or assistance from younger family members. Calls for a more extensive pension system were rare. Indeed, the public viewed most any program administered by the federal government as prone to corruption and fraud; few wanted the government to extend soldier's pensions to the rest of the population. All this changed dramatically, however, with the Great Depression of the 1930s.

The Social Security Act of 1935

The stock market crash of 1929 and unprecedented unemployment in the years to follow—up to one-third of the labor force—destroyed sources of support for many elderly. Frances Townsend, a physician working for the California Health Department described the misery caused by the depression for the elderly: "I stepped into such distress, pain, and horror; such sobbing loyalties under the worse possible circumstances as to shake me even today with their memory."[3] In a letter to a newspaper in 1933, he proposed an old-age pension plan in which each person over age 60 would receive $200 a month. The proposal soon gained a wide following. Townsend became the leader of a national crusade for an old-age pension that at one time had at least 10 million supporters.

Congress and President Franklin Roosevelt also recognized the plight of the elderly and the need for government programs to help. Laws passed soon after Roosevelt's election in 1932 helped find jobs for the unemployed but did little for the elderly and retired. Passed a few years later in 1935, the Social Security Act set up a system to award elderly retired workers with a public pension. The benefits were modest. The law set the minimum monthly benefit at $10 and the maximum benefit at $85. It excluded workers who did not receive formal wages such as agricultural workers, domestic servants, and casual laborers (also federal government employees and railroad workers who had their own pension systems). The first benefits in 1937 took the form of a one-time or lump-sum payment, while the first monthly payments did not begin until 1940.

Social Security was set up to be self-funding. To qualify for benefits, workers had to reach age 65, have worked for five years from the date of the act to the time of retirement at age 65, and have received at least $2,000 in wages. Funding for the program came from contributions or, more precisely, taxes on wages of 1 percent from the employee and 1 percent from the employer. In principle, each person would make contributions from their wages while working to support current retirees; in turn, they would later receive retirement benefits from contributions of younger workers. This structure relied on an assumption that seemed reasonable at the time: There would be many more workers contributing taxes than elderly retirees drawing benefits. Since contributions exceeded the payouts, the law set up a reserve account or trust fund for unspent contributions. The Treasury Department invested the trust fund for use in the future.

Modeled on an insurance system, Social Security linked the contributions or taxes paid on wages to the benefits received during retirement. It made workers paying taxes for Social Security feel they were simply saving money now for their later retirement. However, the relationship between contributions made and benefits received was not exact. Rather than getting back the funds they contributed plus interest, retirees received different benefits based on their wages and salaries: Those most in need, low-income workers, received more benefits relative to their contributions (or a higher rate of return) than did high-income workers.

As in any insurance program, the benefits received depended on length of life. Some might die before getting many benefits, while others who lived a long time might get more in benefits than they contributed. The first recipient of monthly Social Security benefits, a retired legal secretary named Ida Fuller, illustrates the nature of the system. Because she retired in 1940, soon after the passage of the Social Security Act, she contributed $100 into the system through payroll taxes. However, she lived for another 35 years, receiving $22,000 in benefits (more than $100,000 in today's dollars).

The act also helped elderly persons with special needs. Because of unemployment or health problems, some older persons would not contribute sufficiently to qualify for Social Security benefits. The Social Security Act authorized federal grants to states for the needy aged (and other groups such as single mothers and the blind). The responsibility for this assistance remained with the states, but they received funds and guidance from the federal government. The act thus created a dual system of federal benefits for the aged. On one hand, long-term workers received retirement benefits from the federal government based on their contributions; on the other hand, more disadvantaged elderly not eligible for such benefits relied on old age assistance from state governments.

Changes to follow the original legislation expanded benefits:

- In 1939, Social Security added benefits for dependents of retired workers or survivors of workers who die early.
- In 1950, Congress increased benefits by 77 percent with passage of a cost-of-living adjustment (COLA).
- In 1956, a new insurance program for disabled workers 50 years and older extended the program for old age and survivors; Social Security now became Old Age, Survivors, and Disability Insurance or OASDI.
- In 1961, the law was adjusted so early retirees could receive benefits at age 62, although at a lower rate than for normal retirement at age 65.
- In 1972, Congress passed legislation that automatically increased or decreased benefits based on changes in the Consumer Price Index. With inflation shooting upward in the late 1970s, benefits increased significantly.
- In 1974, Supplemental Security Income (SSI) revised the benefit program for older and disabled persons with limited income.
- In 1984, legislation set new rules to gradually raise the normal retirement age for generations retiring in the future; for example, those born after 1959 will have a normal retirement age of 67 (to be reached beginning in 2026).

Despite these many changes, however, Social Security today maintains the structure set up in 1935.

Welfare and Pension Plans Disclosure Act of 1958

This federal legislation took a first step in establishing private pension rights of workers and older retirees. It mandated that administrators of pension plans covering 25 or more participants file a description of their plan with the Labor Department. The description, which must also be made available to participants, should include information on benefits and copies of key documents (large plans must also include an annual financial statement). Other laws later replaced this one, but the early disclosure requirements reduced the misuse and mismanagement of pension plans.

The legislation responded to the tremendous growth in pensions during the 1950s. The huge surpluses paid into private pension plans, but to be paid out only decades later when current workers reached old age, created the potential for embezzlement, poor investments, and underpayment of beneficiaries. Complaints about problems brought passage of this legislation. However, President Dwight D. Eisenhower, who signed the bill into law, wanted something more comprehensive. Although willing to sign, he stated that the bill demanded too little documentation on the financial soundness of the plans and allowed corrupt administrators to hide abuses. He also criticized the bill for failing to give a government agency the power to investigate problems and enforce remedies. A few years later, in 1962, the Department of Labor received powers to investigate and prevent mismanagement and abuse of plan funds.

Older Americans Act of 1965

President Lyndon Johnson signed the Older Americans Act on July 14, 1965, just weeks before he signed Medicare legislation. The Older Americans Act stated that older Americans are entitled to secure equal opportunity for the free and full enjoyment of:

- an adequate retirement income;
- the best possible physical and mental health that science can make available;
- suitable housing for the needs of elderly residents that they can afford;
- full services for those requiring institutional care;
- opportunities for employment with no discrimination based on age;
- retirement in health, honor, and dignity;
- pursuit of meaningful activity;
- efficient community services to provide social assistance;
- immediate benefit from proven research to sustain health and happiness; and
- freedom and independence in planning and managing their lives.

Although meant as a guiding philosophy rather than a set of specific objectives, this list of rights expressed the ambitious intent of the legislation and the concern of leaders about problems of the elderly.

The programs set up by the legislation were more modest. It created the Administration on Aging as part of the Department of Health, Education, and Welfare (later the Department of Health and Human Services). The new agency would help states more effectively serve the elderly by distributing grants, educational materials, statistical information, and technical assistance. The Administration on Aging would not itself provide services but would fund and coordinate services of state and local agencies across the country.

The grants to states allowed them to set up community programs for the elderly, train staff and volunteers, and evaluate small-scale demonstration projects before recommending widespread use. Many programs offered to elderly persons today come from the Older Americans Act. The legislation sponsors services such as delivering meals to elderly persons who cannot cook, transporting older persons who cannot drive, providing adult day care when other family members are at work, and offering legal services to elderly persons who cannot afford to hire a lawyer.

Reauthorizations of the act added new provisions through the years. In 1978, amendments required each state to have a Nursing Home Ombudsman Program. The programs train staff and volunteers to protect and represent the interests of older persons in nursing homes. In 1981, amendments extended the ombudsman program to include boarding homes for the elderly and changed the name to the Long-Term Care Ombudsman Program. In 1992, amendments strengthened the program by making local and state ombudsmen advocates for the elderly and giving them responsibility for preventing elder abuse in nursing homes.

Amendments in 1992 made several other changes. Legislation required that the Administration on Aging approve state formulas for distributing funds and that state and local agencies set objectives for improving participation of low-income persons. Congress wanted its funds to better serve low-income elderly, those most in need of aid. Congress also worried about the redirection of funds set aside for nutrition to other services and the use of private companies to deliver services. It put restrictions on both activities. Other provisions focused on preventing elder abuse, neglect, and exploitation. Amendments made funds available to states to educate the public about elder abuse, provide special services to victims, improve reporting systems, evaluate existing state programs, and train caregivers.

Still more programs were added by the Older Americans Act Amendments of 2000 and 2006. Established in 2000, the National Family Caregiver Program helps family members struggling to care for older loved ones who are ill or disabled. New funds also went to help low-income elderly, older persons in rural areas, and Native Americans caring for elders. In 2006, new attention went to helping older persons to live independently as long as possible. One demonstration project called Choices for Independence directs funds to help moderate- and low-income individuals remain in their homes and delay entry into nursing homes.

Medicare Act of 1965

The Medicare Act of 1965, signed into law by President Lyndon Johnson on July 30, 1965, amended the Social Security Act to provide medical benefits to the elderly. The new law created a program of hospital insurance and supplementary medical insurance for persons age 65 and over. The program, called Medicare in short but Health Insurance for the Aged and Disabled more formally, helped pay bills for hospital stays and doctor visits. Medicare aimed to cover basic rather than all medical costs. Like Social Security, funding came from payroll taxes on earnings from employees, matched by contributions from employers.

The passage of Medicare followed many decades of political struggle. As far back as 1912, President Theodore Roosevelt called for national insurance to protect against the hazards of sickness. In 1927, President Calvin Coolidge appointed a Committee on the Cost of Medical Care, which reported severe and widespread problems paying the costs. The problems worsened with the Great Depression of the 1930s. President Franklin Roosevelt initially hoped to include some form of health insurance in the Social Security Act. Worried that opposition to health care insurance would block passage of old age and survivors insurance, he decided to only study health insurance options. In 1949 and 1950, President Harry Truman proposed a national health insurance act, but Congress failed to pass it.

Many European nations by that time had adopted national health insurance, and labor unions strongly favored doing the same in the United States. However, opposition remained strong. The major opponent to national health insurance, the American Medical Association (AMA), expressed concern over the potential for government control of the medical profession that might follow. After the 1948 election of Truman to the presidency, the AMA "voted a special assessment of members to 'resist the enslavement of the medical profession.'"[4]

Proposals in the 1960s took a different form. Health insurance programs would be set up for the elderly, those most likely to face high medical costs, rather than for all citizens. President John F. Kennedy supported legislation for such a program but did not get it passed before his assassination. The 1964 landslide election victory of Democratic presidential candidate Lyndon Johnson and a huge Democratic majority in Congress finally led to passage. The legislation gave health care rights to the elderly that others did not receive.

The Medicare Act divided the program for payment of medical costs of the elderly into two parts: Part A for Hospital Insurance and Part B for Supplementary Medical Insurance. Hospital Insurance offers premium-free benefits for persons age 65 or over who are eligible for Social Security or other government-based retirement programs such as Railroad Retirement. Persons who have been entitled to Social Security disability benefits for 24 months are also entitled to Medicare benefits. Otherwise ineligible aged and disabled persons can voluntarily pay a monthly premium for coverage. By 2001, 34 million aged and 6 million disabled persons participated in Medicare Part A.

The program covers a variety of hospital costs. For hospital inpatients, it pays for a semi-private room, nursing services, lab tests, and intensive care; for those recently leaving hospitals, it pays for rehabilitation and short-term stays in skilled nursing homes. Home and hospice care are also covered under certain circumstances. However, Medicare does not pay for nursing home care that lasts more than 100 days.

Supplementary Medical Insurance or Part B covers services of physicians and surgeons, and some services offered by chiropractors, podiatrists, dentists, optometrists, clinical psychologists, social workers, physician assistants, and nurse practitioners. Costs occurring outside of the hospital, including same day surgery and ambulance services, fall under this program. Costs for radiation, renal (kidney) dialysis, bone-marrow transplants, physical, occupational, and speech therapy, and medical equipment such as oxygen equipment and wheelchairs do as well.

Unlike hospital insurance, Medicare Part B has cost sharing. Anyone eligible for Medicare Part A or, if not eligible for Part A, is age 65 or over can purchase Part B. Enrollment in the program is optional and requires a monthly fee, but more than 90 percent of those participating in Part A also enroll in Part B. In addition, covered services for Part B are subject to a 20 percent copayment and deductible payments.

The 1965 act did not foresee the increasing demands for medical services. As the gaps in coverage for needed services became apparent, private insurance supplemented the public program. Today, millions of Medicare beneficiaries purchase Medigap Insurance. This short-hand term for Medicare supplemental insurance pays for costs that Medicare does not. Congress has tried over the years, not always successfully, to standardize these policies so that buyers get full value for their money. With costs for deductibles, copayments, and Medigap insurance, and with continued efforts to pare costs, Medicare offers modest benefits. On average, Medicare pays just over half of health care costs for its beneficiaries.

For those too poor to qualify or cover out-of-pocket expenses for Medicare, the 1965 legislation created another medical care program for the poor—elderly or not—called Medicaid. Medicare and Medicaid together cover nearly all older persons with some form of public medical insurance. For example, older persons qualifying for Supplemental Security Income (SSI) also qualify for Medicaid, while others can qualify by demonstrating they have low income and few assets. Medicaid differs from Medicare in that it is administered by individual states (though within federal guidelines). Funding from states is matched by the federal government under most circumstances, but the states have leeway in determining eligibility and benefits.

Medicaid covers services that Medicare does not. Of special significance to the elderly, Medicaid covers long-term care. Since Medicaid is considered a safety net, however, most older persons do not qualify for benefits. Even those with modest income and assets (such as owning their own house) must spend down most of their assets to get Medicaid benefits. A short-lived effort to fund long-term care for nearly all elderly came with the Catastrophic Health Care Act of 1988. Objections to the funding formula, however, led to repeal of the act. More recently, Congress changed eligibility rules to allow spouses of those needing care to keep some of the couple's assets.

Age Discrimination in Employment Act (ADEA) of 1967

The Age Discrimination in Employment Act (ADEA) of 1967 originally did not include the elderly. It protected persons ages 40 to 65 working in companies with 20 or more employees and involved in interstate commerce. For those approaching old age, the ADEA banned use of age in hirings, firings, promotions, wages and salaries, job advertisements, and benefits for health, retirement, and unemployment. Congress excluded those over age 65 because older persons, unlike those ages 40 to 65, could rely on pensions if they lost a job. Mandatory or forced retirement policies remained in place.

Congress extended the 1967 ADEA with amendments in 1978 and 1986. The 1978 amendment raised the covered ages to 70 for private sector workers. The 1986 amendment removed the limit for nearly all workers, effectively abolishing mandatory retirement (institutions of higher education were allowed to keep mandatory retirement for another seven years). The law still contained some exceptions. High-level policy makers such as corporate executives with generous pensions could be forced to retire (and make room for new leaders). Pilots and bus drivers in positions involving public safety could be forced to retire. Employers can use age in hiring when it is a legitimate requirement (such as for actors). And, based on a Supreme Court decision, *Kimel v. Florida Board of Regents*, the law does not cover state employees.

Age discrimination under the ADEA takes two major forms. First, discrimination by disparate treatment involves motives for discrimination that lead to less favorable treatment of older workers and job applicants than younger workers and job applicants. This type of intentional discrimination follows from beliefs about the poor skills of older workers rather than from the evaluation of the skills of particular individuals. Second, discrimination by disparate impact involves policies that do not intentionally favor one age group over another but have unequal consequences for young and old groups. However, policies based on seniority, wage and salary levels, and years of experience that adversely affect some age groups more than others are generally exempt from the ADEA. Policies prohibited by the ADEA because of their disparate impact must lack reasonable justification based on factors other than age.

Employee Retirement Income Security Act (ERISA) of 1974

Commonly known as ERISA, the Employee Retirement Income Security Act of 1974 sets minimum standards for private pension plans. The standards require reporting financial details to participants, vesting employees after a specified number of years, and including provisions to continue benefits for surviving spouses after the death of a pension recipient. The law does not specify minimum benefit levels or require a company to adopt a private pension plan. Rather, it sets standards for those that choose to provide a plan for employees.

ERISA aimed to prevent some well-publicized abuses of vesting rules. Defined-benefit pension plans sometimes required 10 years of employment before a worker qualified for pension benefits. Employees fired or quitting after working nine years and 11 months might not receive a pension. With the law, vesting now occurs fully within five years or in increments (20 percent after three years, 40 percent after four years, and 100 percent after seven years).

It also aimed to protect participants from mismanagement and misuse of pension funds. Plan fiduciaries, those administering the plan, controlling the assets, and making investments of its funds, must run the plan solely in the interest of participants. The fiduciaries must diversify investments to avoid the risk of large losses and avoid conflict of interests such as investing in a company that benefits them or the plan sponsor. Improper use of pension assets can make fiduciaries personally liable for losses and subject them to legal action. Informing plan participants about investment of assets, expected benefits, and procedures for appeals also helps limit mismanagement.

Most important, ERISA created an independent agency of the federal government to protect employees from fund mismanagement or employer bankruptcy. The Pension Benefit Guaranty Corporation (PBGC) serves workers whose pension plans are ended by financial problems of their employers. Using insurance premiums paid by companies with defined-benefit plans and assets of companies that default on its pensions, the PBGC assumes pension benefits when companies cannot. It does so when a company proves to a bankruptcy court that it either can no longer stay in business or can no longer stay in business unless the pension plan is terminated. The PBGC then steps in to pay pension benefits (up to certain limits) at normal retirement age and also pays (again up to certain limits) most early retirement benefits, survivor benefits, and disability benefits.

Age Discrimination Act of 1975

A law related to the ADEA, the Age Discrimination Act of 1975, extends protection against age discrimination that occurs outside employment. It states that "no person in the United States shall, on the basis of age, be excluded from participation, be denied the benefits of, or be subjected to discrimination under, any program or activity receiving Federal financial assistance."[5] The act does not apply to programs or activities which, by law, provide benefits or assistance based on age or establish criteria for participation based on age. It thus excludes Social Security, Medicare, and other age-based programs from violation of the act. It does include, for example, use of age in accepting students into universities and professional schools that receive federal funding. Violators of the law face loss of assistance from federal programs.

Retirement Equity Act of 1984

The Retirement Equity Act of 1984 amended ERISA to address concerns about gender inequality in private pension benefits. Women who entered the labor force early but withdrew to have children typically lost their rights to pensions by not completing vesting periods. Also, widowed and divorced women sometimes lost rights to their former husband's benefits. The law addressed these problems with several new rules. It lowered the minimum age needed to participate in a pension plan, thus permitting women to earn more pension credits during the early years of work (before childbearing). It further required plans to count maternity and paternity leave toward vesting and to provide survivor benefits to widows.

In signing the legislation, President Ronald Reagan summarized its goals: "This important legislation is the first private pension bill in our history to recognize explicitly the importance of women both to the American family and to the Nation's labor force. It contains significant measures to enhance women's ability to earn pensions in their own right. It improves and protects the vital role of pensions as retirement income to widows."[6]

Nursing Home Reform Act of 1987

This legislation, part of the Omnibus Budget Reconciliation Act of 1987, established rights of nursing home residents. It required that, to obtain Medicare and Medicaid payments for patients, nursing homes must promote and protect those rights. The law followed concerns about the poor quality of many nursing homes and a 1986 report from the Institute of Medicine entitled *Improving the Quality of Care in Nursing Homes*. The report called for new performance standards, regular assessment of patients, better training of nursing home staff, and a stronger federal role in nursing home oversight.

As summarized by lawyer Hollis Turnham, the law requires nursing homes to:

- Attend to the quality of life of residents and help with daily activities such as walking and bathing.
- Develop individualized assessment and care programs for each resident.
- Put staff through five hours of training and testing.
- Offer special services for residents with mental illness or retardation.
- Give residents the opportunity to safely maintain personal funds within the nursing home.
- Allow return to the nursing home after leaving for a stay at a hospital or overnight visit with family.
- Allow choice in personal physician and access to medical records.
- Eliminate unnecessary use of physical and chemical restraints.[7]

Enforcement efforts changed as well. Along with interviewing staff and checking records, state inspectors would, based on the law, interview patients and observe their treatment.

The Nursing Home Reform Act changed the lives of many nursing home residents for the better. According to Turnham, "There have been significant improvements in the comprehensiveness of care planning. Antipsychotic drug use declined by 28–36% and physical restraint use was reduced by approximately 40%."[8] Despite the law, however, protection of nursing home residents remains incomplete. According to a report from the AARP in 2001, "Ten years after the passage of the Nursing Home Reform Act, however, a series of research studies and Senate hearings called attention to serious threats to residents' well-being. These problems were attributed to weaknesses in federal and state survey and enforcement activities."[9] Critics call for expanding the law to include more inspections and harsher punishments for violators.

Older Workers Benefit Protection Act of 1990

This legislation amended the ADEA to clarify the protection of benefit plans for older individuals. A Supreme Court decision, *Oubre v. Entersy Operations*, held that the original law allowed use of age in determining employee health benefits and costs (unless the age-based rules were intended to hide other forms of age discrimination). In light of this ruling, the legislation aimed to restore the original intent of the ADEA—to prohibit age discrimination in employee benefits. The ADEA now encompasses benefits included as part of a bona fide employee plan.

With the law, companies no longer can require older workers to pay more than younger workers for health insurance. They also no longer can favor younger workers over older workers in hiring or to justify involuntary retirement because of the high cost of health care programs for older workers. However, the law still allows the use of legitimate seniority plans, as long as they do not attempt to circumvent the ban on age discrimination or require involuntary retirement. Lastly, companies no longer can get around ADEA requirements by enticing employees to sign a waiver in return for early retirement or severance benefits. The law prohibits waiving rights or claims under the ADEA by individuals unless the waiver is done voluntarily and with knowledge of its meaning and consequences. A valid ADEA waiver needs to be in writing, made understandable to the employee, list the specific rights being waived, advise the employee to obtain a lawyer, and allow the waiver to be revoked within a week after signing.

Patient Self-Determination Act of 1990

This legislation addressed a concern with incapacitated patients who cannot make their treatment desires known to medical professionals and may undergo unwanted treatment. There are several ways to deal with this possible problem. Living wills state a person's desire for treatment or nontreatment when unable to make a decision; they often prevent the use of life-extending medical procedures when death is imminent. Power-of-attorney documents give authority for such decisions to someone else. In the 1970s, states began to pass laws (and 42 did so by 1988) advocating the use of living wills or other documents to make treatment wishes known. The federal government followed suit with the Patient Self-Determination Act of 1990.

The act requires hospitals, nursing homes, HMOs, hospice programs, and home health agencies that receive Medicare and Medicaid funds to give patients information on their treatment rights. At the time of enrollment or admission, patients should be told of their rights to participate in treatment decisions, refuse medical or surgical procedures, and complete an advance directive. An advance directive consists of written instructions on what medical treatment to give should the patient become unable to make such decisions. The advance directive generally takes the form of a living will, durable power of attorney, or appointment of a health care proxy. It may also take the form of a simpler nonlegal document administered by health care providers. The law does not require advance directives and, in fact, specifies that patients without advance directives should not face discrimination in health care. Rather, it requires health care providers to inform patients of their rights and the importance of an advance directive.

Rights of the Elderly

The Retirement Protection Act of 1994

Congress attempted to stiffen requirements for funding private pensions with this act. At the time, private pension plans in aggregate had shortages—the difference between their obligations and assets—of $71 billion. The 1994 law forced companies with more than 100 employees and less than 90 percent of the assets needed to pay its promised benefits to send letters to its employees warning of the shortfall. Northwest Airlines and Westinghouse, for example, had to send such letters. In addition, the law forced companies with underfunded plans to increase their contributions. Problems would persist, however, and new legislation would follow 12 years later in the Pension Protection Act of 2006.

Senior Citizens Freedom to Work Act of 2000

This act guarantees the right of qualified persons retiring at normal ages to receive full Social Security benefits while working. Until the act, Social Security had an earnings test that reduced Social Security benefits of many retirees who continued to earn income in the labor force. For example, persons ages 65 to 69 lost $1 in Social Security benefits for every $3 in earnings above $17,000. By limiting Social Security benefits of workers, the earnings test intended to encourage full retirement and open up jobs for young people. Yet it also penalized older persons who wanted to continue working. The law ended the earnings test for persons retiring at normal ages but not for early retirees.

With passage, the law increased the Social Security benefits of some 800,000 workers at ages 65 to 69. Although the change increased the estimated cost of Social Security by $22.7 billion over 10 years, encouraging older persons to work ideally will balance the added costs with more payroll tax contributions. Regardless of the cost, the law seems fairer to retirees and has advantages for the economy. President Bill Clinton said in signing the legislation, "As the baby boomers begin to retire, it is more important than ever that older Americans who are willing and able to work should not have their Social Security benefits deferred when they do."[10]

Medicare Prescription Drug Improvement and Modernization Act of 2003

The largest reform in Medicare since its establishment occurred in 2003, when legislation gave new assistance to program participants in buying prescription drugs. The new prescription benefit set up by the law began January 1, 2006. Relying on a mix of government funding, cost-sharing from beneficiaries, and service from private insurance companies, the program addressed a health care problem that particularly affected the elderly: the rising prices of and demand for prescription drugs.

The prescription drug plan, called Medicare Part D, allows those eligible for Medicare to voluntarily enroll. Enrollees can select from plans offered by private insurance companies. By dealing with private insurance companies, Medicare participants do not receive benefits directly from the government. Instead, insurance companies provide discounts for drugs and receive reimbursement from the government. Having private companies compete for participants with the drug plans they offer aims to keep costs low. The private plans, which vary in the costs they charge and the drugs they cover, also give consumers some choices.

Members of prescription drug plans pay a monthly premium that entitles them to savings of 10–25 percent on the drugs they buy. The premium varies depending on the plan and the company but on average equals $22 a month. Costs for drugs also include deductibles and copayments. The plans thus lower but do not pay totally for the cost of prescription drugs. Low-income groups get additional subsidies to help with out-of-pocket expenses.

Alternatively, those who belong to Medicare Advantage receive prescription drug benefits through these plans. Their drug discounts come as part of HMO membership rather than Medicare Part D. Others receive drug coverage through employer or union plans but must choose between private and public plans. Retirees who have prescription drug coverage from an employer or union lose these benefits if they join Medicare Part D. To encourage participation of the private sector, employer and union-sponsored plans receive government subsidies for the prescription-drug discounts they offer to members.

Medicare Part D appears popular among the elderly. According to figures from the Centers for Medicare and Medicaid Services, about 39 million Medicare participants, more than 90 percent of those eligible, have enrolled in prescription drug plans. About 8.3 million have done so through Medicare Advantage plans. By some estimates, older persons save an average of $1,200 per year through the program (at the cost to the government of about $558 billion over a 10-year period).

Critics point out some limitations, however. The law does not allow the federal government to negotiate lower prices for drugs with pharmaceutical companies—a condition needed to get support for the legislation from some lawmakers. It also has high out-of-pocket costs to participants. The plans vary widely in costs, coverage, and drugs provided, which makes it hard for enrollees to understand the differences and select the best plan. For example, if the preferred list of drugs used by the plan (called the formulary) does not include a desired drug, participants pay the full cost. More generally, critics say that the reliance on profit-seeking insurance companies and Medicare Advantage HMOs for prescription drug benefits rather than reliance on direct government payments raise costs to elderly consumers.

Rights of the Elderly

Social Security Protection Act of 2004

This legislation amended the Social Security Act and the Internal Revenue Code to protect beneficiaries from misuse of their payments by their representatives. Because about 10 percent of Social Security recipients and about 34 percent of SSI recipients are considered incapable of managing their own funds, a family member or friend serves as the representative payee. The Social Security Administration lacked means to monitor the funds paid to representatives and ensure they actually used the benefits for the incapacitated elderly recipient. The law imposes stricter standards on individuals and organizations representing Social Security beneficiaries and makes them liable for civil damages if they misuse the funds.

Pension Protection Act of 2006

Called the most sweeping reform of America's pension laws in 30 years, this legislation strengthened the protection of private pension rights. It does so by requiring companies to shore up the funding of their pension plans and build sufficient assets to pay promised pension benefits. The legislation sets targets for full pension funding that companies must meet within a seven-year period starting in 2008. The law raises the cap on contributions to the pension fund so companies can build assets during financially good times that cover shortfalls during hard times. In addition, companies receive tax subsidies for improving funding of their pension plans and tax penalties for failing to do so. Helping to balance the subsidies, companies must contribute more in premiums to the pension insurance program operated by the PBGC.

Besides toughening standards for companies, the legislation makes it easier for individuals to add to their own retirement accounts. It removes barriers so that companies can automatically enroll workers in defined-contribution plans such as 401(k)s and IRAs. It ensures workers receive more information about how their accounts perform, gives them more control over investing funds in their accounts, and allows for greater contributions to the accounts. In doing more to fund their own retirement, individuals ideally will better supplement funds from employers and Social Security during old age. The act also sets up a legal test to ensure that cash-balance conversion plans do not discriminate against older workers. The change should make this hybrid pension more attractive to those approaching retirement.

STATE LAWS AND REGULATIONS

Many federal laws guaranteeing rights of the elderly have counterparts at the state level. Responsibilities for preventing age discrimination, adding to Supplemental Security Income (SSI), paying Medicaid benefits, and protecting against elder abuse often fall to the states. Although they generally follow the guidelines set forth in federal legislation, states vary in the specifics of the laws they pass and the regulations they enforce.

In the area of age discrimination in employment, some state laws mirror the federal ADEA, which covers persons ages 40 and over and working in a company with 20 or more employees. However, most state laws are broader, also protecting employees of smaller firms from age discrimination. Colorado, Washington, D.C., Michigan, Montana, New Jersey, North Dakota, Oregon, Vermont, and Wisconsin specify no company-size minimum needed to file an age discrimination claim under state law. Many other states have limits well below 20 employees, thus encouraging workers in small companies to work through the state in bringing age discrimination claims.

SSI—the program designed to help low-income elderly persons—is based first on benefit levels set by federal law and the Social Security Administration. However, most states add to the federal benefits with their own supplements (Arkansas, Georgia, Kansas, Mississippi, Tennessee, and West Virginia are exceptions). Some states provide a supplement through the Social Security Administration, which combines the federal and state payments in a single check. For example, New Jersey supplements the SSI payment of $959 a month by $25 for a couple living in their own household. Other states administer the supplement through a state agency, which sends out a separate state check. For example, Wisconsin supplements payments of $1,036 a month with $132 for a couple living independently in their own household.

Medicaid is a state program based on state laws and regulations. However, it involves a partnership with the federal government, which sets program requirements and approves state plans. Despite federal efforts to standardize programs, states have flexibility in setting funding levels that match their particular needs, costs, and finances. As a result, states vary widely in benefits, eligibility, and covered expenses. This is particularly true for long-term care, the part of Medicaid costs that most help the elderly. According to a fact sheet from Georgetown University, "Per capita spending for Medicaid long-term care in 2004 ranged from $833 in New York to about $100 in Utah and Nevada."[11] Still further, states differ in how they allocate Medicaid funds. As the Georgetown University report states, "The proportion of Medicaid long-term care spending devote to home and community-based care ranges from 70.1 percent in Oregon to 12.7 percent in Mississippi."[12]

States also differ in their rules on who qualifies for Medicaid long-term benefits. The federal government sets guidelines for Medicaid eligibility based on SSI eligibility. However, 11 states use more restrictive rules for Medicaid eligibility than for SSI, while a few others use less restrictive rules. For example, some states have low asset limits that reduce the number eligible while others have high asset limits that raise the number eligible. A person thus might be eligible for Medicaid in one state but not another.

Elder abuse falls primarily within the oversight of state law enforcement and social service agencies. These agencies often rely on different definitions of elder abuse. For example, Louisiana defines elder abuse to include physical abuse, emotional or mental abuse, sexual exploitation, financial exploitation, neglect, abandonment, and self-neglect. Indiana defines elder abuse less comprehensively to include physical abuse, financial exploitation, and neglect. Perhaps more important than the general definitions used for elder abuse, state laws and regulations have varied criteria used by Adult Protective Services to determine if abuse has occurred. In some states such as California and Georgia, all persons age 65 and over are eligible for protection from elder abuse. Other states such as Alabama and Delaware require that victims have some sort of impairment or lack of ability to care for themselves.

States also differ in reporting requirements for elderly abuse.[13] For example, Missouri and Nevada require health professionals, human services professionals, clergy, law enforcement officers, and long-term care facility employees to report elder abuse. Louisiana, New Mexico, North Carolina, Tennessee, Texas, Utah, and Wyoming, in contrast, require all persons to report elder abuse rather than specifying particular groups. The sanctions for not reporting differ as well. Alabama, California, the District of Columbia, Louisiana, South Carolina, Vermont, and West Virginia include jail time, while most other states include fines. A few states—Iowa, Michigan, and Minnesota—make those not reporting elder abuse liable for suits.

COURT CASES

Court decisions involving rights of the elderly most often address issues of age discrimination. Other decisions address issues of rights to private pensions and protection from elder abuse. A review of some major cases follows.

Supreme Court Decisions

MASSACHUSETTS BOARD OF RETIREMENT V. MURGIA 427 U.S. 307 (1976)

Background

As an officer in the Massachusetts state police, Robert Murgia was forced by state law to retire at age 50. The state law recognized the arduous duties of uniformed police officers, including responding to civil emergencies and natural disasters, apprehending criminals, controlling disorder, and dealing with prisoners. Advancing age and decreasing physical ability limit the ability to respond to the demands of this job. Up to age 50 and mandatory retirement, officers had to prove their fitness to continue on the job by passing physical exams; after age 50, problems become serious enough in the view of the state to require retirement of all officers. Officer Murgia had passed a physical exam four months before his retirement and claimed that his excellent physical and mental health allowed him to continue on the job.

Murgia sued the Massachusetts Board of Retirement on the grounds that his forced retirement violated the Fourteenth Amendment to the Constitution by denying him equal protection under the law. The Massachusetts district court dismissed the complaint, but an appeals court appointed a three-judge court to consider the constitutional question. The court ruled for the plaintiff. The opinion stated that the mandatory retirement law did not sufficiently further the state's interest to justify the law's interference with a fundamental constitutional right. The U.S. Supreme Court agreed to hear the case.

Legal Issues

The case raised two key issues on employment rights under the Constitution. The first issue concerned whether mandatory retirement violated a fundamental right of citizens. The plaintiff viewed the right to work and earn a living as an essential component of individual freedom. The Fourteenth Amendment guarantees equal protection of the laws to all persons. Given the difficulty older persons have in finding new jobs, mandatory retirement deprives them of the equal opportunity to work and therefore violates the amendment. Mandatory retirement further reflects broader mistreatment of the elderly that the constitution prohibits. The defendant, the Massachusetts Board of Retirement, disagreed. It argued that the Constitution provides no fundamental right to employment. The existence of unemployment throughout the history of the nation demonstrates that the decisions of employers and employees in the labor market rather than the Constitution determine work and retirement. Although courts have interfered in the labor market as a way to protect racial and ethnic minorities, the circumstances for retirement at age 50 differ. Unlike African Americans, the elderly have not experienced a history of extreme employment discrimination that defines a need for special protection.

The second issue concerned whether the age-50 limitation on work for police officers had a rational justification. The plaintiff argued that no sudden change in physical skills occurred at age 50—officers differ little if at all on the day before their 50th birthday when they can work from the day of their 50th birthday when they must retire. Compulsory retirement therefore is irrational, particularly given that the annual exams of the officers could more directly determine their physical skills for the job. In contrast, the defendants argued that the risk of physical failure increases with age (and brought in expert testimony to support the claim). Even if some individuals can perform their duties after age 50, the higher potential for failure rationally justified the policy.

Decision

The Supreme Court majority ruled in favor of the Massachusetts Board of Retirement. First, its ruling concluded that older workers do not have a constitutional right to continued employment. The equal protection amendment to the Constitution specifies a fundamental right only under a crucial condition: The violation of the right must operate to the disadvantage of a class of people who have been subject in the past to purposeful unequal treatment and political powerlessness. However, the elderly have not been subject to the unequal treatment and powerlessness of minority race and ethnic groups. Under these standards, compulsory retirement and discrimination against older workers differ in degree and seriousness from, for example, restrictions on voting and discrimination against blacks. If not based on a fundamental right to work, judging the mandatory retirement law depends on whether it uses rational means to pursue stated goals.

Second, the decision concluded that a rational basis existed for mandatory retirement at age 50. Deterioration of physical skills can in many cases make officers unfit for their duties. In setting mandatory retirement at age 50, the state may not have chosen the best means to identify those unsuited for the job. The opinion indeed makes clear that the court recognized the potential for mistreatment of older workers. The procedures used by the state of Massachusetts may not be wise, efficient, or just, and changes in the law may be warranted. But the Court ruled that imperfect procedures are not necessarily irrational, and only demonstrated irrationality in this case would violate the right to equal protection. Whether ideal or not, the mandatory policy had a rational justification and did not violate the Constitution.

Impact

With this decision, the Supreme Court limited the legal remedies available to older workers for fighting age discrimination. They cannot sue for violation of constitutional rights, a remedy that well served racial and ethnic minorities alleging discriminatory policies. Instead, the elderly would have to rely on age discrimination laws. The ADEA had in fact passed before this case, and Murgia might have brought suit under this law. Since this case, hundreds of thousands of older workers have brought charges of age discrimination to the Equal Employment Opportunity Commission and sued employers under the ADEA. Victims also brought charges and suits under state laws. Such suits have not had a high success rate, however, so the lack of a constitutional challenge has restricted the options of age discrimination victims.

HAZEN PAPER COMPANY, ET AL., PETITIONERS V. WALTER F. BIGGINS 91-1600 (1993)

Background

The Hazen Paper Company, a manufacturer owned by Robert and Thomas Hazen, hired Walter F. Biggins as their technical director in 1977. When Biggins was fired in 1986 at age 62, he sued Hazen Paper in the District Court of Massachusetts. He claimed that Hazen Paper fired him based on age rather than performance, which violated the ADEA. He also claimed that his firing, which occurred just a few weeks before he would meet the 10-year vesting requirement of the company and become eligible for a retirement pension, violated the ERISA. The Hazens denied the allegations. They claimed to have fired Biggins for conducting business with competitors and offered to hire him as a consultant until he qualified for his pension.

A jury trial ruled in favor of Biggins. On appeal brought by Hazen Paper, the court of appeals also ruled against the company. The court concluded that a jury could reasonably find that both age and the closeness to pension vesting were linked to the firing. In addition, the court concluded that the company's interference in Biggins's pension eligibility was willful; that is, it showed reckless disregard for potential violation of the ADEA. The damages awarded to Biggins by the court reached $419,454. On further appeal, the Supreme Court agreed to hear the case.

Legal Issues

The Supreme Court considered two questions. First, does interfering with vesting requirements for pensions violate the ADEA? Second, how do rules for damages under the ADEA apply when the company does not have a discriminatory policy but instead used age in a single, informal employment decision?

The first question raises issues about the use of age by employers. Age is associated with vesting for pensions or years of service but is not identical. The Court might reason that years of service so closely relate to age that firing an employee for the former involves the latter. If not for having reached an older age, Biggins would not have nearly reached the 10-year vesting requirement. The firing would implicitly involve age discrimination. Alternatively, the Court might say that the ADEA focuses specifically on use of age in hiring and firing decisions. Seniority and years of experience differ enough from age that they are not subject to ADEA restrictions.

The second question involves the awarding of damages to Biggins on the basis of willful disregard of age discrimination and pension laws by Hazen Paper. The Supreme Court had earlier established that ADEA violations involving reckless disregard warranted payment of damages, while other violations did not. In this case, the appeals court concluded that Hazen Paper knew the ADEA might apply and therefore showed reckless disregard in firing Biggins. Other courts had interpreted the meaning differently, however. Some had concluded that informal discrimination—in contrast to formal discrimination through a written policy—was not willful or reckless. Hazen Paper argued for this approach by claiming that, if it used age in this case, it occurred just once rather than forming a consistent policy. The company therefore should not be liable for damages. The Supreme Court needed to address the varied interpretation of willful or reckless disregard in assessing damages for age discrimination.

Decision

In a unanimous decision written by Justice Sandra Day O'Connor, the Court vacated (or set aside) the decision of the court of appeals and sent the case back for reconsideration based on its ruling. On the first question—did firing before a vesting deadline constitute age discrimination—the opinion reasoned that interfering with pension benefits does not by itself demonstrate age discrimination. The employer's decision did not rely on inaccurate and stigmatizing stereotypes about the productivity of older workers—the key concern of the ADEA. The dispute involved factors related to seniority and experience rather than age directly. The firing may have been improper but not for reasons directly based on age and ageism. Even if violating pension laws, Hazen Paper did not exhibit disparate treatment by age.

On the second question—were criteria for awarding damages based on age discrimination properly applied—the opinion accepted the reasoning of the appeals court on reckless disregard. It stated that willful or reckless disregard as a condition for awarding damages in age discrimination cases could occur on an informal as well as a formal basis. Since the decision set aside the judgment against Hazen Paper, the company would not face damages. However, the decision supplied guidance for other courts and cases dealing with the issue.

Several justices added a brief concurrence to the opinion. They emphasized that the decision applied only to disparate-treatment forms of age discrimination (i.e., intentional) and reached no conclusion about disparate-impact forms of age discrimination (i.e., unintentional). The justices in the concurrence believed that the ADEA allowed only for disparate-treatment claims.

Impact

Although focused in part on technical issues concerning monetary damages, the ruling also had implications for the rights of the elderly. By concluding that use of years of service in employment decisions did not necessarily result in age discrimination, the Supreme Court narrowed the application of the ADEA and made it harder to prove accusations. The Court would some years later expand on this reasoning in *Smith v. City of Jackson, Mississippi.*

The decision did not change the finding that Hazen Paper violated ERISA. Although not a victim of age discrimination, Biggins improperly lost pension rights with the firing. The decision against Hazen Paper on this count stood, making ERISA the central law for protecting pension rights of the elderly.

J. DANIEL KIMEL, JR. ET AL., PETITIONERS V. FLORIDA BOARD OF REGENTS ET AL. 98-791 (2000)

UNITED STATES, PETITIONER V. FLORIDA BOARD OF REGENTS ET AL. 98-796 (2000)

Background

Kimel and others, all age 40 and over, were employed by Florida State University and Florida International University. They sued the Florida Board of Regents under the ADEA for failing to require the two universities to institute a pay-allocation scheme that treated older employees more equitably. The petitioners claimed that the scheme gave smaller raises to workers with more years of service, most of whom were older employees. The Florida Board of Regents moved to dismiss the suit and then, after the district court denied the motion, appealed the decision. Several other state employees, including professors in Alabama and corrections workers in Florida, had also sued state government with similar claims. Like the Kimel case, these cases worked their way up to the appeals court. Further, the United States intervened on the side of the defendants to enforce the ADEA.

The appeals court consolidated the cases to address a key question: Did the ADEA negate the immunity of states from federal lawsuits? Based on the Eleventh Amendment, the Supreme Court had long held that "the Constitution does not provide for federal jurisdiction over suits against nonconsenting states." The appeals court dismissed the Kimel suit on the grounds that the federal law did not have jurisdiction over the state regulations on pay. Given some confusion on the issue and the need for clarification, the Supreme Court agreed to hear the case.

Rights of the Elderly

Legal Issues

The Court did not consider whether the Florida Board of Regents discriminated against Kimel and other employees. Rather, it considered the same question as the appeals court: Does the federal ADEA have jurisdiction over the states? Based on past interpretations of the Eleventh Amendment, it does not and the employees do not have the right to use a federal statute to sue a state. Allowing citizens to do so would give the federal government undue power over the states. Instead, employees might use state laws rather than the federal ADEA to bring their cases. This argument led the defendants to move for dismissal.

In opposing dismissal, the plaintiffs argued that Congress intended the ADEA to overcome state claims of immunity from federal suits. The law affirms that employees can bring action "against any employer (including a public agency)" and defines a public agency as "the government of the state or political subdivision." With such language, Congress authorized age discrimination suits against state employers. The plaintiffs argued that Congress made clear its intent to override the states' constitutional immunity from suit in federal court.

Decision

The decision, delivered by Justice Sandra Day O'Connor, addressed two questions: Did Congress make clear its intent with the ADEA to abrogate the state's immunity from suits in federal court, and did it have constitutional authority to do so? The opinion answered yes to the first question but no to the second. It thus affirmed the appeals court decision to dismiss the suit.

First, the Supreme Court agreed that Congress made its intent clear in the ADEA to subject state agencies to suits by employees. Further, Congress sometimes does have the power under the Fourteenth Amendment of the Constitution to abrogate the states' independence from federal control. For instance, it can do so in order to deter the violation of constitutional rights by states. Second, however, the ruling concluded that Congress did not have the power to impose the ADEA on state governments. Age discrimination neither violates constitutional rights nor falls under the Fourteenth Amendment. Further, Congress had no reason to believe that state and local governments were unconstitutionally discriminating against their employees on the basis of age. It therefore lacked justification for the broad sweep of its wording in regard to states rights.

Impact

The Supreme Court noted in its ruling that state employees are covered by state age discrimination statutes that they can use to obtain monetary damages and stop discriminatory practices. However, many advocates of older workers criticized the decision. It limited the pool of employees able to sue for age discrimination in federal courts on the basis of the ADEA. Millions of state and local government employees lost an option for fighting age discrimination that other employees have.

AZEL P. SMITH ET AL. V. CITY OF JACKSON, MISSISSIPPI, ET AL. 03-1160 (2005)

Background

Azel P. Smith and other petitioners, all police and public safety officers employed by the city of Jackson, Mississippi, objected to a plan for distributing pay raises in 1999. The plan aimed to attract and retain qualified employees by increasing starting and early career salaries. Those having worked less than five years on the job received proportionally higher wage increases than others. Most officers over age 40, the ages covered by the ADEA, had five or more years of experience and received proportionally lower raises.

A group of older officers claimed that, with this plan, the city discriminated against them in two ways. First, the plan intentionally discriminated by giving smaller raises to older workers. Second, the plan unintentionally discriminated by giving raises based on tenure, which indirectly penalized older workers. The former claim involved disparate treatment of older workers, while the latter claim involved disparate impact on older workers. The district court rejected both these claims. On appeal, the court of appeals affirmed the ruling of the lower court. The Supreme Court then agreed to hear the case.

Legal Issues

Much confusion existed over the use of disparate impact claims under the ADEA. Three circuit courts of appeal allowed such claims, while five did not. Disparate impact claims followed from an interpretation of the Civil Rights Act of 1964 (Title VII) put forth in *Griggs v. Duke Power Company*. When policies appear neutral and applied equally to racial, ethnic, or sex groups but have a significantly greater discriminatory impact on members of a protected group, they are illegal. Even when those implementing policies do not intend to discriminate, they may do so anyway if the policies have a disparate impact.

The question concerns whether this principle applies to age. On one hand, the ADEA seems to protect against age discrimination much as the Civil Rights Act protects against race, ethnic, and gender discrimination. The similarity suggests that laws should make policies with disparate impact on older workers illegal just as policies with disparate impact on other protected classes are illegal. The intent of age discrimination legislation thus should protect the older workers in Jackson, Mississippi. On the other hand, the ADEA and the Civil Rights Act differ in a crucial way. The ADEA includes a statement that allows employers to escape liability if the adverse employment action is "based on reasonable factors other than age." Some lower courts used this statement to conclude that the legislation did not cover disparate impact. Under this interpretation, employers could use reasonable factors other than age legally, even if the outcome affected older age groups more than others.

Decision

In addressing competing interpretations of how the disparate impact principle applies to age discrimination, the Supreme Court accepted arguments of both sides. First, the ruling concluded that the ADEA does allow disparate-impact suits. Since the ADEA used language nearly identical to that of the Civil Rights Act, only substituting age for race or sex, disparate impact should apply to both. To quote the author of the ruling, Justice John Paul Stevens, "When Congress uses the same language in two statutes having similar purposes, particularly when one is enacted shortly after the other, it is appropriate to presume that Congress intended that text to have the same meaning in both statutes." The disparate-impact interpretation of the Civil Rights Act as presented in *Griggs v. Duke Power Company* therefore applies to age discrimination. The lower courts were wrong to conclude otherwise.

Second, however, the Court narrowed the scope of disparate-impact liability of the ADEA. Since the ADEA allows use of reasonable factors other than age, many policies with disparate impact failed to meet the grounds for age discrimination. Employers may reasonably include physical strength, for example, as a job requirement. Although use of this trait in hiring may adversely affect older workers, it does not demonstrate age discrimination. As a result, proving disparate impact with regard to age discrimination is more difficult than for race or sex discrimination. Those bringing suit for age discrimination must identify an unreasonable employment practice that leads to age-based differences in outcomes.

Applying the two principles, the Court allowed the disparate-impact claim in general but found it invalid for this case. It rejected the claims of the lower courts that the ADEA disallowed disparate-impact claims. However, it also rejected the claims of the plaintiffs that the employer discriminated against them. According to the opinion, the plaintiffs did not meet the standard of proof for disparate-impact age discrimination. As the defendants argued, making salaries comparable with the market levels involved reasonable factors other than age. It involved use of characteristics of seniority and rank that appeared legitimate in meeting the city's goals of retaining police officers. The plaintiffs merely identified an outcome—different raises—

rather than the illegality of the practices that led to the outcome. They failed to demonstrate that the city acted unreasonably when giving larger raises to junior officers that make them competitive with similar positions in the labor market.

In short, the Supreme Court rejected the reasoning of the lower courts but affirmed its ultimate judgment. It did not change the outcome—the police officers failed in their claim—but supplied reasoning that courts could use in future decisions on age discrimination.

Other justices concurred with the decision but for different reasons. Justice Antonin Scalia argued in a separate opinion that such issues should go before government agencies such as the Equal Opportunity Commission rather than the courts. In a third opinion, three other justices—Sandra Day O'Connor, Anthony Kennedy, and Clarence Thomas—argued that the ADEA does not cover disparate impact and that allowance for other reasonable factors makes it inappropriate for courts to apply disparate-impact arguments. They read the statute to say that discriminatory intent was required to prove age discrimination and that the arguments of the plaintiffs about unintentional discrimination or disparate impact had no validity. Again, the opinion likewise rejected the claims of the plaintiffs but called for a stricter interpretation of the ADEA than the majority did.

Impact

Although it clarified confusing and competing claims by allowing age discrimination suits to be based on disparate impact, *Smith v. City of Jackson* did little to ease the burden of proof for age discrimination cases. Even if allowed to bring disparate-impact claims, victims of age discrimination have a hard time proving them. Requiring plaintiffs to identify a specific employment practice that created the unintentional age discrimination defines a high standard. Employers can rely on the clause allowing "reasonable factors other than age" to defend themselves against age discrimination liability. When employers say that their policy or actions use reasonable non-age factors, it places the burden of proof on the plaintiffs. For example, layoffs of older workers might be justified by their higher salaries and costs to avoid disparate-impact claims against them.

The ruling likely will have mixed effects on the rights of elderly persons bringing age discrimination suits. As Sandra Sperino, a visiting law professor at the University of Illinois, summarizes,

> *On the positive side, the decision recognizes disparate impact as a possible claim under ADEA and thereby provides companies with an incentive to create [termination] policies that do not single out older workers. However, the case also places many obstacles in the way of litigants who want to challenge such policies.[14]*

Federal Appeals Court Decisions

KATHI COOPER, ET AL. V. IBM PERSONAL PENSION PLAN AND IBM CORPORATION, NO. 05-3588 (2006)

Background

Beginning in 1999, IBM changed the structure of its employee pension plan. To replace a defined-benefit plan, it offered employees a cash-balance plan that set up individual accounts for each employee. Rather than placing money into the individual accounts, however, the pension plan gave credits based on past pay and interest. In addition, all employees would receive a 5 percent pay credit per year. A trust would hold assets to pay the amount credited to an employee until retirement. IBM said that it shifted to the cash-balance plan, which allows workers to take their pension credits when they changed jobs, to fit the needs of a modern, mobile workforce.

However, a class of older IBM employees sued on the grounds that the plan violated a subsection of the Employee Retirement Income Security Act (ERISA) prohibiting age discrimination. They complained that younger workers would receive the annual pay credit for more years than older workers and therefore accumulate more credits and a higher payout on retirement. When the district court ruled in favor of the plaintiffs, IBM and the plaintiffs worked out a plan to make up the difference in credits for older workers. However, IBM also appealed the decision to the court of appeals.

Legal Issues

The key legal issue concerns the meaning of the term "accrued benefit" in ERISA. IBM argued that the plan is age neutral—it gives the same accrued benefit or annual increase in credits to young and old workers. In its law, Congress prohibits age discrimination in the form of ending or reducing benefit accumulation because of age. In other words, employers cannot stop making allocations or change the rate of allocations based on age. According to IBM, their plan did neither of these things. By putting the same amount of credits into accounts for all workers, accrued benefits do not differ by age.

The plaintiffs instead argued for a meaning of accrued benefit based on the size of pension outcome rather than pension contribution. The amount put into the account each year may be identical by age, but the amount available for withdrawal at normal retirement differs by age. Consider an example from the opinion. "Someone who leaves IBM at age 50, after 20 years of service, will have a larger annual benefit at age 65 than someone whose 20 years of service conclude with retirement at age 65. The former receives 15 more years of interest than the latter." The extra years of interest for the younger employees give them benefits denied to older employees.

Decision

The opinion for the Seventh Circuit Court of Appeals sided with IBM to overturn the district court ruling. The opinion says, "The phrase 'benefit accrual' reads most naturally as a reference to what the employer puts in." It is a mistake to use the phrase to refer to outputs. This reading makes defined-benefit and cash-balance plans just like defined-contribution plans, where no age discrimination follows from allowing younger employees to accumulate interest for a longer period. The opinion further noted that nothing in ERISA or age discrimination legislation indicates that Congress wanted to treat time to retirement and time to earn interest as aspects of age discrimination. Indeed, the time to retirement falls into the category of reasonable factors other than age that is allowable under judicial decisions on age discrimination. The court of appeals therefore reversed the district court ruling and returned the case to the lower level with directions to enter a judgment in IBM's favor. On further appeal, the Supreme Court declined to hear the case, letting the ruling stand.

Impact

The decision removed the obligation of IBM to pay the $1.4 billion in damages it had agreed to after the initial ruling. It also left IBM employees with the existing cash-balance plan. Older workers at IBM and other companies may lose benefits when changing from defined-benefit pension plans to cash-balance plans. The defined-benefit plans usually base benefit payments on the salary during the last five years before retirement, which favored older workers with seniority and a high salary. Companies in fact used this aspect of pension plans to keep experienced workers from leaving. With a cash-balance plan, credits are based on salary over the full work history of the employee rather than on the last few years. Based on the decision, however, the change does not discriminate against older workers. No protest followed a 2006 announcement from IBM to freeze its U.S. pensions and instead add benefits into 401(k) plans by 2008.

Congress responded to concerns over cash-balance conversions in another way. It passed the Pension Protection Act of 2006, which set up a legal test to ensure that cash-balance conversion plans do not discriminate against older workers. The legislation should allay the concerns that led to the IBM suit.

STATE COURT DECISIONS

PEOPLE V. SUSAN VALERIE HEITZMAN,
NO. S035624 (1994)

Background

Sixty-seven year old Robert Heitzman, had been partially paralyzed by a stroke many years ago and lacked control of his bowels. He lived in a house with his two sons, Robert Jr. and Jerry. On December 3, police summoned to the house discovered Robert, Sr., lying dead on a urine-soaked mattress and in a filthy bedroom. He was dehydrated, covered with bed sores, and suffering from pneumonia, congestive heart failure, and hepatitis. The two sons were charged with involuntary manslaughter.

Until a year earlier, Susan Heitzman, the defendant in this case and daughter of Robert Heitzman, had been the primary caregiver. When she decided to move away, the sons took over. During visits after the move, however, Susan Heitzman noticed that care of her father by Robert Jr. and Jerry had worsened. The house had become filthy and smelly, and her father needed to see a doctor. She spoke to her brothers about these needs but did not make the arrangements herself. She also spent two days in the house shortly before her father died and noted that he seemed weak and disoriented. Although not the primary caretaker of Robert Heitzman, she was charged with willfully permitting an elder to suffer physical and mental pain.

Susan Heitzman moved to have the charges dismissed on the grounds that the law did not specify a duty for her to prevent the harm suffered by her father. The superior court agreed, and dismissed the charges, but the appeals court reversed this decision. The California Supreme Court then agreed to hear the case.

Legal Issues

The basic question under consideration concerns whether California law imposed a duty on Susan Heitzman to protect her father and control the conduct of her brothers. All agreed that Heitzman did not have primary responsibility for care, but the prosecutor and the defendant disagreed on her legal duty. The relevant law, section 368(a) of the California code, imposes criminal liability on "any person who, under circumstances and conditions likely to produce great bodily harm or death, willfully causes or permits any elder or dependent adult, with knowledge that he or she is an elder or dependent adult, to suffer, or inflict thereon unjustifiable physical pain or mental suffering."

The prosecutors argued that Heitzman observed the abuse of her father and even commented on it to her relatives. It was negligent on her part to permit the suffering, especially given that she had once herself taken care of him and knew how much worse his living conditions had become. Even further, father and child have a special relationship that brings expectations of care. Under these conditions, Heitzman willfully permitted the abuse, thus committing a crime of inaction according to California law.

The defendant argued that she had no duty under the law to take responsibility for her father's condition. To permit abuse by inaction, the defendant must have a legal duty to act, but the law does not define who, other than direct caregivers, have such a duty. If the law implied a duty, its vague definition of those required to protect elders from abuse made the law unconstitutional. Citizens should have a reasonable degree of certainty about whether a law applies to them. Otherwise, the innocent tend to be trapped by not having fair warning about what is prohibited. Heitzman claimed the law did not meet the constitutional standards of certainty.

Decision

By a 4-3 decision, the California Supreme Court sided with the defendant. The ruling said that the prosecutors failed to demonstrate that Heitzman had a legal duty to protect her father. If the law is interpreted broadly to include a wide variety of people who might have contact with an abuse victim, then it is overly vague and unconstitutional. If the law is interpreted narrowly to include only those with a special caregiving relationship to the victim, then it excludes Heitzman. Prosecutors needed to show not only that Heitzman had a duty toward her father but also had control over the actions of her brothers, the actual caregivers. That they did not do so meant she was improperly charged.

The opinion pointed out that it in no way approved of the actions of the daughter and her failure to help her father. It criticized the apparent indifference of the defendant to her father's suffering. However, punishment for such indifference must follow from clearly defined laws. Therefore, the ruling reversed the judgment of the court of appeals and the charges brought against Susan Heitzman.

Impact

The decision narrowed the circle of persons who are criminally liable for elder abuse in California. The elder abuse statute worked well in prosecuting those caregivers directly responsible for abuse but worked less well for other persons knowing about the abuse. Generally, states hold people criminally liable if they have assumed responsibility for victims of elder abuse through words or deed. For others, laws in many states have become more precise in listing those persons who have responsibility to report elder abuse, even if they have no legal duty to prevent it. If decisions such as this one limit those responsible for elder abuse, state laws can widen the circle of persons needing to report abuse to appropriate authorities and allow the government to take action.

THERESA SIENARECKI V. STATE OF FLORIDA, NO. SC94800 (2000)

Background

Patricia Sienarecki had suffered through the death of her husband from lung cancer and two hip surgeries when her disposition changed markedly. She became disoriented, asking where her husband was, mixing up the names of her children, and refusing to try to walk. She became a picky eater, needing help with her food and falling to a weight of 68 pounds. It was decided that Mrs. Sienarecki would move into an apartment with her daughter, Theresa Sienarecki, and her daughter's boyfriend.

According to the petitioner in the case, Theresa Sienarecki, caring for her mother was difficult. The mother needed diapers, scratched her legs and face, and often refused to eat or drink. When urged by her daughter to see the doctor, the mother refused.

When the mother died unexpectedly, police came to the apartment. They found the deceased wearing nothing but a polo shirt, her body smeared with feces, and her mattress filthy. An autopsy found severe dehydration, sores on her body, and infected organs. The coroner ruled that dehydration and malnutrition caused her death. Based on a Florida law that requires caregivers of elderly persons or disabled adults to provide supervision and services needed for mental and physical health, a jury convicted Theresa Sienarecki of neglect of a disabled adult. Sienarecki appealed the conviction, arguing that the law was unconstitutional. The Florida Supreme Court agreed to hear the appeal.

Legal Issues

The appeal made three constitutional claims. First, the law says nothing about the intent to abuse. The Florida Supreme Court had found earlier that a statute prohibiting negligent treatment was unconstitutional because it was overly broad. In this case, Sienarecki claimed that law wrongly included innocent behavior in its definition of criminal behavior. Second, the law is unconstitutionally vague. It does not make clear how, in this case, the caregiver should respond to her mother's stubborn resistance to being helped. Given the attitude of her mother and lack of resources for nursing home care, Sienarecki did all she could to provide care. Third, the law violated the mother's right to privacy. Because the mother had the right to refuse medical treatment, the daughter was wrongfully convicted for not providing treatment.

The Law and Rights of the Elderly

Decision

The Florida Supreme Court rejected all claims of unconstitutionality put forth by Sienarecki and reaffirmed her conviction. First, in regard to the claim that the neglect was not willful or intentional and therefore not criminal, the opinion cited precedent that neglect can occur either willfully or by culpable negligence. This case involved culpable negligence, and the court had ruled earlier that culpable negligence is constitutionally acceptable.

Second, in regard to the claim that the neglect law was unconstitutionally vague, the ruling concluded that the law met the test of vagueness. A constitutional law in Florida should give notice to a reasonably intelligent person of the conduct it forbids. Based on evidence in this case, the mother was impaired or disabled, and Sienarecki had taken the role of caregiver by bathing her, changing diapers, and bringing food. The law required caregivers of disabled adults to provide supervision and services needed for mental and physical health. Sienarecki had a responsibility clearly laid out by the law to address her mother's basic needs.

Third, in regard to the mother's right to privacy in refusing treatment, the court ruled that Sienarecki cannot use her mother's right to privacy to defend her own behavior.

Impact

This decision affirmed the constitutionality of the tough antielder abuse law in Florida and strengthened its prosecution. As in most other states, laws prohibiting elder abuse in Florida include neglect as a punishable offense. As this case makes clear, defendants need to do more than claim they intended no harm for the victim, faced difficulties in care, and protected the privacy rights of the victim.

---

[1] See Jennifer L. Gross, "Civil War Pensions." In *Encyclopedia of the American Civil War*, David S. Heider and Jeanne T. Heider, eds. Santa Barbara, Calif.: ABC-CLIO. Also available online. URL: http://www.civilwarhome.com/pensions.htm. Downloaded in March 2007.

[2] "Act of February 6, 1907," Civil War Pension Acts. Available online. URL; http://www.blackcamisards.com/sc-usct/pension/penacts.html. Downloaded in March 2007.

[3] Francis Townsend, *New Horizons: An Autobiography*. Chicago: J.L. Stewart, 1943, p. 131.

[4] "National Health Insurance," Answers.com. Available online. URL: http://www.answers.com/topic/national-health. Downloaded in March 2007.

[5] "Age Discrimination Act of 1975," Department of Labor. Available online. URL: http://www.dol.gov/oasam/regs/statutes/age_act.htm. Downloaded in March 2007.

[6] "Statement on Signing the Retirement Equity Act of 1984: August 23, 1984." Reagan Archives. Available online. URL: http://www.reagan.utexas.edu/archives/speeches/1984/82384b.htm. Downloaded in March 2007.

[7] Hollis Turnham, "Federal Nursing Home Reform Act from the Omnibus Budget Reconciliation Act of 1987 or Simply OBRA '87 Summary," Ombudsman Resource Center. Available Online. URL: http://www.ltcombudsman.org/uploads/OBRA87summary.pdf. Downloaded in March 2007.

[8] Turnham, "Federal Nursing Home Reform Act."

[9] Bernadette Wright, "Federal and State Enforcement of the Nursing Home Reform Act," AARP Policy and Research. Available online. URL: http://www.aarp.org/research/longtermcare/nursinghomes/aresearch-import-686-FS83.html. Posted in February 2001.

[10] "House Passes Bill Lifting Social Security Earnings Limit," CNN.com. Available online. URL: http://archives.cnn.com/2000/ALLPOLITICS/stories/03/01/social.security/index.html. Posted on March 1, 2000.

[11] "Medicaid and Long-Term Care," Georgetown University Long-Term Care Financing Project. Available online. URL: http://ltc.georgetown.edu/pdfs/medicaid2006.pdf. Posted in January 2007.

[12] "Medicaid and Long-Term Care," Georgetown University Long-Term Care Financing Project.

[13] "Facts about Law and the Elderly," American Bar Association. Available online. URL: http://www.abanet.org/media/factbooks/eldt1.html. Downloaded in March 2007.

[14] Quoted in Mark Reutter, "High Court Decision a Setback for Older Workers, U of I Professor Says," News Bureau, University of Illinois at Urbana-Champaign. Available online. URL: http://www.news.uiuc.edu/NEWS/06/0324age.html. Posted March 24, 2006.

CHAPTER 3

CHRONOLOGY

This chapter presents a timeline of significant events related to rights of the elderly in the United States. It lists passages of laws, significant court cases, and news events involving age discrimination, private pension rights, Social Security, Medicare, nursing home care, and elder abuse.

1861

- In an early example of forced retirement, Congress requires naval officers below the rank of vice admiral to resign their commission on reaching age 62. Private companies over the next decades would begin to adopt similar policies.

1862

- Congress passes legislation intended to attract men into the military during the Civil War by promising pensions to war veterans. Soldiers whose later disability or disease was caused by or could be traced back to a combat injury could collect a pension when older. The pensions will serve as a major source of support for older persons in the late 19th century.

1889

- Setting a precedent that many other European nations soon follow, Germany establishes a pension program for retired workers. The United States rejects such an approach and continues to rely on veterans' pensions.

1890

- The Dependent Pension Act expands pension benefits by allowing all disabled veterans and their widows to receive benefits, not just those disabled by a war injury. The law still places some limits on the benefits:

The veteran's disability must prevent manual labor and limit earned income.

1900

- With average life expectancy of 47.3, 3.1 million or 4 percent of the American population reaches age 65 or over.

1907

- Congressional legislation changes the rules for veterans' pensions so that old age alone, even without disability, becomes sufficient to qualify for benefits. Such efforts widen support for older veterans and their widows but leave other older persons without a public pension.

1912

- President Theodore Roosevelt calls for national health insurance to protect against the hazards of sickness. Despite the need for such protection, particularly for the elderly, Congress does not act on the request.

1927

- President Calvin Coolidge appoints a committee on the cost of medical care, which reports severe and widespread problems paying health care costs. However, no action follows from Congress to help the elderly or other groups with the costs.

1933

- ***September 30:*** In a letter to a newspaper, Francis Townsend proposes an old age pension plan that would give $200 a month to each person over age 60. The proposal soon gains widespread support, with at least 10 million supporters joining a crusade for a national pension.

1935

- ***August 14:*** President Franklin Roosevelt signs the Social Security Act, which sets up a system to award elderly retired workers with a public pension. To qualify for benefits, workers need to reach age 65, have worked for five years from the date of the act to the time of retirement at age 65, and have received at least $2,000 in wages. Funding for the program comes from contributions in the form of taxes on wages. Worried that opposition to health care insurance will block passage of old age and survivors insurance, President Roosevelt decides not to include health insurance in his proposed Social Security program.

Chronology

1938

- A report from the New York State Legislature describes the harm of age discrimination, noting that many older persons forced to retire or let go before retirement want to work but cannot find jobs.

1939

- Social Security extends benefits to include dependents of retired workers and survivors of workers who die early.

1940

- Ida Fuller, a retired legal secretary, receives the first monthly Social Security benefit. Because she retired soon after the passage of the Social Security Act, she contributed only $100 dollars into the system through payroll taxes. However, she will live for another 35 years, receiving $22,000 in benefits (more than $100,000 in today's dollars).

1948

- After the election of Harry Truman to the presidency, the American Medical Association (AMA) votes a special assessment of members to lobby against national health insurance.

1949

- President Truman proposes a national health insurance act, which would help cover increasingly costly medical bills, but Congress fails to pass the proposed legislation.

1950

- Concerned about the low level of Social Security payments, Congress increases the amounts by 77 percent with passage of a cost-of-living adjustment (COLA).

1956

- Civil services rules ban age discrimination in employment by the federal government.
- Social Security adds a new insurance program for disabled workers 50 years and older and changes its official name to Old Age, Survivors, and Disability Insurance (OASDI).

Rights of the Elderly

1958

- Dr. Ethel Percy Andrus founds the American Association of Retired Persons (AARP) to advance the interests of older persons through lobbying and help individual elderly persons defend their rights.
- Responding to the growth of private pensions in the 1950s and the misuse and mismanagement of the funds, the Welfare and Pension Plans Disclosure Act takes a first step in establishing pension rights of workers and older retirees. It mandates that administrators of pension plans covering 25 or more participants file a description of their plan with the Labor Department.

1959

- The finding that more than one of three Americans age 65 and over have income below the poverty line creates concern about the failure of the nation to protect its elderly.

1961

- Congress allows early retirees to receive Social Security benefits at age 62, although at a lower level than for normal retirement at age 65.

1962

- In his book on poverty, *The Other America*, Michael Harrington reports that an elderly retired couple on average receives only $804 a year from Social Security.

1963

- Studebaker automobile manufacturer goes out of business, denying some 4,000 workers all or part of their promised retirement benefits. The large number of workers affected reveals the risks of private pensions.

1965

- Preceding federal legislation, 23 states have passed laws making it illegal to use age as a criterion in the hiring and firing of workers between the ages of 40 and 60.
- *July 14:* President Lyndon Johnson signs the Older Americans Act, which aims to help the elderly realize their full rights to a secure old age by creating the Administration on Aging. The new agency will help states more effectively serve the elderly by providing grants, educational materials, statistical information, and technical assistance.

- **July 30:** President Johnson signs the Medicare Act, which amends the Social Security Act to provide medical benefits to the elderly. The new law creates a program of hospital insurance and supplementary medical insurance for persons age 65 and over that helps pay bills for hospital stays and doctor visits. Like Social Security, funding comes from a combination of payroll taxes on employee earnings and contributions from employers.
- The Medicare Act creates another medical care program for the poor of all ages called Medicaid. Medicare and Medicaid together cover nearly all older persons with some form of public medical insurance.

1967

- **January 23:** In a speech decrying job discrimination against older persons, President Lyndon Johnson says, "approximately half of all private job openings were barred to applicants over 55."
- **December 15:** President Johnson signs the Age Discrimination in Employment Act (ADEA), which prohibits employment discrimination based on age against persons ages 40 to 65 by employers with 20 or more employees and involved in interstate commerce. The law does not cover persons over age 65.

1969

- Robert N. Butler, a physician and first head of the National Institute on Aging, coins the term *ageism* in 1969 to highlight the denigration of the elderly and draw parallels with the treatment of women and African Americans.
- Congress passes legislation that automatically increases or decreases benefits based on changes in the consumer price index. With inflation shooting upward in the late 1970s, benefits will increase significantly because of the legislation.

1974

- Creation of the Supplemental Security Income (SSI) program offers benefits for older and disabled persons with limited income.
- **September 2:** President Gerald Ford signs the Employee Retirement Income Security Act (ERISA). The legislation sets minimum standards for private pension plans and creates the Pension Benefit Guaranty Corporation (PBGC) to cover pensions of workers whose companies default on their pension payments. The legislation aims to curb abuses of vesting rules and mismanagement of pension funds.

1975

- The Medicare program and Congress attempt to control costs by limiting payments to hospitals and doctors.
- Congress passes the Age Discrimination Act of 1975, which prohibits "discrimination on the basis of age in programs or activities receiving Federal financial assistance." The act excludes programs for which age defines eligibility, such as Social Security and Medicare for the elderly and Head Start and school programs for children.

1976

- In a case involving mandatory retirement at age 50 of Massachusetts state police officers, the Supreme Court rules that the constitution does not give protection against age-based job discrimination; the protection must come from age discrimination laws.

1978

- An amendment to the ADEA extends the ages covered by the law to 70 for most workers.
- Amendments to the Older Americans Act require each state to have a Nursing Home Ombudsman Program. The program will train staff and volunteers to protect and represent the interests of older persons in nursing homes.

1981

- A House Committee on Aging calls for the creation of emergency shelters for victims of elder abuse.
- Amendments to the Older Americans Act extend the Nursing Home Ombudsman Program to include boarding homes for the elderly and change the name to the Long-Term Care Ombudsman Program.

1983

- Legislation passes to gradually raise the normal retirement age for generations retiring in the future; for example, those born after 1959 will have a normal retirement age of 67 (to be reached beginning in 2026).

1984

- Colorado Governor Richard Lamm says in a speech that terminally ill elderly people have "a duty to die and get out of the way." He expresses concern that, given the increasing cost of medical care, resources have to be directed toward those who can benefit most from them. This would make it necessary to ration medical resources for the oldest and sickest patients.

- The Retirement Equity Act amends ERISA to address concerns about gender inequality in private pension benefits. The law sets new rules to help women who entered the labor force early but withdrew to have children qualify for pensions. It also sets rules to help widowed and divorced women receive a share of their former husbands' benefits.

1986

- The ADEA is amended to cover nearly all workers age 40 and over, effectively abolishing mandatory retirement policies for all but a few occupations.
- A report from the Institute of Medicine entitled *Improving the Quality of Care in Nursing Homes* calls for a stronger federal role in nursing home oversight, new performance standards, better training of nursing home staff, and regular assessment of patients.

1987

- In his book *Setting Limits*, philosopher Daniel Callahan recommends that the government not pay for expensive life-extending treatments past age 70 or 80. He believes that, without such rationing, the elderly will use resources that should go to those who have yet to live out a normal life span.
- Passage of the Nursing Home Reform Act, part of the Omnibus Budget Reconciliation Act, establishes rights of nursing home residents. Responding to concerns about the poor quality of many nursing homes, the law now requires that, to obtain Medicare and Medicaid payments for their residents, nursing homes must promote and protect those rights.

1988

- Congress passes a law to prevent spouses of persons needing nursing home care from having to spend down nearly all their assets to qualify for Medicaid coverage. The law allows those needing nursing home care to get help from Medicaid and spouses to avoid poverty.
- *July 1:* President Ronald Reagan signs the Catastrophic Health Care Act, which adds long-term care to the services covered by Medicare. However, rather than tax workers (as Medicare and Social Security do), the new program is to be funded by a tax paid largely by high-income Medicare beneficiaries.

Rights of the Elderly

1989

- The Medicare Rights Center is established to help the elderly receive high-quality medical care and full coverage of the services due to them.
- *November 22:* Objections to the funding structure of the Catastrophic Health Care Act of 1988 lead Congress to repeal the law.

1990

- *October 16:* President George H. W. Bush signs the Older Workers Benefit Protection Act, which amends the ADEA to clarify the protection of benefit plans for older individuals. The law prevents companies from requiring older workers to pay more than younger workers for health insurance, or favoring younger workers over older workers because of the high cost of health care programs for older workers.
- *November 5:* President George H. W. Bush signs the Patient Self-Determination Act. It requires hospitals, nursing homes, HMOs, hospice programs, and home health agencies that receive Medicare and Medicaid payments to give patients information on their rights to participate in treatment decisions, refuse medical or surgical procedures, and complete written instructions on desired medical treatment if incapacitated.

1992

- Amendments to the Older Americans Act strengthen the Long-Term Care Ombudsman Program by making local and state ombudsmen advocates for the elderly and giving them responsibility for preventing elder abuse in nursing homes. It also requires states and local agencies to set objectives for improving participation of low-income persons in their programs for the elderly.

1993

- Given a seven-year exemption from 1986 legislation that restricted use of mandatory retirement, institutions of higher education now must comply fully with the ADEA.

1994

- *December 8:* President Bill Clinton signs the Retirement Protection Act, which Congress passed to stiffen requirements for private pension plans. It forces companies with more than 100 employees and less than 90 percent of the assets needed to pay its promised benefits to inform employees of the shortfall. It also forces companies with underfunded plans to increase their contributions.

Chronology

1999

- IBM converts from a defined-benefit to a cash-balance pension plan; older employees claim that the move lowers their pension benefits relative to younger workers and constitutes age discrimination.

2000

- Amendments to the Older Americans Act create the National Family Caregiver Program to help family members struggling to care for their older loved ones who are ill or disabled. New funds also will go to help low-income elderly, older persons in rural areas, and Native Americans caring for elders.
- *April 7:* President Clinton signs the Senior Citizens Freedom to Work Act, which guarantees the right of qualified persons retiring at normal ages to receive full Social Security benefits while working. Until the act, Social Security had an earnings test that reduced benefits of some retirees who continued to earn income in the labor force. The law ends the earnings test for persons retiring at normal ages.

2001

- *October 15:* Bethlehem Steel declares bankruptcy, leaving its pension liabilities of $600 million to the PBGC and its older employees wondering about their promised retirement benefits.
- *December 2:* The Enron Corporation of Houston, Texas, files for bankruptcy, leaving only $321 million from sale of company assets to devote to pensions for some 17,000 workers. In addition, the collapse of Enron stock wipes out the 401(k) accounts of many employees.

2002

- A survey done by the American Health Care Association tells of serious staffing problems at nursing homes. Turnover of certified nurse assistant positions has reached 71 percent and turnover of other staff has reached 50 percent. The shortage of care may lead to neglect and abuse of elderly nursing home patients.
- A California nursing home company, Beverly Enterprises, agrees to settle charges of elder abuse by paying $2.6 million. The company also agrees to improve training of its staff and report on its improvements in care.
- *January:* The Ford Motor Company reports that its U.S. pension plan is underfunded by $7.3 billion, perhaps threatening the future retire-

ment benefits of its workers. The problems at Ford and many other large corporations come from a downturn in the economy in the early 2000s.

- *April:* Delegates to the United Nations Second World Assembly in Madrid, Spain, agree on a plan to help older persons across the world receive pension guarantees, housing and health care rights, and opportunities to work.
- *December 9:* United Airlines files for bankruptcy. The PBGC will take over its $9.8 billion in pension obligations, but former and current United employees worry the change will result in a cut of their promised pension benefits.

2003

- A report from the Centers for Disease Control (CDC) says that 90 percent of older persons fail to get appropriate health screenings and treatment for problems of smoking, poor nutrition, alcohol abuse, and misuse of prescription drugs. The report views these problems as evidence of ageism in the medical care system.
- *March 1:* A court rules that, to save money to prevent bankruptcy, US Airways can liquidate the pensions of its 6,000 pilots, turning over responsibility for the pensions to the PBGC.
- *June 12:* Capital One Financial announces that it has agreed to settle a lawsuit over the alleged use of performance evaluations as a cover to lay off its oldest workers. The company promises to improve its evaluation processes and its awareness of age discrimination.
- *June 16:* The state of Missouri passes the Senior Care and Protection Act, which makes it a felony to conceal abuse or neglect. Legislation such as this in other states strengthens efforts to prevent elder abuse.
- *October 20:* The Senate Special Committee on Aging holds a hearing on the often hidden problem of family elder abuse. Witnesses testify on the severity of the problem and the need for additional legislation. Many of the senators on the committee use the testimony to call for support of the Elder Justice Act.
- *November 14:* The Xerox Corporation announces it agrees to settle a suit by retired workers over the calculation of pension benefits when the company shifted to a cash-balance plan. The former employees sued on the grounds that the changes result in lower benefits for retirees.
- *December 8:* President George W. Bush signs the Medicare Prescription Drug Improvement and Modernization Act, the largest reform of Medicare since its establishment, which gives new assistance to program participants in buying prescription drugs. Those enrolling

in plans sponsored by private insurance companies will pay a monthly premium of about $22 that entitles them to savings of 10–25 percent on the drugs they buy.

2004

- *January 20:* In his State of the Union address, President Bush proposes to allow workers to put part of their Social Security contributions into a personal retirement account. Responding to fears that the partial privatization will disrupt Social Security and threaten benefits for retirees, Congress will not pass legislation recommended by the president.
- *May 21:* A report from the Texas Department of Health and Human Services faults state Adult Protective Services for failing to stop or respond to elder abuse. The report, ordered by Governor Rick Perry, says that one agency in El Paso had improperly investigated more than one-third of reported abuse cases.
- *September 3:* The Department of Health and Human Services announces an increase in premiums for Medicare Part B of 17.4 percent or $11.60 for the next year—the largest dollar increase in the 40-year history of the program. The federal government explains that the rise comes from higher medical costs and payments to physicians and health plans.
- *December 14:* A report released by the Henry J. Kaiser Foundation says that 8 percent of employers surveyed had eliminated subsidized health care benefits for future retirees and another 11 percent planned to do so in the next year. The companies were cutting health care benefits for retirees to deal with rising medical costs.

2005

- With life expectancy of 77.6 years, 35 million Americans (or 12.4 percent of the population) have reached 65 and over. Estimates suggest that by 2050 average life expectancy will reach 81.2 for men and 86.7 for women, the number aged 65 and over will reach 87 million, and the percent of the population age 65 and over will reach 20.7.
- In its annual report, the PBGC announces that it paid out $22.8 billion more than it took in. The deficit indicates problems in the nation's pension protection system and will require changes in the law to improve funding of the government-sponsored corporation.
- *January 14:* The Equal Employment Opportunity Commission sues Sidley Austin Brown & Wood, a law firm with more than 1,500 lawyers, for age discrimination. The firm is accused of demoting or firing 31

lawyers over age 40 because of their age, but it denies the accusations and promises to fight the suit.

- *March 30:* The Supreme Court rules in *Smith v. City of Jackson* that older workers charging age discrimination need not prove intentional discrimination by employers. Instead, they can show that a policy had a disparate impact on older workers. However, employers can counter age discrimination charges by demonstrating that the disparate impact stems from reasonable factors other than age.
- *May 10:* A bankruptcy judge approves the request from United Airlines to end its pension program, which the PBGC will take over. The pension default, the largest in history, leaves $9.8 billion in liabilities. The judge accepts the claims of United that it cannot survive with the pension burden, but many employees protest the decision and the possible cuts in pension benefits they face. A jury later acquits the owners.
- *September 14:* The Louisiana attorney general charges two owners of a New Orleans nursing home with negligent homicide for not moving patients to safety before Hurricane Katrina; 35 elderly residents died afterwards from drowning.
- *November 8:* The National Clearinghouse on Abuse in Later Life reports on the establishment of eight shelter programs for abused elders. Much like shelters for battered women, the elder-abuse shelters offer protection of older persons from abusers. Advocates for the elderly say that the high levels of elder abuse make such shelters an important need for the elderly.
- *November 15:* Senator Orrin Hatch introduces the Elder Justice Act of 2005 to create a new office in the Department of Health and Human Services that will collect and disseminate data on the problem and make grants to state Adult Protective Services agencies. However, the act has not passed Congress.

2006

- The American Medical Association (AMA) reports on results from an online poll of its members showing that, in response to cuts in reimbursements, 29 percent of physicians planned to reduce the number of Medicare beneficiaries they take on. As a result, choices for care available to Medicare patients and their right to quality treatment are becoming more limited.
- *January 1:* The new Medicare Prescription Drug Program begins. Those who enrolled in a plan can start receiving discounts on the prescription drugs they purchase (but also must start paying monthly premiums).

Chronology

- *January 19:* A special committee of the New York Bar Association issues a report opposing mandatory retirement for partners of law firms. Law firms often justify mandatory retirement as a way to create opportunities for younger lawyers and claim that partners are owners rather than employees and thereby exempt from age discrimination laws.
- *May 1:* Trustees of Social Security and Medicare release an annual report saying that the trust funds will run out sooner than expected and predict a looming financial crisis as the baby-boom generation retires.
- *May 15:* Older persons rush to meet the deadline to sign up for Medicare Prescription Drug Coverage in 2007, overloading the ability of insurance providers to meet the demand. The new Medicare law places a penalty on future premiums for those who miss the deadline.
- *July 18:* A doctor and two nurses are arrested in New Orleans on charges that they murdered four severely ill patients (all over age 62) who could not be evacuated from the hospital after Hurricane Katrina hit the city. The three deny any wrongdoing and are later cleared.
- *July 23:* The *New York Daily News* reports on the abuse of 104-year-old Brooke Astor, a well-known New York City socialite and patron of the arts, by her only child, 86-year-old Anthony Marshall—who controls her $45 million fortune. Diagnosed with Alzheimer's disease, Astor suffers from memory loss, heart problems, anemia, and other ailments but, according to the report, is kept inside her dilapidated apartment and prevented from receiving medical care.
- *August 17:* President Bush signs the Pension Protection Act, which he calls the most sweeping reform of America's pension laws in 30 years. The law requires companies to shore up the funding of their pension plans and build sufficient assets to pay promised pension benefits. Companies must meet funding targets within a seven-year period starting in 2008.
- *September 27:* In Orange County, California, officials report on their efforts to identify and prevent elder abuse with new forensic skills. The Orange County's Elder Abuse Forensic Center reviews about 120 cases a year that are considered potential crimes and half of those end up being prosecuted for elder abuse.
- *September 29:* Congress passes amendments to the Older Americans Act that give new attention to helping older persons live independently. One demonstration project called Choices for Independence directs funds to help moderate and low-income individuals remain in their homes and delay entry into nursing homes.
- *October 1:* Great Britain begins to enforce new regulations against age discrimination in employment. The country lagged well behind the United States in formalizing such regulations.

- *December 6:* A ruling from the New York State Supreme Court concludes that claims of elder abuse of 104-year-old Brooke Astor have not
been substantiated. Her 86-year-old son, Anthony Marshall, says the decision vindicates him against the charges of elder abuse, but Mr. Marshall
remains under investigation by the district attorney.

2007

- *January 16:* The Supreme Court declines to hear an appeal of a lower
court ruling that IBM did not discriminate against older workers when
it switched from a defined-benefit to a cash-balance pension plan. Older
IBM workers say the new plan reduced their benefits relative to younger
workers.
- *January 18:* The Federal Reserve chairman, Ben S. Bernanke, warns of
the long-term danger posed by expected future deficits in Social Security
and Medicare. He calls for Congress to deal with the problem of funding
entitlements for the elderly sooner rather than later.
- *February:* President Bush's proposed 2007 budget includes some major
cuts in Medicare that, Democratic opponents say, will impair medical
services for the elderly. The budget also calls for high-income elderly to
pay greater Medicare Part B premiums than others.
- *March 20:* The Alzheimer's Association releases a report on a 10 percent
increase in Alzheimer's disease over the last five years. The disease, which
affects more than 5 million Americans and 42 percent of those age 85 and
over, will become even more common as the population ages and require
greater resources to give quality care to victims.
- *May 6:* Federal and state officials say that some insurance companies
have improperly used hard-sell tactics to convince older Medicare recipients to sign up for private plans. Although insurers disagree, critics
say that the private Medicare Advantage plans offered by the companies
are more expensive for the government and give fewer benefits to plan
members.
- *August 13:* Brooke Astor, age 105, dies in her Briarcliff, New York,
home.
- *October 6:* The EEOC brings an age discrimination suit against the
American Ballet Theatre Company for firing Henry Nowack, a 74-
year-old trumpeter. The EEOC says that Nowack had never been
criticized for his playing, but that an unnamed conductor wanted older
orchestra members to retire. The American Ballet Company denies
any wrongdoing.
- *October 6:* The *New York Times* reports that some private insurers have
improperly denied benefits to tens of thousands of Medicare recipients.
Medicare officials have required the insurers to take corrective actions

and have imposed fines on 11 of them. Critics see these problems as evidence that efforts to privatize Medicare are not working.

- *December 13:* After receiving unanimous support in the U.S. House and Senate, a bill to extend the mandatory retirement age for commercial pilots from 60 to 65 is signed by President George W. Bush. If they pass medical and piloting exams, pilots reaching age 60 can continue to work, and retired pilots between ages 60 and 65 can return to work.
- *December 26:* The Equal Employment Opportunity Commission adopts a regulation that allows employers to eliminate private health benefits for retirees who become eligible for Medicare at age 65. Critics claim that the shift to Medicare coverage represents a loss of benefits and a form of age discrimination.

2008

- *January 1:* Under new rules aimed at reducing costs, Medicare beneficiaries with annual income above $82,000 ($164,000 for couples) will pay higher premiums for Part B than others.

CHAPTER 4

BIOGRAPHICAL LISTING

This chapter contains brief biographic sketches of legislators, activists, government leaders, and scholars who have been involved in issues of elderly rights.

Andrew Achenbaum, historian and gerontologist. Among his extensive writings, Achenbaum offers recommendations for dealing with problems of aging such as the status of older women and minority elderly and the isolation of older persons from community ties. His work also has criticized ageism and discrimination against the elderly in medical care.

Aristotle, ancient Greek philosopher. His writings presented a negative picture of the elderly, one that contrasts with the respect usually given in preindustrial societies to the oldest generation. He viewed aged persons as overly pessimistic and distrustful because of the difficulties they had faced in life and as cowardly and fearful because of their concerns about dying.

Brooke Astor, a famous leader of New York high society and patron of the arts. Before her death in 2007 at age 105, she had been diagnosed with Alzheimer's disease, heart problems, and other ailments, and had been in the center of a controversy over elder abuse. According to a 2006 story in the *New York Daily News,* her only child, Anthony Marshall, controlled her $45 million fortune but refused to spend money for her care. In response to a suit citing abuse, a judge approved moving Astor to a hospital for treatment and later to her estate in Briarcliff Manor, New York.

Michael J. Astrue, commissioner of the Social Security Administration since early 2007. As commissioner, he has responsibility for the $580 billion annual benefits paid to 49 million beneficiaries through retirement, disability, and survivor social insurance programs. He also has responsibility for the Supplemental Security Income (SSI) program that provides cash assistance to more than 7 million people with limited income and assets. During his six-year term, he will face challenges in funding these programs and dealing with rapid growth of beneficiaries.

Biographical Listing

Bradley Belt, executive director of the Pension Benefit Guaranty Corporation (PBGC) from 2004 to 2006 and leading expert on retirement security. He says that the Employee Retirement Income Security Act (ERISA), the main law designed to protect the pension rights of older workers and retirees, has many loopholes and allows companies to avoid its pension obligations to workers. For example, the coverage of pension defaults by the PBGC has encouraged some companies to promise more to workers than they can deliver.

Christopher Bond ("Kit" Bond), Republican U.S. senator from Missouri since 1988. He chaired several hearings and town meetings on the problem of elder abuse and supports stronger federal laws to protect the elderly. He cosponsored an early version of the Elder Justice Act.

George W. Bush, president of the United States since 2000. As president, he signed two major pieces of legislation related to protection of older workers and retirees. First, the Medicare Drug Prescription Act of 2003 newly covered the purchase of prescription drugs by Medicare participants. Second, the Pension Protection Act of 2006 reformed the nation's pension laws to increase funding of the PBGC and require companies to contribute enough to their pension funds to meet obligations to workers and retirees.

Robert N. Butler, a physician, gerontologist, and first head of the National Institute on Aging. He coined the term *ageism* in 1969 to highlight the denigration of the elderly and to draw parallels with treatment of women and African Americans. Along with publishing many scientific articles on healthy aging, his book *Why Survive: Being Old in America* won the Pulitzer Prize in 1976 and brought problems of the aged to the attention of scholars and the public.

Daniel Callahan, philosopher and cofounder of the Hastings Center, a research institute on biomedical ethics. His 1987 book, *Setting Limits*, suggested that the government avoid paying for expensive life-extending treatments for those past age 70. Health care at this age level should encompass little more than routine care and easing of pain. Otherwise, he argues, the elderly will use resources that could go to younger persons who have yet to live out a normal life span.

Josefina G. Carbonell, assistant secretary for aging at the Department of Health and Human Services since 2001. She heads the Administration on Aging, the main federal agency for providing home- and community-based services to the elderly. In her position, Carbonell has worked to improve the network of aging services and access to modern and high-quality long-term care, and foster consumer choice among the elderly.

William J. Clinton (Bill Clinton), president of the United States from 1993 to 2001. During his administration, passage of the Retirement Protection Act of 1994 stiffened requirements for funding private pensions, and passage of the Senior Citizens Freedom to Work Act of 2000 eliminated the earnings test that cut Social Security benefits for many wage earners between ages 65 and 70.

Ken Dychtwald, leading expert, author, speaker on aging-related issues, and president of Age Wave. His writings highlight the changing nature of old age in today's world and the need for policy-makers, businesses, and scholars to recognize the potential revolutionary influence the baby-boom generation will have on old age in coming decades.

Naomi C. Earp, chair of the Equal Employment Opportunity Commission (EEOC). Under her leadership, the EEOC enforces age discrimination regulations set forth in the Age Discrimination in Employment Act (ADEA). In 2006 EEOC investigated 13,569 age discrimination charges. Although only a small number of the charges ended up in court, the EEOC cites figures that it recovered $51.5 million that year in monetary benefits for victims of age discrimination.

Dwight D. Eisenhower, president of the United States from 1953 to 1961. During his years in office, he signed the Welfare and Pension Plans Disclosure Act of 1958, the first major government effort to regulate private pension plans. Although signing the bill, he believed that it demanded too little documentation on the financial soundness of private plans and allowed corrupt administrators to hide abuses. He also criticized the bill for failing to assign power to a government agency for investigating problems and enforcing remedies. Many of his proposals became law in years to come.

Rahm Emanuel, the democratic U.S. representative from the Chicago area of Illinois since 2003. He has cosponsored the House version of the Elder Justice Act of 2006, which aims to create a clearly defined federal role in combating elder abuse and providing resources to states and local agencies. Despite bipartisan support, the legislation has not yet passed Congress.

Karen Ferguson, lawyer, author, and director of the Pension Rights Center since 1976. As director, she made the Pension Rights Center a consumer advocate organization dedicated to protecting retirement security, helping older persons with pension problems, and advocating policy changes in laws and regulations on pensions. The work of the organization gives particular attention to violations of the pension rights of older women.

David Hackett Fischer, eminent historian who has written on the history of old age. In *Growing Old in America,* he argued that the elderly had more than economic resources in colonial America and the decades following the Revolutionary War—they also had respect and reverence. He calls the period in America from 1607 to 1820 one of exaltation of old age. Other historians believe this characterization overstates the status of age, but Fischer's work has had much influence on understandings of changes in the position and rights of the elderly.

Biographical Listing

Benjamin Franklin, famous American patriot, diplomat, and founding father of the new nation. In writing to President George Washington, Franklin at age 83 said, "For my own personal ease I should have died two years ago . . . those years have been spent in excruciating pain." As his blunt statement reveals, the rights and respect of the elderly in colonial times came with physical problems and disabilities.

Raymond Gregory, writer and practicing attorney specializing in employment discrimination law. His book *Age Discrimination in the American Workplace* documents widespread mistreatment of older employees and job applicants. He believes that age discrimination is so common that it adversely affects nearly all middle-aged and older workers at least sometime during their careers.

Alan Greenspan, economist, former secretary of the treasury, and former chairman of the Federal Reserve. From 1981 to 1983, he served as chairman of the National Commission on Social Security Reform. Passage of legislation based on commission recommendations helped avert or postpone a funding crisis in Social Security. Changes that went into effect in 1984 included taxing high-income Social Security recipients and extending the normal age of retirement for future generations.

Michael Harrington, American Democratic Socialist and writer. His 1964 book on poverty, *The Other America: Poverty in the United States*, which documented the plight of elderly persons trying to survive on meager Social Security benefits, helped publicize the need for programs to help those in poverty. Changes in Social Security and other programs that followed in the next decade would do much to reduce poverty among the elderly.

Orrin Hatch, Republican U.S. senator of Utah since 1977. He co-sponsored with Blanche Lincoln the Senate version of the Elder Justice Act of 2006, which aims to create a clearly defined federal role in combating elder abuse and providing more resources to states and local agencies. Despite bipartisan support, the legislation has not yet passed Congress.

Jacob K. Javits, Republican U.S. senator of New York from 1957 to 1981. While serving in the Senate, he took a lead role in passing legislation to protect the elderly and pension recipients. For example, he cosponsored the Age Discrimination in Employment Act (ADEA) of 1967.

Lyndon B. Johnson, president of the United States from 1963 to 1969. During his presidency, several important laws protecting the rights of the elderly passed, including the Older Americans Act, the Medicare Act, and the Age Discrimination in Employment Act (ADEA). With his strong support for new programs and regulations, Johnson did much to expand the rights of the elderly.

John F. Kennedy, president of the United States from 1961 to 1963. Although he supported legislation to provide public health care for the elderly, protect them from age discrimination, and set up community services for those needing help, President Kennedy did not live to see passage of major laws for the elderly. The Older Americans Act, the Medicare Act, and the Age Discrimination in Employment Act (ADEA) would pass within the next five years under President Lyndon Johnson.

Peter King, Republican U.S. representative from the Long Island area of New York since 1993. He cosponsored the House version of the Elder Justice Act of 2006, which aims to create a clearly defined federal role in combating elder abuse and providing more resources to states and local agencies. Despite bipartisan support, the legislation has not yet passed Congress.

Herb Kohl, current chair of the U.S. Senate Special Committee on Aging. This committee studies issues, conducts oversight of programs, and investigates reports of fraud and waste related to aging and the elderly. He has criticized the George W. Bush administration for terminating some popular programs for the elderly and has cosponsored the Elder Justice Act to protect against elder abuse.

Maggie Kuhn, activist and founder of the Gray Panthers. After being forced to retire by her employer, she founded the Gray Panther movement in 1970 at age 66 as a way to fight ageism and advocate nursing home reform. She led the organization until her death in 1995 at age 89. She believed that old people constituted a vast untapped and undervalued source of wisdom and energy, and she encouraged older people to stay active in their later years. In advocating on behalf of the rights of the elderly, she also encouraged close ties across ages and generations.

Richard Lamm, former governor of Colorado and current professor at Denver University. As governor, he famously and controversially said in 1984 that terminally ill elderly people have "a duty to die and get out of the way." This statement followed from his belief in the need to ration finite health care resources by age.

Blanche Lincoln, Democratic U.S. senator from Arkansas since 1988. She cosponsored the Senate version of the Elder Justice Act of 2006, which aims to create a clearly defined federal role in combating elder abuse and providing more resources to states and local agencies. Despite bipartisan support, the legislation has not yet passed Congress.

Charles E. F. Millard, director of the Pension Benefit Guaranty Corporation (PBGC), faces several challenges in meeting the corporation's mission to cover the pensions of workers when employers cannot. With problems of pension funding in the airline and steel industries having already strained the finances of the PBGC, further defaults by large private companies could worsen the situation. Legislation in 2006 intended to improve the financial standing of the public corporation and eliminate its shortfall in funding.

Richard M. Nixon, president of the United States from 1969 to 1974. While in office, a modest reform in Social Security ended up doing much to boost benefits for the elderly. In 1972, a law specified that Social Security benefits would increase automatically each year based on the percentage rise in the consumer price index or inflation. The yearly cost-of-living increase prevented the income of the elderly from falling behind rising prices.

Bill Novelli, CEO of the AARP. With 35 million members and revenues of $1 billion, the organization takes stands on public issues affecting the elderly, sponsors testimony before Congress, and mobilizes elderly members to support or oppose legislation. Novelli and the AARP have recently called for political parties to cooperate in addressing problems of health care, retirement funding, and private pension security.

Erdman Palmore, gerontologist and retired professor at Duke University. He has written extensively on ageism and problems of old age. His work highlights not only negative ageism that harms the elderly but also positive ageism that leads to special benefits and programs for the elderly. His work also demonstrates the prevalence of inaccurate and negative images of the elderly.

Claude Pepper, a Democratic politician who served in the House of Representatives from 1963 to his death in 1989 at age 88. Representing a district in and around Miami, Florida, with many older voters, he became a national spokesman for the rights of the elderly and helped strengthen many programs to help the elderly. For example, he helped amend the ADEA to ban mandatory retirement and helped improve Social Security funding with policy changes in the early 1980s.

Richard Posner, former professor at the University of Chicago Law School, current judge on the U.S. Court of Appeals, and prolific author. His book *Aging and Old Age*, which examines diverse economic, moral, and legal issues related to growing old, presents arguments opposing age discrimination laws. For example, he argues that age-discrimination suits have a low success rate and that courts have shown confusion in interpreting the law.

Henry J. Pratt, political scientist and gerontologist. He coined the term *gray lobby* to describe the many age-based interest groups that act on behalf of older persons. This characterization has led to much debate over the political power of the elderly, with other political scientists denying that persons age 65 and over form a meaningful interest group or have disproportionate power.

Jane Bryant Quinn, contributing editor and columnist for *Newsweek* magazine and well-known expert on money and finances. Quinn has expressed concerns about trends in private pensions, particularly the replacement of defined-benefit plans by cash-conversion, defined-contribution, and 401(k) plans. She believes that the defined-benefit plans are better run and pay more to retirees than the alternatives.

Their decline may weaken the economic well-being of the elderly in decades to come.

Erik Rakowski, professor of law at the University of California, Berkeley, and expert on ethical issues relating to health care. He argues that rationing of medical care resources by age makes sense given the need for young patients to have the same chance at longevity that old patients have already enjoyed. When forced to limit or ration resources, society should give the most help to those with the most potential years of life to live and likely to gain greater long-term benefits from medical care.

Ronald Reagan, president of the United States from 1981 to 1989. During his term, recommendations of the National Commission on Social Security Reform were passed to help avert or postpone a funding crisis in Social Security. Changes that went into effect in 1984 included new taxes on high-income Social Security recipients and raised the age of eligibility for full retirement benefits for future generations.

Franklin Delano Roosevelt, president of the United States from 1933 to 1945. Ranked in a survey of historians as one of the three greatest presidents, his strong support for a national pension program for the elderly led to passage of Social Security in 1935. He wanted to ensure the right to economic security for the elderly, but it took several decades for the new program to expand enough to substantially improve the financial well-being of the elderly.

Robert Samuelson, economist, writer, and contributing editor at *Newsweek* and the *Washington Post*. He has written extensively on the problems created by coinciding trends of early retirement and growing entitlements of the elderly to Social Security and Medicare. He has criticized Congress and several presidents for not doing more to deal with the potential future crisis in funding for these old age programs.

Dan Seligman, journalist and editor at *Fortune* magazine. In an article in *Fortune*, he argued that age discrimination laws have exactly the opposite of the intended effects. The laws lead employers, who worry about frivolous and false claims of age discrimination, to avoid hiring older employers. He also believes that worsening performance during old age justifies use of age in hiring decisions.

Harry S. Truman, president of the United States from 1945 to 1953. An advocate of universal public health care, he could not get his proposals passed by Congress in the face of opposition from the American Medical Association (AMA) and other groups. When Lyndon Johnson signed the Medicare bill in 1965, establishing public health care coverage for the elderly, he held the ceremony at the Truman Library in Independence, Missouri, and gave the first two Medicare cards to Truman and his wife Bess.

Biographical Listing

David Walker, comptroller general of the Government Accountability Office. As the national government's head accountant, Walker has criticized the high level of deficit spending by the government, including spending on entitlements for the elderly. He believes that excessive spending and promises of future spending will gradually erode or even suddenly damage economic growth, the standard of living, and national security. Dealing with the problem requires changes in entitlements (especially Social Security and Medicare), cuts in spending, and tax reform.

Kelly M. Weems, acting administrator, Office of Administrator of the Centers for Medicare and Medicaid Services. He leads an organization that has the second largest budget outlay of the federal government and is responsible for $1 of every $3 spent on health care in the United States. The growth of Medicare and Medicaid costs and the concerns about quality of treatment for elderly patients are among the problems Weems faces as administrator.

CHAPTER 5

—————

GLOSSARY

This chapter defines terms, word meanings, and program titles that those doing research on elderly rights may encounter.

401(k) An account (named after a section of the U.S. Internal Revenue Code) that allows workers to contribute funds toward their retirement and that remains free from taxes until withdrawn.

AARP Formerly the American Association of Retired Persons.

ADEA Age Discrimination in Employment Act.

affirmative action Setting goals to hire members of a class of people facing discrimination, often by giving preferences among qualified persons to underrepresented groups; some have called for affirmative action to hire older workers.

age discrimination The unfair treatment of older persons (defined as age 40 and over by the ADEA) that stems from age bias or ageism.

ageism Prejudiced beliefs about older persons that lead to discriminatory actions, much as racism and sexism lead to discrimination on the basis of skin color and gender; some define the term to include positive treatment of the aged that gives them advantages over the young.

Alzheimer's disease The most common form of dementia, it involves the breakdown of cells and nervous tissue in the brain, loss of intellectual abilities and memory, and changes in personality; it occurs most often in old age.

AMA American Medical Association.

annuity Income paid at regular intervals for a fixed period of time, usually the recipient's life, in return for a premium paid at the start; retirees often purchase an annuity with accumulated retirement savings.

assisted living An arrangement for residents to live in their own house or apartment but also receive services for food preparation, housekeeping, bathing, dressing, and 24-hour emergency aid.

baby boomer Member of the generation born between roughly 1945 and 1964, the years of a rise in fertility (known as a baby boom) in the United

States; the generation comprises a large part of the U.S. population and will produce exceptional growth in the size of the older population in the 21st century.

cash-balance conversion A hybrid pension plan involving the shift from a defined-benefit plan to one more closely resembling a defined-contribution plan.

copayment The amount a beneficiary in Medicare or other health care plans must pay for each (otherwise free) medical service received.

cost-of-living allowance (COLA) A periodic increase in payments (such as Social Security or Supplemental Security Income benefits) meant to keep pace with inflation and based on the Consumer Price Index.

deductible The initial amount of a covered expense (such as for Medicare services) that the beneficiary must pay before the program or insurance policy pays its part.

defined-benefit pension Fixed monthly retirement payment based on years of service and earnings prior to retirement that usually lasts until death.

defined-contribution pension Retirement payment based on the accumulation of fixed contributions made by employers and employees into an investment account that belongs to the worker.

dementia A term referring to symptoms occurring most often in old age and involving the loss of intellectual functioning and changes in personality.

discrimination The unfair treatment of a group or person—usually based on race, color, sex, national origin, religion, disability, or age—because of prejudices, economic interests, or unconscious bias.

disparate impact A form of unintentional discrimination based on policies or actions that negatively affect protected groups more than others, such as a policy of giving lower raises to experienced workers, who also tend to be older.

disparate treatment A form of discrimination based on intentional actions, such as giving preference to younger workers and job applicants over older workers and job applicants.

early retirement For Social Security, retirement that begins at age 62, several years before normal retirement, and gives recipients lower benefits for a longer period of time than normal retirees.

EEOC Equal Employment Opportunity Commission.

elder abuse The infliction of physical, emotional, financial, or psychological harm on an older adult.

ERISA Employee Retirement Income and Security Act.

euthanasia Mercy killing that puts an ailing person to a painless death or withholds medical measures to allow a person to die.

fee-for-service plan In Medicare, the direct payment of hospitals and doctors for the costs of services and tests provided for Medicare patients.

fiduciary   A person entrusted with power or property, such as for the proper operation and financial safety of a pension plan.

gerontology   The study of the biological, psychological, and social aspects of human aging and the aged.

graying of the federal budget   An expression that refers to the increasing proportion of the federal government budget that goes to programs for the elderly.

Health Maintenance Organization (HMO)   A type of health care plan that covers a full range of services, with treatment given only by providers in the HMO network.

Individual Retirement Account (IRA)   A savings plan for individuals that is protected from taxes until the funds are paid out for retirement.

life expectancy   The average number of years a person can expect to live starting from birth (or other age) according to age-based rates of mortality in a given year.

lump-sum payment   A single sum of money that serves as complete payment; sometimes it is in the form of a pension payout.

mandatory retirement   Retirement forced on workers after reaching a specified age such as 65.

means-test   A way to determine eligibility for a program based on the financial position (or means) and needs of a person or family.

Medicaid   A federal and state partnership to provide health insurance to the needy (or those with low income and assets) that has become a key source of health care support of the elderly.

Medicare   A federal health insurance program for people age 65 and over or younger people with disabilities that partially covers hospital, medical, and prescription drug costs; it consists of the health insurance component of Social Security or OASDHI.

Medicare Advantage   A Medicare-approved private health care plan, such as a Health Maintenance Network or Preferred Provider Organization, that serves as an alternative for Medicare participants to a fee-for-service plan.

Medigap   Medicare Supplemental Insurance or policies to pay for health care costs that Medicare does not cover.

NIA   National Institute on Aging.

NRTA   National Retired Teachers Association.

nursing home   A residential institution that cares for persons unable to look after themselves; skilled nursing homes provide more medical care than custodial nursing homes.

OASDHI   Old Age, Survivors, Disability, and Health Insurance, the formal name of Social Security.

old age   Although commonly meaning age 65 and over, it more generally refers to a stage in life that precedes death and can be used in a variety of contexts to include early retirees in their 50s or only those in their 80s and older who are likely to be slowed by physical deterioration.

oldest old   Older persons over age 84, those least likely to be healthy and active; the term helps make distinctions among the diverse population of those age 65 and over.

ombudsman   A person who investigates and attempts to resolve complaints and problems.

PBGC   Pension Benefit Guaranty Corporation.

pension   The regular payment of income to persons for support during retirement and old age; the amount of the payment is generally based on years of previous work, wages or salary, and contributions to a pension system.

population aging   An increase in the average age of a population or in the percentage of the population over age 65.

Preferred Provider Organization (PPO)   A type of health care plan in which a sponsor such as an employer or insurer negotiates prices and treatment options for its members with a network of health care providers.

privatization   Conversion of a state-owned company or public program such as Social Security into a private one.

ration   A restriction on the allotment of goods and services such as medical care.

right   An idea based on values, tradition, or law of what is due or guaranteed to a person or group.

social security   A term commonly used in Europe to refer to a package of programs such as old-age pensions, universal health care, unemployment insurance, and family allowances that helps persons of all ages; its usage differs from that for Social Security in the United States, which refers more narrowly to old-age programs.

Social Security   A program in the United States originally officially entitled Old Age, Survivors, Disability, and Health Insurance (OASDHI) that provides retirement income, health care for the aged, and income support of the disabled.

spouse benefit   For Social Security, the benefit that goes to a person who has not worked enough to be directly eligible but is based on the eligibility of a spouse.

SSA   Social Security Administration.

SSI   Supplemental Security Income.

stereotype   A simplified, often negative belief or image about a group that is inaccurately generalized to all individuals belonging to the group.

Supplemental Security Income   A means-tested program that provides benefits to the elderly with income and assets below specified limits.

survivor's benefit   Payments for a pension, insurance plan, or other program that go to a surviving spouse or children who are minors of the deceased person originally eligible for the benefit.

trust fund   For Social Security, an account that collects the excess of revenues over expenditures, invests the difference in government securities, and holds the funds to cover future shortfalls in revenues.

vest   To grant an employee the right to a specified pension from a company, usually after completing a fixed period of employment.

youngest old   Older persons ages 65 to 84, those in old age most likely to be healthy and active; the term helps make distinctions among the diverse population of those age 65 and over.

waiver   Intentional relinquishment of a right, such as giving up age discrimination claims in return for retirement incentives.

PART II

GUIDE TO FURTHER RESEARCH

CHAPTER 6

HOW TO RESEARCH ELDERLY RIGHTS

The importance of trends that have affected the elderly over the last century—increasing longevity, longer retirement, and expanded spending for Social Security and Medicare—makes information on elderly rights easy to find. Media reports regularly cover topics relating to the elderly, a large audience with interests in issues shaping their lives. Books, articles, and web documents likewise address issues relating to the well-being of the elderly and the impact of aging on society. These issues include:

- mistreatment of older people in the labor force,
- the growing desire of older persons to work longer,
- the success of Social Security in supporting retired persons,
- expected future problems in funding Social Security,
- access of the elderly to government-funded medical care,
- concerns about the quality of that care,
- vulnerability of frail and confused elderly persons to abuse, and
- the growing burden of caring for these elderly.

Since nearly everyone is affected to some extent by these problems or has a parent or grandparent who is affected, elderly rights is a topic of special interest and importance.

CHALLENGES TO RESEARCHING ELDERLY RIGHTS

Although easily accessible, information on elderly rights can also overwhelm those conducting research. As a help to researchers, this chapter offers some general suggestions on using bibliographic resources and more specific suggestions on consulting key sources. Even with these suggestions, however, those researching elderly rights will face several challenges.

First, writings on the topic span a variety of fields of study. Elderly rights relate to the complexities of discrimination, ageism, employment law, private pension plans, retirement, government finances, privatization of public programs, health care delivery, mistreatment of patients, rationing of health care, nursing home regulations, and abuse within families. They further relate to specific knowledge about the Age Discrimination in Employment Act (ADEA), Social Security, Supplemental Security Income (SSI), the Pension Benefit Guaranty Corporation (PBGC), Medicare, Medicaid, and the Administration on Aging. These topics cover diverse and detailed fields of study such as law, ethics, political science, sociology, demography, criminology, medicine, and finance.

Second, the literature on the topic sometimes reflects strong political and moral views that make it hard to separate facts from opinions. Differing viewpoints can lead to widely varying interpretations of the facts and issues. These views come into play, for example, in debates over the proper role of the government in supporting the elderly and the ability of government agencies to aid those in need. On one side, critics view Social Security and Medicare as seriously flawed. They suggest that the government does not do well in administering these huge programs and that the programs will go bankrupt without excessive tax increases in decades to come. They call instead for more reliance on the market in supporting the elderly and limiting the entitlements granted by the government to the elderly. On the other side, many see Social Security and Medicare as two of the country's most successful programs, ones that have eliminated most poverty among the elderly and contributed to longer and healthier lives. The government should expand and protect these programs by investing more resources rather than diverting resources to the private sector. They claim that forecasts of bankruptcy are exaggerated and designed to reduce the public support for the programs. With proper leadership, government organizations perform effectively in protecting the rights of the elderly.

Third, elderly rights relate to complex legal and policy issues. Writings on the topic are filled with so many names and acronyms of government programs, departments, and laws that regulations and responsibilities easily can get blurred. Even those with the most at stake are daunted by the complexities. As noted by critics of age discrimination laws, courts often have trouble interpreting the meaning of relevant legislation. As noted by critics of Medicare, physicians often have trouble determining what treatments the program covers and what rights their elderly patients have. And as noted by critics of private pension plans, workers often have trouble understanding what financial rights they have to retirement benefits from employers.

How to Research Elderly Rights

How can researchers overcome these challenges? Here are some tips:

- **Define the topic and questions carefully.** Rather than researching general elderly rights, the following topics would allow for more focused and in-depth research: changes in the social status of the elderly, ageism in social life, laws prohibiting age discrimination, future Social Security funding, income of the elderly, violations of private pension rights, quality of health care services for the elderly, the pros and cons of health care rationing for the elderly, and strategies to prevent elder abuse. With so many choices available, making the research manageable requires care and precision in selecting topics. A narrowly defined topic can prevent feeling overwhelmed by the material and allow for in-depth treatment.

- **Consider the underlying perspectives.** Relying on a variety of sources will help make sense of the differing values and beliefs that shape views on elderly rights. Toward that end, the annotated bibliography in the next chapter includes a wide selection of readings that represent diverse perspectives. In addition, however, it helps to consider the background and potential biases of the authors. Given the heated disputes over the costs and benefits of government funding for retirement and health care, information on the underlying perspectives of authors can separate opinions and emotion from facts and reason.

- **Evaluate your sources.** In reviewing books and articles, check the date of publication to make sure the information is recent, check the qualifications of the author and the citation of sources to make sure the information is reliable, and check for the presentation of alternative views to make sure the information is presented fairly. Books and articles often differ in their audience, with some more focused on popular audiences and some more focused on scholarly audiences. Both popular and scholarly information is useful, but it helps to recognize how they differ in the depth of information, citation of sources, and year of publication. In reviewing Internet sources, use even more care. Nearly anyone can post documents online, and many lack checks on the reliability of their information. Evaluate the qualifications of the author, the legitimacy of the sponsoring organization, and the potential for bias.

- **Master the basic facts and terms.** Few can make sense of the material on elderly rights without having some familiarity with common names, organizations, and acronyms in the area. Try to learn the basic terminology; careful and precise usage lends authority to research.

- **Search for balance.** Since complex questions about elderly rights seldom have simple answers, do not accept controversial claims of fact and suggested solutions to problems at face value. It is easy to assign blame for problems in support of the elderly and advocate simple solutions. To avoid this tendency, search for balanced presentations based on evidence—even if highly technical—and careful weighing of the alternatives. Researchers should seek to understand the complexity that underlies the topic and treat all sides of the debates fairly.

The rest of this chapter reviews various types of research resources. It considers online resources, print resources, and resources related to law and legislation.

ONLINE RESOURCES

GENERAL SITES

Given its ease in providing information, the Internet offers a good place to begin research on elderly rights. The Web contains a wide variety of research, reference, and opinion pieces on the topic that can be easily accessed with an Internet connection. One can find useful facts and perspectives on nearly any aspect of elderly rights by patiently working through even a small portion of available web pages. Finding one suitable site suggests links to others, which in turn leads in new directions. Innovative ideas and fresh information emerge in this process. Indeed, many web documents are updated or created anew to keep up with recent events and the latest information.

However, the extraordinary wealth of information that the Internet makes available to researchers can be overwhelming. Most searches return an impressive but dauntingly large number of "hits." The advice to define narrow research topics applies particularly to using the Internet. Otherwise, combing through all the web sites listed by searches can result in wasted effort. In addition, the information obtained does not always meet high standards of reliability and balance. Unlike books and articles, web documents generally do not go through a process of review and editing before publication. In some cases, they offer little more than the opinions of strangers.

Users must take care in relying on materials obtained from web sites and inquire into the background of the site sponsors. Is the organization sponsoring the page reputable, or does the author have expertise? Does the web page aim for objectivity? Is it written well and based on careful thinking? Those web pages where one can answer these questions affirmatively will be the ones to rely on the most. With these qualifications in mind, Internet research can proceed in several ways.

Popular and general search engines such as Google (http://www.google.com), Yahoo! (http://www.yahoo.com), Alta Vista (http://www.altavista.com), Excite (http://www.excite.com), Lycos (http://www.lycos.com), Ask (http://www.ask.com), MSN (http://www.msn.com), and many others can find web sites with information on elderly rights. Using these search engines effectively requires thoughtful selection of search terms and patient effort but can lead to unexpected and intriguing discoveries. Broad searches that focus on "elderly" and "rights" will work less well than narrower searches on age discrimination, Social Security, Medicare, and elder abuse.

Wikipedia (http://en.wikipedia.org/wiki/Main_Page), a free web-based encyclopedia, has entries for most major laws and programs related to elderly rights. Created in 2001, Wikipedia allows readers to collaboratively make and revise entries, which is particularly helpful in keeping up-to-date with current events. Critics point out that the entries lack an authority or known author to ensure reliability, and many schools prohibit use of Wikipedia as a source for student papers. Sometimes the objectivity of writers and editors is disputed. While recognizing these limitations, the entries for topics relating to elderly rights can be useful, in combination with other sources, to researchers.

ORGANIZATION SITES

Knowledge of key organizations—government, advocacy, service, professional, and research—is crucial for researching elderly rights. Chapter 8 lists a variety of such organizations, but consulting the home pages of a few of them can help in starting research.

The federal government agencies that deal most directly with seniors have web pages with information on topics related to elderly rights. Check the Administration on Aging (http://www.aoa.gov), the Social Security Administration (http://www.ssa.gov), and the Centers for Medicare and Medicaid Services (http://www.cms.hhs.gov). Although less directly focused on the elderly, the Employee Benefits Security Administration of the Department of Labor (http://www.dol.gov/ebsa) and the Pension Benefit Guaranty Corporation (http://www.pbgc.gov), a federal government corporation, offer information on pension plan rights and protections. In addition to the federal government, each state government will have offices or departments that deal with Medicaid, adult protective services, and nursing home regulation. Finding the office or department requires a search within a state government website, but a search can locate useful material. Among private organizations, the AARP webpage (http://www.aarp.org) has sections on health, money and work, and family, home, and the law that discuss issues relating to elderly rights. A United Nations organization, Global Action on Aging (http://www.global aging.org/index.htm) covers elder rights from an international perspective.

SITES ON SPECIFIC ELDERLY RIGHTS TOPICS

Along with getting resources from broad—and perhaps overwhelming—general searches and from organizations with wide-ranging goals, it helps to begin a search from particular sites. Here are some recommendations organized by the major topics on elderly rights.

General Treatments: The web is filled with pages that present statistics on longevity, retirement, and aging. One useful overview from the Administration on Aging, "A Profile of Older American: 2006" (http://www. aoa.gov/prof/Statistics/profile/2006/2006profile.pdf) has key charts and tables that describe the elderly population. For a set of international statistics, see "World Population Aging: 1950–2050" from the United Nations (http://www.un.org/esa/population/publications/worldageing19502050).

Work and Age Discrimination: In "Job Loss Help: Age Discrimination at Work" (http://www.aarp.org/money/careers/jobloss/Articles/a2004-04-28-agediscrimination.html), the AARP aims to help its members with information on the ADEA and the options available to age discrimination victims. With its clear advice and links to other resources (including help in finding legal representation), this web page offers an excellent starting place to learn about age discrimination. For a less practical but still helpful resource, see "Equal Employment Opportunity" from the U.S. Department of Labor (http://www.dol.gov/dol/topic/discrimination/agedisc.htm).

Pensions, Income, and Social Security: For an introduction to the topic of private pension rights, the Department of Labor has posted its booklet on "What You Should Know About Your Retirement Plan" (http://www.dol.gov/ebsa/publications/wyskapr.html). With a style that nicely melds attention to detail with a presentation geared to nonexperts, it describes different types of pension plans, how to receive retirement pension benefits, and how divorce or employment changes might affect retirement benefits. For an introduction to Social Security rights, the Congressional Budget Office has prepared "Social Security: A Primer" (http://www.cbo.gov/ftpdoc.cfm?index=3213&type=0&sequence=0). Although it has much information, the document is fair-minded in its description of the problems faced by Social Security and the proposed reforms to address the problems.

Medical Care, Medicare, and Medicaid: A description of how ageism violates the medical care rights of the elderly can be found in "Ageism: How Health Care Fails the Elderly" (http://www.agingresearch.org/content/article/detail/694). Descriptions of the complex rules for Medicare and Medicaid and the rights of the elderly under these programs can be found in two documents: "Medicare and You 2007" from the Centers for Medicare and Medicaid Services (http://www.medicare.gov/publications/pubs/pdf/10050.pdf), and "Medicaid: A Primer" from the Kaiser Commission on Medicaid and the Uninsured (http://www.kff.org/medicaid/7334-02.cfm). The AARP complements these two documents with a short listing of "Your Medicare Rights" (http://www.aarp.org/health/medicare/traditional/a2003-04-28-medicarerights.html).

Elder Care and Protection against Abuse: The American Psychological Association introduces readers to the problem of elder abuse in "Elder Abuse and Neglect: In Search of Solutions" (http://www.apa.org/pi/aging/eldabuse.html). It defines key terms, gives several real life examples, discusses causes, and offers solutions to the problem. "Residents' Rights" from the National Citizens' Coalition for Nursing Home Reform (http://www.nccnhr.org/public/50_156_449.cfm) lays out a long list of rights and problems of nursing home residents.

PRINT SOURCES

Despite the ease of obtaining information from the Internet, books and articles available from libraries and bookstores remain essential sources. Good books integrate material that is otherwise scattered, present information in a logical and understandable format, and allow for a comprehensive approach to the issues. Edited volumes provide multiple perspectives on a topic but usually with a meaningful framework, while other books present a single but in-depth viewpoint. Exploiting these advantages requires use of catalogs, indexes, bibliographies, and other guides.

BIBLIOGRAPHIC RESOURCES

Besides using catalogs at a city or university library, researchers can consult the comprehensive bibliographic resource of the Library of Congress catalog (http://catalog.loc.gov). To browse holdings by subject, click Basic Search, then type in age discrimination, private pensions, Social Security, Medicare, Medicaid, elder abuse, or other specific terms and highlight the subject browse. A variety of subject headings will be listed, some deserving further investigation. Alternatively, a keyword search of "elderly rights" returns a list of 9,697 references. The list can be narrowed by adding limits to search results.

A listing of catalogs for specific libraries can be found through Yahoo! (dir.Yahoo.com/Reference/Libraries). A large list of libraries allows users to browse catalogs outside their local library and discover new references. Each library will have its own search procedures but the general rule of searching for more specific keywords will work best in finding relevant materials.

Bookstore catalogs not only allow for searches of books currently in print on any variety of topics but also have another advantage. They often include summaries and reader reviews of books that can help determine their relevance and value. In some cases, one can browse through an electronic version of parts of a book. At the same time, bookstore catalogs will not have as many books that are out-of-print, but still valuable, as libraries. Overall, electronic bookstores such as Amazon.com (http://www.amazon.com) and Barnes and Noble (http://www.barnesandnoble.com) are good bibliographic resources.

Periodical indexes used to search for print articles are available at most libraries. *OCLC First Search* contains an electronic version of *Reader's Guide Abstracts* that will list titles and abstracts from a large number of magazines (and sometimes allow access to the full text). However, users generally need access to a subscribing library for this database. *InfoTrac* also compiles articles for general interest audiences and sometimes includes an abstract with the citation, or an abstract and a full text article. It again requires library privileges. *Ingenta Connect* (http://www.ingentaconnect.com) allows a search of scholarly works from more than 22 million articles and reports and more than 30,000 publications. Searching *Ingenta* is free but delivery of an article sometimes requires a fee. Magazines such as *Time* (http://www.time.com/time) often have a web site that allows users to search for articles.

Libraries usually subscribe to catalogs of newspaper articles. In addition, many newspapers maintain a web page with an archive of past articles. The *New York Times*, for example, allows searches of its stories (and presents the day's major news) at its web page (http://www.nytimes.com). Most articles from the last seven days are free but premium articles and access to earlier articles requires a fee. The *Washington Post* also provides a web page with a search option (http://www.washingtonpost.com) but also requires purchase of older articles. Otherwise, Yahoo! (http://dir.yahoo.com/News_and_Media/Newspapers) lists links to many newspapers that can be accessed via the Web. Local libraries will offer a better source for finding past articles without a fee. For all these sources, a search on the elderly or rights will typically return too many stories to sort through, and narrower searches will provide more useful information.

SPECIFIC BOOKS AND ARTICLES ON ELDERLY RIGHTS

Along with general bibliographic resources for print materials and an annotated bibliography, it helps to have a few books and print articles to get started. Here are some recommended books and articles organized by the major topics of elderly rights.

General Treatments: A classic history of old age, *Growing Old in America* by David Hackett Fischer (Oxford: Oxford University Press, 1978) introduces readers to the broad sweep of change in the status of the elderly over the last several centuries. Revisionist scholars have disputed some of his arguments and offered more nuanced understandings of the history of old age, but this remains a fascinating and credible source. For a recent view of the future of aging and ways to make it better, see *Older Americans, Vital Communities: A Bold Vision for Societal Aging* (Baltimore, Md.: Johns Hopkins University Press, 2005) by historian Andrew Achenbaum. For a more popularized and positive book on the future of the elderly, see *Age Wave: How the Most Important Trend in Our Time Will Change Your Future* (New York: St. Martin's Press, 1989) by Ken Dychtwald and Joe Flower.

Two articles contrast positive and negative views about the future of old age. On the positive side, Peter Coy argues in "Old. Smart. Productive" (*Business Week*, no. 3939, June 27, 2005, pp. 78–84, 86) that the elderly in the future will become a productive force rather than an economic burden. One the negative side, Marti G. Parker and Mats Thorslund argue in "Health Trends in the Elderly Population: Getting Better and Getting Worse" (*The Gerontologist*, vol. 47, 2007, pp. 150–158) that increases in chronic disease will lead to greater health problems in old age and devotion of more resources for health care.

Work and Age Discrimination: A book by employment lawyer Raymond Gregory, *Age Discrimination in the American Workplace: Old at a Young Age* (New Brunswick, N.J.: Rutgers University Press, 2001), presents statistics mixed with personal stories to illustrate that the problem of age discrimination is much worse than people realize. An article by Ira Carnahan, "Removing the Scarlet A" (*Forbes*, vol. 170, no. 3, August 12, 2002, p. 78) also describes the growth of age discrimination suits but cautions that the suits can backfire by creating a new incentive for employers not to hire older workers.

Pensions, Income, and Social Security: *Social Security, Medicare and Government Pensions: Get the Most of Your Retirement and Medical Benefits* (Berkeley, Calif.: NOLO, 2007) by Joseph L. Matthews and Dorothy Matthews Berman offers a guide through the maze of Social Security and Medicare options and serves as a reference for those wanting to understand the rights older persons have in these programs. *Protecting Your Pension for Dummies* (New York: For Dummies, 2007) by Robert D. Gary and Jori Bloom Naegele does much the same for private pensions. "More Risk— More Reward: Retirement Guide" (*Business Week*, no. 3944, July 25, 2005, pp. 100–101) by Howard Gleckman and Rich Miller describes changes in public and private funding for retirement income and what older workers need to do to prepare for a costly old age.

Medical Care, Medicare, and Medicaid: A broad resource on the legal rights of the elderly, particularly in relation to health care, can be found in *American Bar Association Legal Guide for Americans Over 50: Everything about the Law and Medicare and Medicaid, Retirement Rights, and Long-Term Choices . . . and Your Parents* (New York: Random House Reference, 2006). Jeanne M. Hannah and Joseph H. Friedman in *Taking Charge: Good Medical Care for the Elderly and How to Get It* (Traverse City, Mich.: Old Mission Press,

2006) give practical advice on how older persons can act on their own to get health care rights. Information on the specific problem of obtaining long-term care and getting Medicaid rights can be found in K. Gabriel Heiser, *How to Protect Your Family's Assets from Devastating Nursing Home Costs: Medicaid Secrets* (Superior, Colo.: Phylius Press, 2007).

Elder Care and Protection against Abuse: Two different kinds of books introduce readers to the problem of elder abuse and ways to prevent it. One book for popular audiences, *Ending Elder Abuse: A Family Guide* by Diane S. Sandell and Lois Hudson (Fort Bragg, Calif.: QED Press, 2000), offers advice to family members, caregivers, and legislators on how to prevent and stop the problem of elder abuse. A scholarly book from the National Research Council, *Elder Mistreatment: Abuse, Neglect, and Exploitation in an Aging America* (Washington, D.C.: National Academy Press, January 2003), presents an in-depth review of studies and knowledge on the topic.

LEGAL RESEARCH

A search for federal laws on elderly rights must first identify specific rights, laws, and terms. Age discrimination law rests primarily in the ADEA (see Appendix A). Regulations of private pension come from the ERISA and its amendments (http://finduslaw.com/employee_retirement_income_security_act_erisa_29_u_s_code_chapter_18). However, the Pension Protection Act of 2006, all 393 pages (http://www.dol.gov/ebsa/pdf/ppa2006.pdf), has added much to the law on pension rights. The Social Security Act, a compilation of 21 sections, is easily found (http://www.ssa.gov/OP_Home/ssact/comp-ssa.htm) but less easy to read and understand. The Social Security Act contains Medicare and Medicaid regulations, but for the recent addition of the prescription drugs to Medicare, see the Medicare Modernization Act of 2003 (http://www.cms.hhs.gov/MMAUpdate).

For more detail—and more complexity—a search of the U.S. Code will locate a variety of more specific laws on other topics relating to elderly rights. Go to the Cornell Law School search web page (http://www4.law.cornell.edu/uscode/search/index.html) and type elderly. Then scroll through the 358 (at last count) separate listings of the code to find those of most interest. Finding the codes for individual states or cities requires separate searches. A FindLaw web page helps in the searches by listing links to each state (http://www.findlaw.com/11stategov/indexcode.html). Although difficult, state searches are required to research elder abuse laws, which are the responsibility of the states rather than the federal government.

Court decisions on elderly rights usually involve aspects of age discrimination but also involve pension rights and elder abuse (see chapter 2).

The suits usually involve individuals suing over mistreatment in the work-place, cuts in promised pension benefits, or abusers seeking an overturn of their convictions. Information on the suits, jury decisions, awards, appeals, and final judgments can be found through searches of newspapers such as the *New York Times* (http://www.nytimes.com) and general search engines such as Google, Yahoo!, and Ask. To obtain the written decisions in cases involving elderly rights, electronic law libraries such as Westlaw (http://www.westlaw.com) and LexisNexis (http://www.lexisnexis.com) include court opinions but require a subscription. Opinions of the Supreme Court can be obtained from the Legal Information Institute (http://www.law.cornell.edu).

CHAPTER 7

ANNOTATED BIBLIOGRAPHY

The following annotated bibliography on rights of the elderly contains five sections:

- general information on aging and ageism,
- rights involving work and freedom from age discrimination,
- rights involving pensions, income, and Social Security,
- rights involving medical care, Medicare, and Medicaid, and
- rights involving elder care and protection against abuse.

Within each of these sections, the citations are divided into subsections on books, articles, and web documents. The topics and citations include technical and nontechnical works, in-depth and short treatments, and research and opinion pieces (see chapter 6 for an overview on how to most effectively use these materials).

GENERAL INFORMATION ON AGING AND AGEISM

BOOKS

Achenbaum, W. Andrew. *Older Americans, Vital Communities: A Bold Vision for Societal Aging*. Baltimore, Md.: Johns Hopkins University Press, 2005. A respected historian considers the future of aging rather than its past. He describes how changes in longevity and demographic characteristics of the elderly will transform the nature of aging in the coming decades and offers recommendations for making that future better. The chapter on reforming the U.S. health care system to serve an aging population better has special importance to elderly rights.

Annotated Bibliography

Achenbaum, W. Andrew, Steven Weiland, and Carole Haber. *Key Words in Sociocultural Gerontology*. New York: Springer Publishing, 1996. Each of the 40-plus entries in this short book is 2–3 pages long, which allows the authors to discuss definitions and meanings more thoroughly than do dictionaries or glossaries. Terms such as age discrimination, ageism, elderly, gray lobby, Older Americans Act, old-age entitlements, retirement, and Social Security relate closely to issues involving elderly rights.

Altman, Stuart H., and David I. Shactman, eds. *Policies for an Aging Society*. Baltimore, Md.: Johns Hopkins University Press, 2002. Participants in a 1999 conference considered the financial challenges facing nations with aging populations. Based on the conference papers, the chapters in the book offer recommendations for dealing with the challenges. With each chapter linked to another chapter that offers an alternative viewpoint, readers get a sense not only of the problems governments face in paying the costs for retirement and medical care of a large aged population but also the disagreements over needed reforms. Readers get an even-handed presentation of contrasting policies.

Butler, Robert N. *Why Survive? Being Old in America*. Baltimore, Md.: Johns Hopkins Press, 2002. The theme of this book is that modern medicine has allowed persons to live to older ages, but the mistreatment of the elderly makes a longer life less satisfying than it should be. Butler, a physician, gerontologist, and former director of the National Institute on Aging, describes problems of the elderly involving Social Security, health care, housing, and nursing homes. He believes the nation needs a concerted and coordinated national policy on aging to address these problems and give the elderly the rights they deserve. However, this newly released version of the original 1975 publication has become somewhat dated.

Campbell, Andrea Louise. *How Policies Make Citizens: Senior Political Activism and the American Welfare State*. Princeton, N.J.: Princeton University Press, 2003. This case study of senior citizens and their political activity describes how older Americans emerged as a powerful interest group. The book focuses most on political activism involving Social Security but more generally illustrates the political influence of the elderly on broad public policies and entitlements. Although the book says little directly about elderly rights, it does explain how the elderly gained political power that expanded their rights.

Cassel, Christine K., ed. *The Practical Guide to Aging: What Everyone Needs to Know*. New York: New York University Press, 1999. Most of the chapters in this volume, while of interest to older persons, have little to do with elderly rights. Yet chapters on managing medicine, the law and the elderly, and achieving financial security touch on related topics. Because the book aims to give practical advice to the elderly rather than discuss academic issues, it complements other books on elderly rights.

Coyle, Jean M., ed. *Handbook on Women and Aging*. Westport, Conn.: Praeger, 1997. As a disproportionate percentage of the elderly population and a group subjected to discrimination earlier in their lives, older women deserve special study. This edited volume compiles existing research on the topic with the goal of providing an accurate picture of older women and understanding their social treatment, psychological change, and experience of widowhood.

Disch, Robert, Harry R. Moody, and Rose Dobrof, eds. *Dignity and Old Age*. New York: Haworth Press, 1998. Based on the premise that people have the right to age with dignity, the chapters in this edited volume cover topics such as assuring dignity in means-tested programs, paying for programs to support the elderly, and the role of spirituality and community in the last years of life. While most books on rights of the elderly focus on economics, work, and health care, this book focuses on rights that are less concrete but equally important.

Dychtwald, Ken, and Joe Flower. *Age Wave: How the Most Important Trend in Our Time Will Change Your Future*. New York: St. Martin's Press, 1989. Age wave refers to the aging baby-boom generation and the changes it will bring in future decades to society and to the experience of growing old. The authors dispute negative views that overstate problems of poor health, poverty, and rigid beliefs in old age. They instead see the potential for new activities, a high standard of living, and strong relationships across generations. In decades to come, the new elderly will demand protection of their rights and have the power to realize their goals.

Fischer, David Hackett. *Growing Old in America: The Bland-Lee Lectures Delivered at Clark University*. Expanded Edition. Oxford: Oxford University Press, 1978. An esteemed scholar presents a history of old age in America from colonial times to the 20th century. Covering changes in the treatment of the aged from veneration centuries ago to current discrimination and lack of respect, the history is vividly presented and filled with fascinating examples. Revisionist scholars have disputed some of his arguments and offered more nuanced understandings of the history of old age, but this remains a classic text and is well worth reading.

Freedman, Marc. *Prime Time: How Baby Boomers Will Revolutionize Retirement and Transform America*. New York: Public Affairs, 1999. Aging may change drastically in the 21st century according to this book. The author argues that old age in the future will involve intense social activism, volunteering, and lifelong learning. Accustomed to leadership roles and using their skills to change society, the elderly will demand more rights for themselves in decades to come and participate in community activities to help others. These positive changes will contradict views of the elderly as a drain on public resources.

Gillick, Muriel R. *The Denial of Aging: Perpetual Youth, Eternal Life, and Other Dangerous Fantasies.* Cambridge, Mass.: Harvard University Press, 2006. A Harvard professor disputes common beliefs that diet and exercise can preserve youth. She encourages greater acceptance of old age and the changes it brings.

Haber, Carole, and Brian Gratton. *Old Age and the Search for Security: An American Social History.* Bloomington: Indiana University Press, 1994. This book examines many of the same issues about changes in the status of the elderly examined by David Hackett Fischer and sometimes comes to different conclusions. It has the advantage of relying on a flurry of research that followed Fischer's early work but is oriented more for academics than the general public.

Harper, Sarah. *Aging Societies.* London: Hodder Education, 2006. A variety of textbooks on aging and gerontology can supply background information on demographic, social, and psychological aspects of aging for those researching elderly rights. This one by the director of the Institute on Ageing at the University of Oxford gives special attention to demographic trends in aging and how they affect retirement and family relationships.

Harper, Sarah, and Peter Laslett. "The Puzzle of Retirement and Early Retirement." In Anthony F. Health, John Ermisch, and Duncan Gallie, eds., *Understanding Social Change.* Oxford: Oxford University Press, 2005, pp. 224–254. The puzzle referenced by the title of this chapter is that early retirement grew during decades when the size of the aged population and the need for more workers grew. The authors explain the puzzle by suggesting that retirement has emerged as a right and a new stage of life that continues independently of labor force demand for older workers. Older persons now view retirement as a period of funded leisure, even though governments may have trouble paying for early retirement of large portions of the labor force.

Hudson, Robert B., ed. *The New Politics of Old Age Policy.* Baltimore, Md.: Johns Hopkins Press, 2005. Along with debates over the form Social Security and Medicare should take, the chapters in this volume consider topics such as the political power of the elderly and the use of age rather than the need to entitle persons to public benefits. The chapter by Angela O'Rand on when old age begins and what implications the definition has for public policy is particularly useful in relation to elderly rights.

Levin, Jack, and William C. Levin. *Ageism: Prejudice and Discrimination against the Elderly.* Belmont, Calif.: Wadsworth Publishing, 1980. One of the first to develop the idea of ageism and give detailed examples of how it affects the elderly, this dated book remains informative. The authors criticize the field of gerontology for emphasizing the decline in abilities with old age, an emphasis that, like race and racism, can lead to blaming the elderly rather than society for their problems. The book is more one-sided than Palmore's more recent book on the same topic, *Ageism: Negative and Positive*, but useful for its critical viewpoint.

Lynch, Julia. *Age in the Welfare State: The Origins of Social Spending on Pensioners, Workers and Children*. New York: Cambridge University Press, 2006. Some nations such as the United States devote more government spending to the elderly than other nations. The author of this book says these differences result not from political activities of the elderly. Rather they stem from the way programs are set up. Those systems based on work contributions such as in the United States tend to favor funding for the elderly over programs for other age groups. To make its case, the book presents case studies of Italy and Japan as well as the United States.

Morris, Charles. *The AARP: America's Most Powerful Lobby and the Clash of Generations*. New York: Times Books, 1996. This book uses a case study of the AARP to launch a discussion of funding for Social Security and Medicare and the influence of lobbying organizations on the programs. The author sees the AARP as one of the most responsible lobbies in Washington, D.C., and argues that modest reforms rather than major change can best address funding problems for the programs.

Onyx, Jenny, Rosemary Leonard, and Rosslyn Reed, eds. *Revisioning Aging: Empowerment of Older Women*. New York: Peter Lang, 1999. The contributors to this collection have a common aim: to challenge negative and devaluing images of older women. They discuss how social and economic forces discriminate against women and how more positive and empowering images can help counter the discrimination. As women face special problems in old age, a volume devoted specifically to older women helps round out the literature on elderly rights.

Palmore, Erdman B. *Ageism: Negative and Positive*. 2nd Edition. New York: Springer Publishing, 1999. Although focused primarily on how older people are undervalued by negative ageism, Palmore also notes that positive ageism attributes valued traits to the elderly. The book describes the sources of ageism in society and gives examples of ageism in the economy, government, family, housing, and health care. Appendices include a facts-on-aging quiz and a selection of ageist humor that reveals the misleading beliefs most people have about the elderly. Overall, the book helps readers understand the problems of the elderly in obtaining their rights in many areas and the justification for giving the elderly special rights in other areas.

Price, Matthew C. *Justice between Generations: The Growing Power of the Elderly in America*. Westport, Conn.: Praeger, 1997. A political scientist argues that being old in America today means wealth and power. With this wealth and power, the elderly have the ability to defend Social Security and Medicare from attacks but also to use their resources at the expense of the young. Price discusses debates over the battle between generations and describes the shift in the position of the elderly from veneration to burden and then to power.

Quadagno, Jill. *Aging and the Life Course: An Introduction to Social Gerontology.* 4th Edition. Boston: McGraw Hill, 2007. This text emphasizes that understanding aging requires understanding how it relates to experiences, choices, and opportunities at early stages of the life course. Although not directly related to elderly rights, the book's overview of knowledge and research on social aspects of aging makes it a helpful resource.

Sember, Brette McWhorter. *Seniors' Rights: Your Guide to Living Life to the Fullest.* Second Edition. Naperville, Ill.: Sphinx Publishing, 2006. This book covers a comprehensive set of issues faced by seniors, including retirement, age discrimination, income, health care, estate planning, long-term care, and disability benefits. Although it is less detailed than other works that concentrate on only one of these issues, the book offers a broad guide to help seniors plan for getting their rights during old age.

Thane, Pat, ed. *A History of Old Age.* Los Angeles: J. Paul Getty Museum, 2005. Understanding problems of the elderly and their rights today requires some understanding of the past. This volume has chapters that cover old age in Greek and Roman civilizations through old age in the 20th century, and the authors of the chapters offer insightful comments on changes that have occurred over past centuries. Of most value, however, is the artwork contained in the volume. How the elderly have been depicted throughout history gives special insight into their changing status.

Thomas, William H. *What Are Old People For? How Elders Will Save the World.* Acton, Mass.: VanderWyk and Burnham, 2004. A Harvard-trained physician argues that the obsession with youth damages young and old alike, and he offers an alternative vision that celebrates old age. The book aims to counter negative images of old age with recommendations for radical change such as abolishing nursing homes and encouraging group living among otherwise isolated older persons. More philosophical reflection and anecdote than systematic research, the book reads well and has an uplifting message about aging.

ARTICLES

Aaron, Henry J. "Longer Life Spans: Boon or Burden?" *Daedalus*, vol. 135, no. 1, Winter 2006, pp. 9–19. While most view longer life spans as a boon, the author notes some of the difficulties the trend brings: social costs of care are high, the elderly face more years of infirmity, and the young have to pay higher tax rates. Consideration of both the burden and the boon leads to more realistic predictions about aging in future decades and allows society to take steps to address impending problems. The author outlines some of these steps in the article.

Achenbaum, W. Andrew. "What Is Retirement For?" *The Wilson Quarterly*, vol. 30, no. 2, Spring 2006, pp. 50–56. The author argues that the traditional concept of retirement, a period of rest and enjoyment after decades of hard work, is outdated. With older persons living longer than ever, the high cost of pensions to the government and the wasted resources of retirees, society should reconsider the goals, ages, and activities of retirement. According to the author, the right to retire at age 65 no longer fits the needs of society and abilities of older people.

Binstock, Robert H. "Old-Age Policies, Politics, and Ageism." *Generations*, vol. 29, no. 3, Fall 2005, pp. 73–78. Although needs of the elderly have on one hand encouraged the creation of government old-age programs, they have on the other hand led to negative stereotypes of the elderly. The author discusses how both aspects of ageism have affected the political behavior of the elderly and perceptions of this political behavior by others. He also discusses the future of ageism in policy and politics.

Bongaarts, John. "Population Aging and the Rising Costs of Pensions." *Population and Development Review*, vol. 30, no. 1, March 2004, pp. 1–23. The analysis presented in this study confirms that aging of the population in the United States and other high-income nations will bring huge increases in pension spending. The high spending results from an expectation that the number of pension recipients per worker will double from 0.7 in 2000 to 1.5 in 2050. Pay-as-you-go schemes based on current workers paying for current retirees are not sustainable under these demographic circumstances. The author says that reductions in the generosity of public pensions in the future seem inevitable. This conclusion highlights the link between population change and elderly rights.

Butler, Robert N. "Declaration of the Rights of Older Persons." *The Gerontologist*, vol. 42, no. 2, April 2002, pp. 152–153. Dr. Butler presents the text of the declaration presented at the United Nations World Assembly on Aging held in Madrid, Spain, in 2002. He calls for using the declaration as a basis for action to help older persons throughout the world.

Cairncross, Frances. "Grey Power." *The Economist*, vol. 370, March 27, 2004, pp. 17–18. As part of a special section on retirement, this British weekly news magazine presents its view of the political power of the elderly. The author says that they have far more power than younger counterparts because they vote at higher rates. Despite this power, however, the elderly will need to accept changes in their entitlements to deal with the economic problems created by aging populations.

Coy, Peter. "Old. Smart. Productive." *Business Week*, no. 3939, June 27, 2005, pp. 78–84, 86. In arguing that the elderly in the future will become a productive force rather than an economic burden, the author makes an intriguing prediction about the rights of the elderly: "If society can tap boomers' talents, employers will benefit, living standards will be raised, and the funding problems of Social Security and Medicare will be easier to solve. This logic is so powerful that it is likely to eliminate many of the legal obstacles and corporate practices that currently prevent older workers from achieving their full productive potential." Although perhaps overly optimistic, this prediction should encourage advocates of elderly rights.

Crimmins, E. M. "Trends in the Health of the Elderly." *Annual Review of Public Health*, vol. 25, 2004, pp. 79–98. Also available online. URL: http://www.usc.edu/projects/rehab/private/docs/advisors/crimmins/10_Crimmins_trends_2004.pdf. Downloaded in May 2007. The article reviews findings on improvements in the health of the elderly. Not only has mortality declined but so has disability. Since older persons live longer than in the past, they face more disease. Yet having a disease appears less disabling to the elderly today than in the past.

Cuddy, Amy J. C., Michael I. Norton, and Susan T. Fiske. "This Old Stereotype: The Pervasiveness and Persistence of the Elderly Stereotype." *The Journal of Social Issues*, vol. 61, no. 2, 2005, pp. 267–285. Some young people view the elderly as warm and friendly but also as incompetent and low status in society. This statistical study of 55 college students investigates the nature of these views. It also finds that students in many other nations besides the United States often hold these stereotypes.

Deets, Horace B. "The Graying of the World: Crisis or Opportunity." *Modern Maturity*, vol. 43R, no. 1, January/February 2000, p. 82. This short article puts social changes stemming from population aging in a world context. It suggests the need for nations across the world to make old-age support a central part of their policies.

Dominus, Susan. "Life in the Age of Old, Old Age." *New York Times Magazine*, February 22, 2004, pp. 26–33, 46, 58–59. Noting that predictions of future life expectancy have consistently been too low, the author suggests that the elderly population will grow even more than expected. The experience of aging will change as a result. For example, the increasing purchasing power of older consumers will lead retirement homes to target this new market, upgrade their quality, and add style to their formerly utilitarian designs.

Goulding, M. R., M. E. Rogers, and S. M. Smith. "Public Health and Aging: Trends in Aging—United States and Worldwide." *MMWR Weekly*, vol. 52, no. 6, February 14, 2003, pp. 101–106. Also available online. URL: http://www.cdc.gov/mmwr/preview/mmwrhtml/mm5206a2.htm. Posted on February 14, 2003. The population pyramid charts in this article contrast the age structure and size of the aged population in developed and developing countries. The article also reviews the major causes of population aging and its impact on health care and public services.

Rights of the Elderly

Hackler, Chris. "Troubling Implications of Doubling the Human Lifespan." *Generations*, vol. 25, no. 4, Winter 2001/2002, pp. 15–19. The author suggests that lifespan extension may cause problems of social displacement. New problems for families, work careers, and prisons would emerge, and inequalities in access to medical care would worsen considerably. Doubling of the human lifespan will not come quickly but can adversely affect the rights of the elderly.

Hagestad, Gunhild O., and Peter Uhlenberg. "The Social Separation of Old and Young: A Root of Ageism." *The Journal of Social Issues*, vol. 61, no. 2, 2005, pp. 343–360. This article on age segregation notes that persons tend to have friends and interact with others of the same age. This pattern reinforces negative images of other age groups. The authors suggest several ways for social policies to reduce age segregation in social life and foster better understanding across age groups.

Henretta, John C. "The Future of Age Integration in Employment." *The Gerontologist*, vol. 40, no. 3, June 2000, pp. 286–292. The article focuses on making the labor market and jobs more suitable for older workers and thereby integrating young and old in the workforce. It describes trends supporting continued work of older persons and changes in job characteristics and employer policies that will help keep older persons interested in work.

Kinnon, Joy Bennett. "A New Look At 'Old Age.'" *Ebony*, vol. 69, no. 10, August 2006, pp. 124, 126, 128, 130. This concise review of the facts about population aging argues that the aged population not only will grow but also will be healthier and more active than in the past. Better health and more activity in turn may alter negative stereotypes about aging.

Kressley, Konrad M. "Aging and Public Institutions." *The Futurist*, vol. 39, no. 5, September/October 2005, pp. 28–32. The author believes that social organizations and institutions need to change in response to the growing size of the aged population. Schools, prisons, businesses, and health care organizations have traditionally focused on the young, but given new demographic conditions, they may need to do more to meet the needs of older clients. The article discusses each of these types of organizations and the changes they need to implement.

Mboya, Pamela. "Addressing Exclusion and Denial of Equal Rights." *UN Chronicle*, vol. 39, no. 2, June/August 2002, pp. 58–59. This article discusses efforts of the United Nations to include problems of population aging in its programs against poverty and isolation. By neglecting the importance of the elderly and the problems they face, programs fail to recognize the human rights of the elderly. The author offers several recommendations for raising the profile of the elderly in UN programs.

McConatha, Jasmin Tahmaseb, Frauke Schnell, Karin Volkwein, Lori Riley, and Elizabeth Leach. "Attitudes toward Aging: A Comparative Analysis of Young Adults from the United States and Germany." *International Journal of Aging and Human Development*, vol. 57, no. 3, 2003, pp. 203–215. This study finds that young Americans view aging less negatively than Germans but also consider themselves to be old at a younger age. Women in both countries express more concern than men do about physical changes in old age.

Miller, Tim. "Increasing Longevity and Medicare Expenditures." *Demography*, vol. 38, no. 2, May 2001, pp. 215–226. This article contrasts two competing views about the economic effects of increasing longevity. On one hand, Medicare projections assume that a longer life will increase medical expenditures for the elderly. On the other hand, a longer life may merely postpone health problems to a later age rather than cause greater health problems. The author advocates this latter view and predicts smaller increases of Medicare costs than many others do.

Morgan, Russell E., Jr., and Sam David. "Human Rights: A New Language for Aging Advocacy." *The Gerontologist*, vol. 42, no. 4, August 2002, pp. 436–442. This research article suggests that ideas developed by the international human rights movement could be used on behalf of the elderly. Protection of the elderly should come not from rights due only to those of a certain age but from rights due to all humans.

Parker, Marti G., and Mats Thorslund. "Health Trends in the Elderly Population: Getting Better and Getting Worse." *The Gerontologist*, vol. 47, 2007, pp. 150–158. This article notes that, although the elderly have enjoyed improvements in disability, increases in chronic disease will require greater resources for health care.

Pethokoukis, James M. "7 Reasons Not to Retire: 2. The Economy May Face a Shortage of Qualified Workers." *U.S. News & World Report*, vol. 140, no. 22, June 12, 2006, pp. 46–47. Part of a longer section on reasons not to retire, this article lays out the facts about work. It says that slow growth in the size of the workforce will create new shortages for employers and new employment opportunities for seniors.

Rosenbloom, Stephanie. "Here Come the Great Grandparents." *New York Times*, November 2, 2006, p. G1. Also available online. URL: http://www. nytimes.com/2006/11/02/fashion/02parents.html?ex=1320123600&en=3 47a355f9cc19a33&ei=5088&partner=rssnyt&emc=rss. Family relations across generations have shifted over the last century toward greater independence of older family members. As this article describes, a more recent trend is the survival of older persons to see their great-grandchildren born. According to one estimate, about 70 percent of 8 year olds will have a living great-grandparent by 2030. This great-grandparent boom makes family relations of the elderly both more rewarding and more complex.

Schieber, Sylvester J. "Paying for It." *The Wilson Quarterly*, vol. 30, no. 2, Spring 2006, pp. 62–69. This article considers how European nations with large elderly populations have managed to deal with the high cost to governments of supporting this age group. The author suggests that those nations able to encourage older persons to continue working have dealt best with the problem. The policies for generous and universal retirement support in Sweden and Germany present interesting alternatives for dealing with the problem in the United States.

Tergesen, Anne. "Three Generations, One Roof." *Business Week*, no. 3957, October 31, 2005, pp. 92–94. The long-term trend in family relations has moved toward more independent living among the elderly. According to this article, rising housing prices have started to reverse the trend. Homes with three or more generations living together rose by 38 percent from 1990 to 2000. Although such homes make up only 4 percent of the population, cost pressures may lead more older persons to begin living with (or take in) their children and grandchildren.

Wentworth, Seyda, and David Pattison. "Income Growth and Future Poverty Rates of the Aged." *Social Security Bulletin*, vol. 64, no. 3, 2001/2002, pp. 23–37. The authors qualify their conclusions by noting the many factors that will affect the poverty of the elderly in decades to come. However, based on increases in earnings and other income, they expect poverty among the elderly to decline to 7.2 percent by 2020.

Wilmoth, Janet M., and Charles F. Longino, Jr. "Demographic Trends that Will Shape U.S. Policy in the Twenty-First Century." *Research on Aging*, vol. 28, no. 3, May 2006, pp. 269–288. In describing expected trends, the authors emphasize the diversity of the aged population and the need for public policies to target groups of the elderly with special needs. They also emphasize the importance of changes in families and women's participation in the labor force for old age in the future.

WEB DOCUMENTS

"The Aging of the U.S. Labor Force: Employer Challenges and Responses." Ernst and Young LLP Human Capital Practice. Available online. URL: http://www.ey.com/global/download.nsf/US/Arnone_Aging_US_Workforce/$file/AgingUSWorkforceEmployerChallenges.pdf. Posted in January 2006. This report from a successful accounting firm points to a lack of awareness among employers of the problems expected from an aging workforce but identifies some actions that organizations can take to help deal with potential shortages of skilled workers in years to come.

"The Aging Workforce: Testimony of Vice Chairman Donald L. Kohn before the Special Committee on Aging, U.S. Senate." Federal Reserve Board. Available online. URL: http://www.federalreserve.gov/boarddocs/testimony/2007/200702282/default.htm. Posted on February 28, 2007. The Federal Reserve and the U.S. Senate are concerned about how the growth of the retired population and the potential decline in the size of the workforce may affect the economy. Vice Chairman Kohn tells the Senate in this testimony that a decline in the number of workers may lower economic output and growth, but he also suggests several ways to keep older persons in the labor force longer. His testimony comes with several charts on the trends and projections.

"Baby Boomers Worried about Money for Retirement." Senior Journal. Available online. URL: http://www.seniorjournal.com/NEWS/Features/ 3-06-18delweb.htm. Posted on June 18, 2003. This summary of results from the 2003 Baby Boomer Report presents many figures on plans for relocation after retirement and expected finances in old age. For example, 43 percent of baby boomers plan to continue working during retirement and 76 percent are not confident they will have enough income in retirement. A link gives access to the full report and statistical details.

Dittman, Melissa. "Fighting Ageism." Monitor on Psychology, APA Online. Available online. URL: http://www.apa.org/monitor/may03/fighting. html. Posted in May 2003. A good introduction to the nature of ageism and its harmful consequences for the elderly, this document reports on a survey in which 80 percent of older respondents claimed to have been victims of ageism. Negative views of the elderly unfortunately make it harder for older persons to receive mental health treatment. The article calls for doing more to meet these mental health needs of the elderly.

"Federal Budget." Concord Coalition. Available online. URL: http://www. concordcoalition.org/issues/fedbudget. Downloaded in May 2007. This organization advocating greater fiscal responsibility from the federal government presents statistics and projections on likely government deficits. It argues that the nation cannot sustain the status quo for Social Security and Medicare.

Friedberg, Leora. "The Recent Trend toward Later Retirement." Center for Retirement Research at Boston College. Available online. URL: http://www.bc.edu/centers/crr/issues/wob_9.pdf. Posted in May 2007. A dramatic reversal of trends toward early retirement during most of the 20th century has occurred recently. This article reviews the evidence of the reversal and offers possible explanations for its occurrence. It presents the material clearly and gives background information needed to help understand the income and work potential for elderly persons in the coming decades.

Lee, Ronald, and Ryan Edwards. "The Fiscal Impact of Population Aging in the US: Assessing the Uncertainties." Center for the Economics and Demography of Aging, University of California, Berkeley. Available online. URL: http://repositories.cdlib.org/iber/ceda/papers/2002-0001CL. Posted on November 5, 2000. The details of this analysis can be overwhelming, but the conclusion stemming from the details is more straightforward: Changing demographics involving aging of the population will require substantial tax increases, substantial cuts in benefits, or restructuring of federal government programs for the elderly.

"Life Expectancy." Fast Stats, National Center for Health Statistics. Available online. URL: http://www.cdc.gov/nchs/fastats/lifexpec.htm. Updated on January 24, 2007. The trends in life expectancy at birth reported on this web page show remarkable progress in longevity. Of special interest for issues of aging, the page also lists figures on life expectancy at ages 65 and 75. Based on mortality rates in old age during 2004, a person reaching age 65 can expect on average to live 18.7 more years and a person reaching age 75 can expect to live 11.9 more years.

Miniño, Arialdi M., Melonie Heron, and Betty L. Smith, "Deaths: Preliminary Data for 2004." National Center for Health Statistics. Available online. URL: http://0-www.cdc.gov.mill1.sjlibrary.org/nchs/products/pubs/pubd/hestats/prelimdeaths04/preliminarydeaths04.htm. Updated on January 11, 2007. Figures on mortality in the United States are released only after a lag of several years. This report on 2004 mortality lists record lows of age-adjusted morality and a record-high life expectancy of 77.9 years.

"A Profile of Older Americans: 2006." Administration on Aging, Department of Health and Human Services. Available online. URL: http://www.aoa.gov/prof/Statistics/profile/2006/2006profile.pdf. Downloaded in May 2007. For those wanting to research beyond the summary description of trends and look at the figures directly, this brochure highlights key statistics on aging. It presents charts and tables on the number of older persons and their expected growth in the next several decades. It also emphasizes diversity among the aged population in marital status (most men are married and most women are widowed) and living arrangements (19 percent of men and 38 percent of women live alone). A variety of other statistics on income, disability, and health care also highlight diversity among the elderly.

"A Profile of Older Americans: 2006. Geographic Distribution." Administration on Aging, Department of Health and Human Services. Available online. URL: http://www.aoa.gov/prof/Statistics/profile/2006/8.asp. Downloaded in May 2007. This subsection of a larger profile of the elderly presents interesting information on the size of the elderly population in each of the 50 states. For example, Florida (16.8 percent), West Virginia (15.3 percent), and Pennsylvania (15.2 percent) have the largest percentages of persons age 65 and over.

Purcell, Patrick. "Older Workers: Employment and Retirement Trends." Congressional Research Service. Available online. URL: http://digital.library.unt.edu/govdocs/crs//data/2005/upl-meta-crs-7258/RL30629_2005Sep14.pdf?PHPSESSID=173a32e169a869a84f943895667a0cf5.

story tells of a Manhattan hairstylist, Michael D'Amico, who barred women customers over age 45 from his shop. He changed his policy of cutting the hair of only the young after threatened by fines from the city government.

Carnahan, Ira. "Removing the Scarlet A." *Forbes*, vol. 170, no. 3, August 12, 2002, p. 78. This article cites facts on the growth of age discrimination suits and the high level of awards (compared to awards for race and gender suits). It cautions, however, that age discrimination suits can backfire by creating a new incentive for employers not to hire older workers.

Deets, Horace B. "Age Discrimination Still on the Rise." *Modern Maturity*, vol. 42R, no. 3, May/June, 1999, p. 80. Noting that older workers are reluctant to file age discrimination charges despite the pervasiveness of the practice, this article outlines the services offered by the AARP and other organizations to help victims of age discrimination.

Garstka, Teri A., Michael T. Schmitt, and Nyla R. Branscombe. "How Young and Older Adults Differ in Their Responses to Perceived Age Discrimination." *Psychology and Aging*, vol. 19, no. 2, June 2004, pp. 326–335. The reference to a rejection-identification model and the use of complex statistical terms make this article difficult reading, but its findings are interesting. It presents evidence that perceptions of age discrimination by older persons lower their psychological well-being. However, strong age-group identification of the elderly can help counter the harm of age discrimination.

Graves, John. "Age Discrimination: Development and Trends." *Trial*, vol. 35, no. 2, February 1999, pp. 58–63. Protecting the employment rights of the elderly often comes down to proving age discrimination in court. The author suggests that recent trends in age discrimination law and court cases "should give ammunition to plaintiff lawyers seeking to assist older workers who are ejected from the workplace." He believes both plaintiffs and the lawyers representing them will find age discrimination suits profitable.

Greenhouse, Linda. "Justices Remove Hurdle to Suits Alleging Age Bias." *New York Times*, March 31, 2005, p. A1. This summary of an important 2005 Supreme Court decision on age discrimination highlights the illegality of disparate-impact as well as disparate-treatment forms of age discrimination. Advocates of the rights of the elderly call the decision a victory because it allows older workers to bring claims based on unintentional age bias and end policies with disparate impact on older workers. At the same time, others point out that the decision allows employers to defend policies with disparate impact by showing that reasonable factors other than age justify the policies.

Harris, Diane. "Age Discrimination Case Involving Disability Benefits." *AARP The Magazine*, vol. 46, no. 4A, July/August, 2003, pp. 64–70. This article describes the largest age-discrimination settlement in American history. Disabled public safety officers sued CalPERS, the California Public Employees' Retirement System, over the payments of benefits to disabled public safety officers. CalPERS had given reduced disability benefits to police and firefighters hired after age 30. The settlement involved repayment of benefits to the officers.

Helyar, John. "50 and Fired." *Fortune*, vol. 151, no. 10, May 16, 2005, pp. 78–80. The author tells stories of successful senior executives who, after losing their jobs, had trouble finding other ones. Part of the problem comes from age discrimination—older managers are often viewed as less flexible and unwilling to work with young people. The problem appears especially serious in the high-tech industry, where many hold negative views about older workers. The article also tells of an age-discrimination suit against Capital One that was settled in terms favorable to the older workers who brought it.

Hoffman, Ellen. "Age Discrimination: How Real a Problem?" *New Choices*, vol. 42, no. 2, March 2002, pp. 57–59. The author describes the difficulties in proving age discrimination but notes that the high number of complaints filed with the Equal Employment Opportunity Commission indicates widespread concern about the problem. Despite difficulties in offering proof, victims should fight back against age discrimination, and the author offers tips for presenting a successful claim.

Kurland, Nancy B. "The Impact of Legal Age Discrimination on Women in Professional Occupations." *Business Ethics Quarterly*, vol. 11, no. 2, April 2001, pp. 331-348. Older working women face problems from both gender and age discrimination. According to this article, women entering the labor force at a young age are aware of age discrimination and therefore feel the need to establish their careers before they have a family. They worry that having children first and entering the labor force late will make it hard to become successful in professional occupations. In this way, age discrimination against older women may affect the career choices of younger women.

Lardner, James. "Too Old to Write Code." *U.S. News & World Report*, vol. 124, March 16, 1998, pp. 39–40. Although many years old, this article describes a source of age discrimination that persists today—the bias toward younger workers in the information-technology industry. At the time of the article, many leaders of the high-tech industry were decrying a shortage of skilled programmers and wanting to hire foreign workers. The article points out that many skilled older programmers could not find jobs. Despite claims that the skills of programmers become outdated quickly, the article argues that experience makes for better and more productive workers.

Lavelle, Marianne. "On the Edge of Discrimination." *New York Times Magazine*, March 9, 1997, pp. 66–69. The author predicts that age dis-

crimination will become a major civil rights cause as activist baby boomers reach old age. She cites several cases of older workers who successfully
sued for age discrimination and who represent the beginning of efforts to
better protect the employment rights of middle aged and older persons.
With ten years hindsight, age discrimination has not become a major civil
rights issue, but recognition of the problem has grown.

Muhl, Charles J. "Age Discrimination." *Monthly Labor Review*, vol. 123, no.
4, April 2000, pp. 28–29. This short article nicely summarizes some of the
major legal issues and court decisions involving age discrimination. Of
most importance is the case involving Florida State University employee
Daniel Kimel, who sued the state on grounds of age discrimination. The
Supreme Court ruled that Congress did not have the power to allow
workers to sue state governments in federal courts. State workers must
instead find remedies in state laws and courts. The article also presents
short summaries of other important age discrimination cases.

Neumark, David. "Age Discrimination Legislation in the United States."
Contemporary Economic Policy, vol. 21, no. 3, July 2003, pp. 297–317. Pre-
dicting that the problem of age discrimination will grow as the population
ages, this article reviews the history of age discrimination legislation and
evolving case law. The author concludes that the legislation has increased
employment and reduced retirement of older workers. He believes that
these benefits outweigh any negative consequences of the legislation.

Pear, Robert. "Agency to Allow Insurance Cuts for the Retired." *New York
Times*, April 23, 2004, p. A1. This news story reports on a decision of the
Equal Employment Opportunity Commission to permit companies to
reduce or eliminate health care benefits at age 65 (when workers or retirees become eligible for Medicare). Advocates of the aged such as the
AARP object to the ruling as an unwarranted exception to the ADEA and
a step that will reduce health care coverage of 12 million Medicare beneficiaries who had also relied on support from former employees.

Seligman, Dan. "The Case for Age Discrimination." *Forbes*, vol. 164, no. 14,
December 13, 1999, pp. 116–120. The heading to this story asks a provocative question: "Thirty-two years after Congress enacted the controlling law, the courts still haven't decided what constitutes illegal age
discrimination. Could that be because the law is irrational?" Seligman
answers yes. The article presents clear arguments in favor of this viewpoint and backs up the arguments with scientific evidence on physiologi-
cal and mental changes during old age. Few share this viewpoint,
however.

Weiss, Elizabeth M., and Todd J. Mauer. "Age Discrimination in Personnel
Decisions: A Reexamination." *Journal of Applied Social Psychology*, vol. 34,
no. 8, August 2004, pp. 1551–1562. This recent study replicates one done
25 years earlier in which subjects who reviewed several work-related sce-

narios gave older workers lower ratings than younger workers. However, the replication finds that subjects gave similar ratings to older and younger workers. The authors suggest that the new results indicate more positive attitudes toward older workers today than in the past.

Weiss, Giselle. "Age Bar Forces Europe's Senior Researchers to Head West." *Science*, vol. 302, December 12, 2003, pp. 1885–1886. In contrast to the United States, several European nations such as France and Sweden have mandatory retirement laws for public employees, including university professors and scientists. When forced to retire, distinguished scientists are taking their expertise to universities in the United States. As described in this article, European nations concerned about the exodus of top scholars are considering legislation to raise or abolish the mandatory retirement age.

WEB DOCUMENTS

"Age Discrimination." Workplace Fairness. Available online. URL: http://www.workplacefairness.org/age#7. Downloaded in April 2007. This web page lists answers to 15 questions on age discrimination (e.g., What is age discrimination? What are valid reasons for an employer to fire an older worker?). The clear answers to the questions help in understanding the complexities of age discrimination law. In addition, a link offers information on age discrimination laws in each U.S. state.

"Age Discrimination Case Studies." Age Concern. Available online. URL: http://www.ageconcern.org.uk/AgeConcern/ageism_advisers_cases.asp. Downloaded in April 2007. Although sponsored by a UK organization and based on UK laws, this web page offers something unique. It has stories of older individuals and discusses how their circumstances might or might not involve age discrimination.

"Age Discrimination in Employment Act (ADEA) Charges FY 1997—FY 2006." U.S. Equal Employment Opportunity Commission. Available online. URL: http://www.eeoc.gov/stats/adea.html. Updated on February 26, 2007. This web page contains a table with annual figures for the last 11 years on age-discrimination statistics gathered by the EEOC: the number of age-discrimination charges, the resolutions of the charges, the percent of charges that led to settlements, the percent of charges that led to a conclusion of reasonable cause, and the monetary benefits received. The page offers no interpretation of the data, but the figures show a low proportion of charges leading to conclusions favorable to the victim.

"The Age Discrimination in Employment Act of 1967." U.S. Equal Employment Opportunity Commission. Available online. URL: http://www.eeoc.gov/policy/adea.html. Updated on January 15, 1997. The original 1967 legislation plus amendments guide age discrimination law today.

Annotated Bibliography

After a statement on the unfairness of age discrimination and the need to protect older workers from its harm, this legislation expresses its aim to have workers and applicants evaluated on their ability rather than their age. The law then defines what behaviors it forbids (e.g., refusing to hire or discharging because of age) and allows (e.g., use of a seniority system). Since the law's wording has led to diverse interpretations in court decisions, it helps to read the original text.

"Avoiding Age Discrimination in the Workplace." AllBusiness. Available Online. URL: http://www.allbusiness.com/human-resources/workplace-health-safety-employment/11441-1.html. Downloaded in April 2007. This web page aims to help businesses identify potential problems they may have with age discrimination. It recommends ways to eliminate references to age in hiring practices and use training sessions to raise employee awareness of the problems. The attention to specific action rather than philosophical principles makes the page helpful to employers and those wanting to learn more about steps to take against age discrimination.

DiOrio, Carl. "Writers' Age Discrimination Case Heats Up." The Hollywood Reporter. Available online. URL: http://www.hollywoodreporter-esq.com/thresq/labor/article_display.jsp?vnu_content_id=1003565338. Posted on March 30, 2007. An interesting case of alleged age discrimination involves 150 veteran TV writers. Although successful earlier in their careers, they now say their age prevents them from getting work and have sued the Hollywood studios. The case, first brought in 2000, has moved slowly and involves many legal complexities but publicizes mistreatment of older workers in creative fields.

"Equal Employment Opportunity." U.S. Department of Labor. Available online. URL: http://www.dol.gov/dol/topic/discrimination/agedisc.htm. Downloaded in April 2007. This web page sponsored by the Department of Labor has links to the main laws and regulations such as the Age Discrimination Act of 1975 and to the Civil Rights Center that enforces the act. It supplements other web pages on the ADEA.

"Facts about Age Discrimination." U.S. Equal Employment Opportunity Commission. Available online. URL: http://www.eeoc.gov/facts/age.html. Updated on January 15, 1997. This brief description of what the ADEA forbids covers topics such as job notices, preemployment inquiries, benefits, and waivers. Although short, the web page contains key facts.

"Filing a Charge." U.S. Equal Employment Opportunity Commission. Available online. URL: http://www.eeoc.gov/facts/howtofil.html. Updated on June 10, 1997. For those who believe they have been victims of age discrimination, the guidelines for filing a charge with the EEOC are simple. Possible victims should contact their local EEOC office (the web page helps locate the nearest one). The web page reminds readers that age discrimination charges have strict time limits and should be filed soon after the event.

Greenberg, David H., and Jeremy Pasternak. "Age Discrimination in the Workplace." Law offices of David H. Greenberg. Available online. URL: http://www.discriminationattorney.com/article-age.shtml. Downloaded in April 2007. Written by two attorneys specializing in employment law, this article suggests that employers have good reason to be concerned about age discrimination lawsuits. A successful suit can charge for lost wages, a new job search, emotional distress, and punitive damages; the awards often exceed those made for race and sex discrimination. The authors recommend that employers protect themselves by recognizing the unfairness of age discrimination and the value of older workers.

"Job Loss Help: Age Discrimination at Work." AARP. Available online. URL: http://www.aarp.org/money/careers/jobloss/Articles/a2004-04-28-agediscrimination.html. Downloaded in April 2007. The AARP aims to help its members with information on who the ADEA covers, what the ADEA forbids, and what victims of age discrimination can do. The web page's advice is practical, clear, and filled with links to other resources (including help in finding legal representation). An excellent starting place to learn about age discrimination.

Preston, Peter J. "Ageism in the Workplace: Understanding the ADEA." ThinkAvenue. Available online. URL: http://thinkavenue.com/articles/hr/article07.htm. Downloaded in May 2007. An attorney specializing in employment law explains the basic provisions of the ADEA. A sample case illustrates the application of the law and a section on penalties explains what victims can receive if a court determines that an employer has violated the law.

RIGHTS INVOLVING PENSIONS, INCOME, AND SOCIAL SECURITY

BOOKS

Ambachtsheer, Keith P. *The Pension Revolution: A Solution to the Pensions Crisis.* Hoboken, N.J.: Wiley, 2007. The author proposes The Optimal Pension System, used now by several pension plans, as a model for others to adopt. He suggests that, because private pension plans have been run ineffectively for decades, workers cannot be certain they will receive their promised benefits in retirement. The details of the proposed system to overcome this crisis are complex but sound intriguing. To support his thesis, the author presents much research on pension systems in other countries and on the history of pensions in the United States.

Annotated Bibliography

Béland, Daniel. *Social Security: History and Politics from the New Deal.* Lawrence: University of Kansas Press, 2007. This history of Social Security aims to provide background information needed to understand current debates over privatization. The author promises a balanced perspective that will help readers understand and evaluate competing views about reforming Social Security. He also gives special attention to issues of gender equality, an important component of reform proposals. However, the book has most value as a resource on the historical development of Social Security.

CCH. *Pension Protection Act of 2006: Explanation and Analysis.* Chicago: CCH, 2006. This legislation aims to protect the private pension rights of retirees. The book presents a detailed analysis of the act that pension plan administrators, benefit consultants, and tax and legal professionals can use. Although the jargon and technical detail make it less well suited for general researchers, the book can help in understanding the goals of the legislation and the causes of the problems it addresses.

Clark, Gordon L., Alice H. Munnell, and J. Michael Orszag, eds. *The Oxford Handbook of Pensions and Retirement Income.* Oxford: Oxford University Press, 2006. This comprehensive volume includes chapters by experts on topics such as future funding for pensions, retirement income, and the implications of demographic aging. The contributors, all well-known experts, provide both a reference work for scholars and a guide for policy makers.

Clark, Robert Louis, Lee A. Craig, and Jack W. Wilson. *A History of Public Sector Pensions in the United States.* Philadelphia: University of Pennsylvania Press, 2003. Starting with colonial times, this history follows the development of pension plans for public sector employees through the 20th century and compares developments in the United States with those in Europe. The book gives much attention to military pension plans and the development of plans for federal, state, and local government employees. The slow emergence of pension rights for government employees in the United States offers lessons on pension rights for private employees.

Diamond, Peter A., and Peter R. Orszag. *Saving Social Security: A Balanced Approach.* Washington, D.C.: Brookings Institution Press, 2005. Contrasting views about the seriousness of Social Security funding problems and the need for reforms are related to contrasting views on the rights of the elderly to a decent retirement income. In this book (a recently revised edition), two economists avoid the extremes—privatizing Social Security or leaving things as they are—in offering recommendations for change. The balanced approach they offer suggests ways to both cut benefits and raise revenues without a major overhaul. The book will most help those wanting to learn about the current policy debates over Social Security reform.

Evandrou, Maria, and Jane Falkingham. "Will Baby-Boomers Be Better Off than their Parents in Retirement?" In John A. Vincent, Chris R. Phillipson, and Murna Downs, eds., *The Futures of Old Age*. London: Sage Publications, 2006, pp. 85–97. A short answer to the title question is yes: Baby boomers on average will be better off. However, the authors also demonstrate that because baby boomers will depend more on private retirement income than older generations, more potential exists for disparities in support. Those with stable, high-paying jobs and participating in a private pension plan will do much better than their parents; those in opposite circumstances will do worse. The authors conclude that increasing public income support in old age will help address problems of inequality.

Gary, Robert D., and Jori Bloom Naegele. *Protecting Your Pension for Dummies*. New York: For Dummies, 2007. Current problems with underfunded private pension plans combined with the complexities of understanding the workings of the plans make this nontechnical and friendly guide an excellent resource. It covers changes in pensions due to the 2006 Pension Protection Act and translates legal material into tips on what actions older workers can take to protect themselves.

Matthews, Joseph L., and Dorothy Matthews Berman. *Social Security, Medicare and Government Pensions: Get the Most of Your Retirement and Medical Benefits*. 12th Edition. Berkeley, Calif.: Nolo, 2007. Called a guide through the maze of Social Security and Medicare options, this book can serve as reference for those wanting to understand the rights older persons have in these programs. For beneficiaries, it shows how to identify and demand what they have accrued through Social Security and other programs. For researchers, it describes the many benefits available to older persons—Social Security retirement and disability benefits; Social Security dependents and survivors' benefits; Supplemental Security Income; federal, state, and local government pensions; Medicare and Medicaid; Medigap managed care plans; veterans' benefits; and prescription drug coverage.

Mimms, Richard. "The Future of Stock Market Pensions." In John A. Vincent, Chris R. Phillipson, and Murna Downs, eds., *The Futures of Old Age*. London: Sage Publications, 2006, pp. 98–105. The author argues that the shift from state financing of retirement to financing by private accounts invested in the stock market has resulted in an increasingly risky system. In a strongly worded conclusion, he says, "The market is a poor provider of security in old age: the evidence from around the world points to continuing disaster." He sees the shift as one based on political beliefs rather than economic efficiency. While many disagree with these conclusions, the chapter presents one pessimistic forecast of the future of economic rights of the elderly.

Annotated Bibliography

Monk, Abraham, ed., *The Columbia Retirement Handbook*. New York: Columbia University Press, 1994. This comprehensive volume reviews knowledge (as of 1994) on retirement and covers a variety of topics relevant to elderly rights. Chapters on Social Security, private pensions, individual retirement accounts, health-care options, housing assistance, and government financing are clearly written and apply to concerns of older persons. The dated material requires supplementing the information with more recent sources, but the inclusion of so many topics in a single volume makes it valuable.

Powell, Lawrence Alfred, Kenneth J. Branco, and John B. Williamson. *The Senior Rights Movement: Framing the Policy Debate in America*. New York: Twayne Publishers, 1996. This "history of the struggle for old-age justice in America as it has unfolded since Colonial times" defines senior rights mostly in terms of economic well-being. It ends the history with consideration of the current politics of Social Security and Medicare legislation and debates about the solvency of the programs. The book views these debates as part of a larger struggle of elderly persons to get and protect their economic rights.

Santow, Leonard J., and Mark E. Santow. *Social Security and the Middle-Class Squeeze: Fact and Fiction about America's Entitlement Programs*. Westport, Conn.: Praeger, 2005. Advertised as a primer for citizens concerned about Social Security and other government programs, the book emphasizes the importance of the programs for the middle class, not just the poor. The authors believe that keeping Social Security as a broad-based program requires reforms that cut across ideological debates. Although each represents a different political viewpoint, the authors try to integrate their perspectives in making recommendations for change.

Schulz, James H. *The Economics of Aging*. 7th Edition. Westport, Conn.: Auburn House, 2000. This readable textbook covers basic knowledge needed to understand elderly economic rights. It reviews research on the decision to retire, the economic status of the elderly, the varied sources of income during old age, and government programs for the elderly. It fairly presents both sides of controversial issues and lists many helpful statistics.

Tomkeil, Stanley, III. *Social Security Benefits Handbook*. 5th Edition. Naperville, Ill.: Sphinx Publishing, 2007. The author, an attorney and former Social Security claims representative, intends to explain the complexities of Social Security rules and regulations in a way that allows readers to understand and get what they are entitled to. The Social Security Handbook put out by the Social Security Administration contains such information but in 676 pages. This shorter book of 368 pages covers eligibility, entitlements, applying for benefits, disability benefits, work requirements, benefit amounts, earning limitations, appeals, and special provisions.

Weller, Christian, and Edward N. Wolff. *Retirement Income: The Crucial Role of Social Security*. Washington, D.C.: Economic Policy Institute, 2005. Based on a study of all forms of wealth and income among the elderly, this 66-page book by two economists concludes that Social Security is more important than ever to the finances of the elderly. The program's universality makes it a crucial income source for those most in need of help during retirement. In contrast, the retirement system outside of Social Security has many holes—about one-fifth of the elderly have no source of private retirement income—and exacerbates economic disparities in old age. The authors conclude that Social Security needs protection and expansion more than change.

Wooten, James. *The Employee Retirement Income Security Act of 1974: A Political History*. Berkeley: University of California Press, 2005. The author treats passage of the act as a major improvement in employee pension rights, one that required public officials and Congress to overcome opposition from employers and unions. Employers and unions had great discretion in how they ran their pension programs and often overlooked the interests of workers. According to the history, the efforts of Senator Jacob Javits to publicize horror stories of lost pension benefits helped increase public support for reform, overcome opposition from employers and unions, and help protect the income of workers when they reach old age.

Ziesenheim, Ken. *Understanding ERISA: A Compact Guide to the Landmark Act*. Ellicott City, Md.: Marketplace Books, 2002. As the title indicates, ERISA was indeed a landmark in protecting the private pension rights of older workers. This book describes the basic principles behind ERISA in simple and understandable terms but aims primarily to help organizations and fiduciaries make sure their plans comply with the law. The description of the law can also help others understand its complex details.

ARTICLES

Achenbaum, W. Andrew. "What Is Retirement For?" *The Wilson Quarterly*, vol. 30, no. 2, Spring 2006, pp. 50–56. The right to retire around age 65 has become outdated according to this respected historian. He argues that the expected longevity of baby boomers, their educational and job skills, and the great cost of supporting large numbers of older persons for many years require rethinking of retirement. The current model of retirement was developed haphazardly over past decades and relies on vague conceptions of the appropriate age for rest and leisure. Society now needs to reevaluate the meaning of retirement and the appropriate age for leaving the labor force.

Andrews, Michelle. "Whatever Happened to the Golden Years? Case of the Beltram Family." *Reader's Digest*, vol. 166, February 2005, pp. 154–160.

This case illustrates the loss of public pension rights and the increasing number of private companies that fail to honor their pension commitments. As illustrated by the Beltram family, the failure forces older persons into poverty or continued work.

Barlett, Donald L., and James B. Steele. "Where Pensions Are Golden: Government Employee Pensions." *Time*, vol. 166, no. 18, October 31, 2005, pp. 34–35. According to this article, state and local government employees such as teachers and police officers face problems with funding of their defined-benefit pension plans, just as many private-sector employees do. The difference is that public employees can count on taxes to make up shortfalls, while private employees risk losing benefits. That puts public employees in a superior position. Private-sector employees face not only loss of pension benefits but also higher taxes to ensure pension benefits for public employees.

Bernstein, Aaron. "The Undoing of a Done Deal?" *Business Week*, no. 3971, February 13, 2006, p. 54. This article about a proposed cost-cutting agreement between the United Auto Workers union and General Motors Corporation illustrates the dilemma older workers face. On one hand, the agreement involves loss of health care benefits that the company has provided to retirees, a change many union members oppose. On the other hand, without the agreement, General Motors may have to declare bankruptcy and reduce its retirement benefits even more. The threat of bankruptcy and the risk of greater cuts in benefits led the union to accept the change.

Borrus, Amy. "The Case of the Vanishing 401(k)s." *Business Week*, no. 3894, August 2, 2004, p. 62. In light of the loss of stock-based assets in 401(k)s by Enron employees, Congress has debated how to better protect these kinds of retirement accounts. As noted in the article, many companies make contributions to employee 401(k)s in the form of company stock but 36 percent of the companies allow workers to trade their employer-match shares. Such opportunity can protect workers from an Enron-like collapse in a company's stock.

"A Bridge to Higher Social Security Benefits." *Kiplinger's Retirement Report*, vol. 13, no. 1, January 2006, pp. 12–13. Those qualifying for Social Security have the right to retire at age 62 with lower benefits, and more than two-thirds of retirees claim the benefits early. This article says that waiting to get full benefits at the normal retirement age (somewhere between 65 and 67) can make more money for retirees. Longer life expectancy means that normal retirees will receive higher benefits for extra years and will get more over the long run than early retirees will.

Colvin, Geoffrey. "Living the Golden Years without the Gold." *Fortune*, vol. 152, no. 1, July 11, 2005, p. 89. The introduction to a special section on retirement makes a telling point about poverty among the elderly: The dramatic reduction in the last 50 years has been one of America's great achievements. However, the article also notes that the low savings rate of workers threatens to increase poverty in old age as these workers retire.

———. "You're on Your Own." *Fortune*, vol. 145, no. 3, February 4, 2002, p. 42. This article reviews the pension problem faced by Enron employees when the company went bankrupt. Many put their 401(k) assets in Enron stock and lost their savings when the stock price fell to near zero. The author emphasizes that the safety of 401(k) funds cannot be guaranteed.

"The Earnings Test's Squeeze on Benefits." *Kiplinger's Retirement Report*, vol. 13, no. 2, February 2006, p. 12. Along with explaining how the earnings test works—in brief, it reduces Social Security benefits by $1 for each $2 in earnings before age 65—this article also notes a little known fact. The reduction in benefits due to the earnings test during early retirement is offset by an increase in benefits after normal retirement age. Early retirees receive lower benefits for the rest of their retirement, but early retirees who lose benefits because of the earnings make it up faster with larger checks during normal retirement.

Gleckman, Howard, and Rich Miller. "More Risk—More Reward: Retirement Guide." *Business Week*, no. 3944, July 25, 2005, pp. 100–101. This article describes the trend toward shifting retirement income from employers and the government to individuals. That means older persons need to do more to protect themselves from the risk of low income and costly health care, especially given that they can expect to live longer than previous generations. The article also discusses the likely future of private pension and Social Security payments.

Hood, John. "Elderly Feel Entitled to Social Security and Medicare." *National Review*, vol. 52, no. 20, October 23, 2000, pp. 56–59. Reflecting a view that the aged have gained too much in the way of income entitlements, largely at the cost to younger generations, this article in a conservative magazine says that politicians pay too much attention to the elderly and their rights. With the elderly doing better financially than ever before, the attention given to caring for them makes little sense to the author. He believes that other issues of more concern to the average voter, particularly those related to the relatively worse situation of children, deserve more attention.

Lowenstein, Roger. "The End of Pensions?" *New York Times Magazine*, October 30, 2005, pp. 56-63. After describing the inadequate funding of pensions by large corporations and the problems of the Pension Benefit Guaranty Corporation (PBGC) in covering for corporations that default, this articles reaches a discouraging conclusion: "If the pension system continues to fail, it will be easy to envision a darker future in which many of the elderly would have to keep working to stave off poverty."

Annotated Bibliography

Maldonado, Culberto Jose. "Income Security for Our Older Citizens." *Vital Speeches of the Day*, vol. 72, no. 5, December 15, 2005, pp. 144–147. In this speech given at the International Conference on Aging in Mexico City, a board member of the AARP discusses solutions to the problem of caring for a growing world population of older persons. Although Maldonado recognizes that different countries will choose different solutions, he generally opposes efforts like those in the United States and some other countries to privatize Social Security.

Maynard, Micheline. "United Air Wins Right to Default on Its Pensions." *New York Times*, May 11, 2005, p. A1. This story provides details on the controversial bankruptcy court decision to free United Airlines from $3.2 billion in pension obligations. The airline, under bankruptcy protection since 2002, claimed it could not survive with its liabilities for paying pensions to older workers. The decision now gives the PBGC responsibility for paying the pensions.

Quinn, Jane Bryant. "A Requiem for Pensions." *Newsweek*, vol. 148, no. 1/2, July 3–10, 2006, p. 53. This well-respected financial columnist worries that the trend away from traditional defined-benefit pension plans and toward defined-contribution and 401(k) plans will hurt workers when they retire. She believes the guaranteed lifetime income provided by defined-benefit plans and the management of these plans by investment professionals make them superior to the alternatives. However, the 2006 Pension Protection Act may intensify the trend away from the traditional plans by requiring companies to invest more in them. The companies may instead replace the plans.

Regnier, Pat. "Can You Live Long and Prosper?" *Money*, vol. 35, no. 10, October 2006, pp. 96–100. One risk to a decent income during old age is the increasing number of years that retirees can expect to live. This article reports that by 2050 there will be more than a million persons age 100 or older. It offers practical advice on how to make retirement income last for a full, long life.

Shuey, Kim M., and Angela M. O'Rand. "New Risks for Workers: Pensions, Labor Markets, and Gender." *Annual Review of Sociology*, vol. 30, 2004, pp. 453–477. This review of scholarly studies makes the point that responsibilities for pension security have shifted from employers to employees. Further, women face special income security risks during old age because of their irregular labor force history. The authors describe how these changes have widened differences in economic risks during old age.

Shulman, Beth. "Sweating the Golden Years." *The Wilson Quarterly*, vol. 30, no. 2, Spring 2006, pp. 57–61. The author says that the dream of a dignified old age is a mere fantasy for some. Even now, many elderly are forced to work because of limited retirement income. She argues that support from Social Security and private pensions is collapsing and calls for strengthening Social Security and safeguarding private pensions.

Sloan, Allan. "The Big Value of Small Increases." *Newsweek*, vol. 148, no. 19, November 6, 2006, p. 17. How much is Social Security worth to retirees? This article gives an answer that allows comparisons with defined-benefit pension plans: "It would cost you well over $700,000 to buy a benefit to match what Social Security pays a married couple with one high lifetime earner and a stay-at-home spouse." In clear language, the article explains how annuities work and how an annuity like Social Security—one that goes up with inflation—has become a valuable resource for retirees.

Steuerle, Eugene. "Social Security and the Poor: Budget Should Be Reoriented to the Older of the Elderly." *America*, vol. 183, no. 21, December 23–30, 2000, pp. 8–11. The author points out an interesting fact about old age today: The elderly retire five years earlier and live five years longer than they did in 1940. With older persons spending an additional ten extra years in retirement, the meaning of old age has changed. To respond to this change, Steuerle argues that retirement income should go only to those ages 75 and over and that special elderly rights be limited to the oldest age groups.

Tanner, Michael. "Social Security Shortchanges African-Americans." *USA Today*, vol. 130, no. 2674, July 2001, pp. 12–14. Although African Americans rely more on Social Security benefits than others, they get a worse rate of return on the contributions they make. This inequity results from the shorter life expectancy of African Americans and the fewer years they have to collect benefits. The author argues that opportunity for this deprived group to invest retirement funds in personal accounts would lead to more equitable treatment.

Walsh, Mary Williams. "I.B.M. to Freeze Pension Plans to Trim Costs." *New York Times*, January 6, 2006, pp. A1. The facts summarized in this story—that IBM will by 2008 replace its traditional pension plan with 401(k)s—have implications for the support of older workers during retirement. The change will save IBM money but will cut benefits for many current employees. Retirees will depend more on personal accounts, which give more freedom in investing but also lead to new risks in saving for old age.

Wang, Penelope. "A Law Bulks up the 401(k)." *Money*, vol. 35, no. 10, October 2006, p. 29. In describing the key provisions of the Pension Protection Act of 2006, the most recent effort to protect the private pension rights of older workers, this article highlights the strengths and weaknesses of the legislation. One strength is that it encourages private savings for retirement by making it easier to contribute to 401(k)s. One weakness is that it may accelerate the decline of traditional defined-benefit plans by demanding more funding from companies.

Annotated Bibliography

WEB DOCUMENTS

Anrig, Greg, Jr. "Ten Myths about Social Security." The Social Security Network. Available online. URL: http://www.socsec.org/publications. asp?pubid=507. Posted on January 26, 2005. An opponent of major reform of Social Security, the author says that the program is not in crisis, offers retirees a good deal, and can be sustained. Many others disagree with these claims, arguing instead that reform of Social Security is needed soon to deal with the costs of retired baby boomers. The document disputes such arguments.

"Bush Signs Massive Pension Overhaul: New Rules Seek to Protect Workers' Retirement Benefits." MSNBC. Available online. URL: http://www. msnbc.msn.com/id/14391251/. Posted on August 22, 2006. The headline of this news story summarizes the goals of the Pension Protection Act of 2006. The legislation requires companies to set aside enough funds to cover the pension commitments they have made to their workers. As described in the article, many see the change as a major improvement in the retirement rights of older workers. However, critics say that it does not do enough to protect workers and might ultimately make things worse by encouraging companies to drop their defined-benefit plans.

"Employment-Based Retirement Plan Participation: Geographic Differences and Trends, 2005." Employee Benefits Research Organization. Available online. URL: http://www.ebri.org/publications/ib/index. cfm?fa=ibDisp&content_id=3761. Posted in November 2006. The facts presented by this organization on participation in private pension plans are discouraging for those concerned about the future economic well-being of the elderly. Only 47 percent of wage and salary employees ages 21–64 participate in a retirement pension plan. In its comparison of workers by age, gender, race, and region of residence, the page also finds that some groups have particularly low pension plan participation.

"Employment Retirement Income Security Act—ERISA—29 U.S. Code Chapter 18." FINDUSLAW. Available online. URL: http://finduslaw.com/ employee_retirement_income_security_act_erisa_29_u_s_code_chapter_ 18. Downloaded in May 2007. This page reproduces the full wording of this important law protecting the private pension rights of workers.

"Find Your Retirement Age." Social Security Online. Available online. URL: http://www.ssa.gov/retirement/retirechartred.htm. Downloaded in May 2007. The normal retirement age of 65, in place since Social Security started, no longer applies to those born after 1937. It increases steadily until reaching age 67 for those born after 1959. This web page lists normal retirement age by year of birth. It also calculates the reduction in benefits retirees will face if they retire at age 62 rather than the normal age.

"Fulfilling the Promises: An Agenda to Restore Retirement Security for Millions of Older Americans." Ad Hoc Coalition to Restore Retirement Security. Available online. URL: http://restoreretirementsecurity.org/pages/agenda.htm. Downloaded in May 2007. This organization opposes changes in private pension plans that involve revising rules of eligibility and benefits, selling divisions to companies that do not honor pension obligations, reclassifying workers as independent contractors without pension rights, and eliminating health care coverage of retirees. The document describes its concerns about violations of pension rights and identifies companies it accuses of the violations.

Hoffman, Ellen. "Why Your Pension Might Need Protection." Business Week Online. Available online. URL: http://www.businessweek.com/bw-daily/dnflash/july2000/nf00713a.htm. Posted on July 13, 2000. The article tells how workers can check if their pension plan remains safe and recommends checking well before retirement. It encourages workers to get help from pension counselors and gives several examples of workers who found employer violations when they checked.

Nader, Ralph. "A Trail of Broken Promises: Pension Rights." CounterPunch. Available online. URL: http://www.counterpunch.org/nader03092004.html. Posted on March 8, 2004. Ralph Nader, founder of the Pension Rights Center more than 30 years ago, criticizes large corporations for trying to avoid the pension obligations they have to their workers. He lists five broken promises related to pension rights such as changing the rules by switching to a cash-balance plan, cutting pensions when selling a division to another company, and cancelling lifetime health insurance.

"Pension Pains." NOW, PBS Online. Available online. URL: http://www.pbs.org/now/politics/pensions05.html. Downloaded in January 2007. This web-based version of a PBS television show is an excellent introduction to the problems of protecting pension plans and fulfilling pension promises made to workers. The overview on this page introduces the topic, while another page describes landmark legislation. The material covers only the basics of the problem, but the web page lists links to more detailed information. For example, users can find an article from *Fortune* magazine on corporations that are cutting their pension payments.

"Pension Rights: Know Your Rights." Legal Aid Society—Employment Law Center. Available online. URL: http://www.las-elc.org/aspensions.pdf. Downloaded in May 2007. A nonprofit organization that gives legal assistance to low-income workers offers clear and valuable advice on the complex topic of pension rights. It starts with an answer to the question "What is a pension plan?" and then answers other questions such as "What must I do to receive a pension?" and "How does a break in my employment affect my pension?" For those who think their pension rights are being violated, the document lists the steps to take to correct the violation.

"Pensions Agency Reports Deficit of $18.1 Billion: Smaller Shortfall Aided by Special Treatment for Airlines." MSNBC. Available online. URL: http://www.msnbc.msn.com/id/15730546. Posted on November 15, 2006. The $18.1 billion deficit of the PBGC for the 2006 fiscal year is lower than the year before but still indicates a problem with private pensions. So many companies defaulted on their obligations that the funding for the PBGC has not kept up with its responsibilities. As discussed in the article, Congress hopes new legislation will correct the funding problem.

"A Predictable, Secure Pension for Life: Defined Benefit Pensions." Pension Benefit Guaranty Corporation. Available online. URL: http://www.pbgc.gov/docs/A_Predictable_Secure_Pension_for_Life.pdf. Posted in January 2000. This document from the PBGC explains how traditional pensions work and how the federal government insures them. The discussion of pension plan provisions and trends aims to help older workers understand the benefits they can expect, and a list of questions at the end of the document helps workers calculate their expected benefits.

"Social Security Benefit Amounts." Social Security Online. Available online. URL: http://www.ssa.gov/OACT/COLA/Benefits.html. Updated on October 18, 2006. This web page explains the complex calculations used to determine a qualified worker's Social Security benefits. Filled with terms such as averaged indexed monthly earnings and primary insurance amount, the treatment is sometimes difficult to follow but nonetheless helps in understanding the logic behind Social Security benefit rights.

"Social Security: A Primer." Congressional Budget Office. Available online. URL: http://www.cbo.gov/ftpdoc.cfm?index=3213&type=0&sequence=0. Posted in September 2001. This introduction to the workings of a major source of income for older persons describes provisions and benefits in the context of proposed reforms to deal with the costs of an aging population. The four chapters, three appendices, four tables, 18 figures, and eight boxes sometimes contain overwhelming information. Still, the fair-minded description of the problems faced by Social Security and the proposed reforms to address the problems do much to clarify the often heated debate over the future of the program.

"Understanding Supplemental Security Income." Social Security Online. Available online. URL: http://www.socialsecurity.gov/notices/supplemental-security-income/text-understanding-ssi.htm. Downloaded in May 2007. This program for elderly persons with limited resources aims to protect them from poverty. The web page explains how the program works and offers information on eligibility criteria, benefit levels, and the application process. The document also contains links to more detailed information on topics such as reporting earnings, Medicaid eligibility, and allowable transfers of resources to qualify for Supplemental Security Income.

"Update: The Pension Protection Act of 2006." Frontline: Can You Afford to Retire? PBS Online. Available online. URL: http://www.pbs.org/wgbh/pages/frontline/retirement/world/fixing.html. Posted on October 30, 2006. A nice summary of the most recent legislation affecting pension rights of older workers. The document, which updates an earlier PBS show, describes the competing goals of the act: on one hand to force companies to better fund their plans, while on the other hand to avoid demanding so much funding that companies must freeze their pensions and turn over their obligations to the PBGC.

"What Are My Pension Rights?" Know Your Pension. Available online. URL: http://www.knowyourpension.org/pensions/pensionrights/pension_rights.aspx. Downloaded in May 2007. This short web page lists seven basic rights of pension plan holders. Most important, the rights require plan administrators to provide information about the plan and any changes they make to it. The page tells what workers should do if their plan appears to be mismanaged.

"What You Need to Know When You Get Retirement or Survivors Benefits." Social Security Online. Available online. URL: http://www.ssa.gov/pubs/10077.html. Downloaded in May 2007. The specifics of what older workers need to do to get their Social Security benefits are explained on this web page. It tells how applications are made, the benefits are paid, and changes in circumstances are reported.

"What You Should Know About Your Retirement Plan." U.S. Department of Labor, Employee Benefits Security Administration. Available online. URL: http://www.dol.gov/ebsa/publications/wyskapr.html. Downloaded in January 2007. This booklet from the federal government agency responsible for enforcing ERISA regulations seeks to help workers and retirees understand their pension plan and get answers to questions they may have. It describes different types of pension plans, how to get retirement pension benefits, and how divorce or employment change might affect retirement benefits. With eight short chapters and six tables, the booklet contains much information. Yet it nicely melds attention to detail with a presentation geared to nonexperts.

Wild, Russell. "Your Money: Now You See It, Now You Don't." AARP Bulletin Online. Available online. URL: http://www.aarp.org/bulletin/yourmoney/see_it.html. Posted on January 27, 2007. The author argues that the switchover to cash-balance pension plans cheats older workers of the benefits due to them. According to one AARP expert quoted in the article, "the companies have pulled the rug out from under their older workers by eliminating promised late-career benefits just as those workers were about to obtain them." The article summarizes the defects of cash-balance plans and efforts of new legislation to correct them.

RIGHTS INVOLVING MEDICAL CARE, MEDICARE, AND MEDICAID

BOOKS

American Bar Association. *American Bar Association Legal Guide for Americans Over 50: Everything about the Law and Medicare and Medicaid, Retirement Rights, and Long-Term Choices . . . and Your Parents.* New York: Random House Reference, 2006. A reference book on legal rights of the elderly, particularly in relation to health care.

Barry, Robert L., and Gerard Bradley, eds. *Set No Limits: A Rebuttal to Daniel Callahan's Proposal to Limit Health Care for the Elderly.* Urbana: University of Illinois Press, 1991. Critics of Daniel Callahan's proposals to ration health care for the elderly present a variety of ethical, legal, and policy arguments in this edited volume. The arguments are linked by their rejection of age as a criterion for distributing limited health care resources. The debate over rationing has lost much of the heat that characterized the late 1980s and early 1990s, but the objections raised in this book have had much influence on public policy.

Begley, Thomas D., and Jo-Anne Herina Jeffreys. *Representing the Elderly Client: Law and Practice. Volume 1.* New York: Aspen Publishers, 2004. Written for lawyers, this book will have too much case law and legal detail for most readers. However, the topics covered include many related to elderly rights. Chapters cover estate planning, nursing homes, and managed care but give particular attention to Medicaid financing of long-term care.

Callahan, Daniel. *Setting Limits: Medical Goals in an Aging Society.* Washington, D.C.: Georgetown University Press, 1995. This reprint of the original 1987 book contains a response to critics by the author. Callahan's main point is that resources are too often used to extend the lives of the elderly without attention to the quality of life they face in their last years. In his words, "The proper question is not whether we are succeeding in giving a longer life to the aged, [but] whether we are making of old age a decent and honorable time of life." The most controversial part of the argument, that medical care resources sometimes should be withheld from the elderly, makes up one part of the book. Another part of the argument, that the goal of medical care of the elderly should be to improve rather than worsen their lives, raises less controversy.

Cassel, Christine K. *Medicare Matters: What Geriatric Medicine Can Teach American Health Care.* Berkeley: University of California Press, 2007. A geriatric physician with 30 years of experience explains how government health care policies affect the everyday experience of doctors and elderly patients. She draws on this knowledge to make recommendations for improving Medicare and the health care of the elderly. Recommended reforms of Medicare may also provide a model for reforming health care for citizens of all ages.

Conklin, Joan H. *Medicare for the Clueless: The Complete Guide to This Federal Program.* New York: Citadel Press, 2005. To protect their health care rights, older persons should understand Medicare. Using the breezy yet informative style of other books in series for the clueless, dummies, or complete idiots, this volume explains the basics of how Medicare works. Chapters on Medicare rules for hospital stays, skilled nursing facilities, home health care, and Medicare Advantage HMOs cover key topics.

Fincham, Jack E. *The Medicare Part D Drug Program: Making the Most of the Benefit.* Sudbury, Mass.: Jones and Bartlett Publishers, 2007. The newness of the Medicare program for prescription drugs and the special rules for joining the program make it useful to have a guide to decision making. This book explains how the program works, who is eligible, and how eligible older persons can join. It promises an easy-to-understand format and simple terminology to help those eligible for but unfamiliar with the program.

Gelfand, Donald E. *The Aging Network: Programs and Services.* New York: Springer Publishing, 2006. A variety of federal, state, and local programs outside of Social Security, Medicare, and Medicaid help the elderly (most are sponsored by the Older Americans Act and the Administration on Aging). This book presents a listing of hundreds of these programs for transportation, law, employment, income support, and other services. Meant largely for providers of services for the elderly, it can also help others understand the many rights to public services that elderly persons enjoy.

Geyman, John. *Shredding the Social Contract: The Privatization of Medicare.* Monroe, Me.: Common Courage Press, 2006. The author, a retired professor of family medicine at the University of Washington, agrees that Medicare is a program in trouble. However, he criticizes current efforts to deal with problems of funding and quality of care by privatizing services. He instead favors returning to the original structure of the program—a public social insurance program.

Hannah, Jeanne M., and Joseph H. Friedman. *Taking Charge: Good Medical Care for the Elderly and How to Get It.* Traverse City, Mich.: Old Mission Press, 2006. The authors encourage older persons to participate actively in their medical care. Even more than doctors and nurses, the elderly and their caregivers can detect subtle changes that signal the beginning of more serious problems and can alert medical personnel to the problems.

The book gives advice on how patients can become an effective member of the treatment team and help doctors and nurses develop treatment strategies. This advice highlights the ability of older persons to act on their own in getting their health care rights.

Heiser, K. Gabriel. *How to Protect Your Family's Assets from Devastating Nursing Home Costs: Medicaid Secrets.* Superior, Colo.: Phylius Press, 2007. This up-to-date volume covers the maze of rules and regulations that govern who can receive Medicaid benefits for long-term care. Older persons have a right to such care but only under restrictive conditions. The attorney author gives information of use not only to lawyers and financial advisors but also to elderly persons dealing with their health problems or those of their spouse.

Kuba, Cheryl. *Navigating the Journey of Aging Parents: What Care Receivers Want.* New York: Routledge, 2006. Based on interviews with older persons receiving care, this book offers recommendations to caregivers. The author disputes the myth that Americans abandon their elderly parents but recognizes that caregivers need good advice and intends to fill this need.

Olson, Laura Katz, eds. *The Graying of the World: Who Will Care for the Frail Elderly.* New York: Haworth Press, 1994. With chapters on the United States, Sweden, Finland, Britain, Canada, Japan, and several other countries, this book compares government responses to the growing problem of a large dependent and frail elderly population. The second chapter on the United States offers a summary of the approaches used to finance long-term care. Other chapters on the different approaches taken by other governments and nations highlight some weaknesses of American programs.

Rai, Gurcharan S., ed. *Medical Ethics and the Elderly: Practical Guide.* Amsterdam, Netherlands: Harwood Academic Publishers, 1999. Arguing that health care personnel face difficult ethical decisions every day, the editor, a London physician, sees ethics as a central part of geriatrics. The articles in the book cover topics such as evaluating the competence of patients to make decisions, getting informed consent and advance directives, and using life-sustaining technology. The book seeks to help students understand ethical issues in medical care and junior physicians apply ethical principles to their practice. In addition, it may help others understand problems in safeguarding the health care rights of the elderly.

Smith, George P., III. *Legal and Health Care Ethics for the Elderly.* Washington, D.C.: Taylor & Francis, 1996. Although dated, this book addresses issues central to the health care rights of the elderly. It defines the meaning of health care rights, problems of financing, and choices of treatment and nontreatment faced by older persons and their families. It gives special attention to the rights of nursing home residents and the problems of long-term care residents.

U.S. Senate. *Ageism in Health Care: Are Our Nation's Seniors Receiving Proper Oral Health Care?: Forum before the Special Committee on Aging, United States Senate, One Hundred Eighth Congress, First Session, Washington, D.C., September 22, 2003.* Washington, D.C.: U.S. Government Printing Office, 2003. Also available online. URL: http://frwebgate.access.gpo.gov/cgi-bin/getdoc.cgi?dbname=108_senate_hearings&docid=f:91118.pdf. Downloaded in May 2007. Several witnesses at this Senate forum stated that millions of elderly patients do not receive the dental care they need, including 8,000 who die each year from cancers of the mouth. The title suggests that this problem stems from mistreatment of the elderly and misunderstanding of their oral health needs.

Wicclair, Mark R. *Ethics and the Elderly.* New York: Oxford University Press, 1993. The ethical issues discussed in this book relate primarily to care and treatment of the sick elderly. It considers questions such as: Is rationing by age justified as a means of controlling costs? What are the responsibilities of adult children toward frail elderly? What precautions are needed to protect sick elderly?

ARTICLES

"Advance Directives." *Mayo Clinic Health Letter,* vol. 23, no. 2, February 2005, p. 6. An advance directive encourages planning for end-of-life care by directing the treatment when a patient is incapacitated. Without the directive, family and physicians end up guessing what the patient would have wanted. This article discusses some of the issues a directive should address and encourages older patients to think ahead about unpleasant subjects such as death and incapacity.

Archer, Diane. "From a Medicare Rights Advocate: Problems and Solutions in Medicare Managed Care." *Generations*, vol. 22, no 2, Summer 1998, pp. 77–78. An early critic of the shift from Medicare fee-for-service to managed-care plans (such as HMOs) sees two major problems in the managed-care approach. First, it attracts healthier and less expensive patients while offering fewer benefits to those who need major, more expensive care. Second, the federal government does not require HMOs to disclose their treatment practices and guidelines. The author calls for changes in Medicare to correct these problems.

Baldauf, Sarah. "A Primer on the New Medicaid Rulebook." *U.S. News & World Report*, vol. 141, no. 20, November 27, 2006, p. 73. Few can keep up with the many rule changes in Medicaid—some legislated by Congress and others mandated by executive branch decisions. This article summarizes the most recent rule changes, many of which affect elderly persons attempting to qualify for long-term care benefits. For example, Congress has made it more difficult to qualify for financial hardship by putting a limit on the housing assets an applicant can have. At the same time, it also has set aside more funds to increase coverage for home care.

Baldwin, William. "Medical Gremlins." *Forbes*, vol. 178, no. 9, October 30, 2006, p. 18. The term medical gremlins refers to the perverse incentives built into Medicare and the medical system more generally. For example, stingy Medicare payments to doctors may lead them to use quick treatments like medication or to order multiple tests that bring in larger payments. Low payments thus may lead to poor health care of the elderly. The author suggests reforms that would make Medicare more like an insurance program for catastrophic health care rather than a source of benefits for routine treatment.

Brockmann, Hilke. "Why Is Less Money Spent on Health Care for the Elderly than for the Rest of the Population? Health Care Rationing in German Hospitals." *Social Science & Medicine*, vol. 55, no. 4, August 2002, pp. 593–608. This study of the costs to insurers of caring for older persons during their last years of life finds, surprisingly, that older patients cost less. Indeed, the oldest patients, particularly older women, receive less costly treatment for the same illness than younger women do. The authors interpret these findings for German hospitals as an indication of informal medical care rationing by age. However, they also note that the evidence of rationing appears stronger in Germany than the United States.

Christian, Cora. "Bringing Health Care Policy into the Information Age." *Vital Speeches of the Day*, vol. 72, no. 18/19, July 2006, pp. 521–525. A member of the AARP Board of Directors, Christian spoke as part of a symposium on Women's Healthy Aging. She suggests ways that health policy and technology can help improve the medical care treatment older women receive and contribute to independence and empowerment during the later years of life.

"The Costs of Aging." *Society*, vol. 41, no. 3, March/April 2004, pp. 3–4. This article gives some precise figures on medical care costs for the elderly: The average cost from age 70 to death was $140,700. Moreover, the costs for those prone to illness and early death are similar to those who live a longer and more active life. The article suggests these findings are good news for Medicare. If true, longer life in the future will not increase per person medical costs for the large baby-boom generation.

Deets, Horace B. "Let's Not Ration Health Care." *Modern Maturity*, vol. 31, April/May 1988, p. 15. Rejecting the claim that devoting health care resources to the elderly worsens care for the young, the author states his opposition to rationing of health care for the elderly. Problems of expensive health care occur at all ages, he argues, and must entail solutions that benefit young and old alike.

Fuchs, Victor Robert. "Medicare Reform: The Larger Picture." *Journal of Economic Perspectives*, vol. 14, no. 2, Spring 2000, pp. 57–70. The author sees innovations in medical treatment as the major source of rising costs for the elderly but also as a source of longer and higher quality lives. If medical innovations and costs continue to rise, transfers from the young to fund Medicare will likely reach a limit and older persons will have to pay for more of their medical care. This need will in turn encourage continued work in old age. These predictions suggest that elderly rights to medical care may diminish in the future.

Gearon, Christopher J. "Navigate the Medicare Maze before Age 65." *Kiplinger's Retirement Report*, vol. 14, no. 3, March 2007, p. 12. Given the complexity of Medicare rules, those becoming eligible for the program can easily miss out on entitlements. This article encourages persons approaching age 65 and retirement to learn how Medicare fits with any private coverage they have, to contact the Social Security Administration three months before becoming eligible, and in general to become an informed consumer of medical care.

Gleckman, Howard. "Providing for Your Own Care." *Business Week*, no. 3891, July 12, 2004, pp. 92–93. Purchasing private insurance for long-term care offers one way to finance the costs of living in a nursing home. As discussed in this article, such insurance is becoming both expensive and necessary. The article offers advice on shopping wisely for nursing home insurance.

Gotthardt, Melissa. "The Cancer Conundrum: Older Patients Not Being Offered Chemotherapy." *AARP The Magazine*, vol. 48, no. 6C, November/December 2005, pp. 11–12. Physicians prescribe chemotherapy less often for older cancer patients than younger cancer patients because they believe that the older body deals less well with the rigors of the treatment. The author and experts quoted in the article argue that older patients benefit more from chemotherapy than doctors think and that older patients should have access to the full range of treatments.

Harmetz, Aljean. "Ageism: The Disease America Won't Cure—and Should." *New Choices*, vol. 36, September 1996, pp. 58–62. Although discussing ageism in general, this article considers in particular how stereotypes and discrimination harm elderly persons receiving medical care. For example, medical personnel tend to talk down to older patients and listen less carefully to what they say. The author hopes that activist baby boomers will end such discrimination by demanding better treatment and disproving stereotypes about old age.

Hoopes, Roy. "When It's Time to Leave: Views of D. Callahan." *Modern Maturity*, vol. 31, August/September 1988, pp. 38–43. In this interview, Daniel Callahan defends his views that modern medicine should be used to achieve a fitting life span rather than to devote excessive expense to extending years of sickness, disability, and pain in old age.

Kane, Robert L., and Rosalie A. Kane. "Ageism in Health Care and Long-Term Care." *Generations*, vol. 29, no. 3, Fall 2005, pp. 49–54. The authors believe that ageism pervades medical care, particularly for long-term care, less for acute care. They strongly oppose ageism but also recognize that legitimate reasons sometimes exist for different treatments by age.

Lachs, Mark S. "Equal Treatment for Older Adults." *Prevention*, vol. 55, no. 5, May 2003, pp. 185–187. Believing that ageism leads to inferior medical care for the elderly, the author offers several recommendations to correct the problem. For example, older patients should ask more questions and prepare for a visit with a physician by writing down symptoms and current medications. In addition, the author, himself a physician, believes medical schools should improve their training programs in geriatrics.

Lamm, Richard D., and Robert H. Blank. "The Challenge of an Aging Society." *The Futurist*, vol. 39, no. 4, July/August 2005, pp. 23–27. The challenge described by the authors is how to pay for the retirement and health care of baby boomers as they reach old age without bankrupting the country or unfairly burdening future generations. The article says that "the current system of funding health care is unsustainable" and Americans must give up a cherished dream of "total, universal care for any ailment freely available on demand." More pessimistic about Medicare than others, the authors call for major changes in health care programs for the elderly.

Lindeman, Bard. "Ageism Is Bad Medicine." *50 Plus*, vol. 27, January 1987, p. 4. According to expert physicians quoted in this article, negative attitudes about the elderly among health care personnel stem from dealing most often with older patients who have the worst health and mental problems. The author believes such attitudes must change. Medical students need to be taught to respect the elderly, and elderly persons need to be more assertive in demanding their right to equality in medical care.

Mandel, Jenny. "Medicaid's Third Rail." *Governing*, vol. 19, no. 4, January 2006, pp. A8–A11. The importance of Medicaid to the elderly shows in several statistics presented in this article. One-third of Medicaid spending goes to long-term care, but it serves only 10 percent of beneficiaries. About two-thirds of long-term care beneficiaries are over age 65, and the costs for this group will almost certainly rise in the future. Plus, state governments bear most of the high expense of Medicaid. These statistics suggest the need to experiment with new approaches that limit costs for long-term care.

Mianowany, Joe. "When Advance Directives Don't Say Enough." *Kiplinger's Retirement Report*, vol. 11, no. 12, December 2004, p. 16. As happened to the author and his father, simple advance directives sometimes do not contain enough information to guide treatment in unforeseen circumstances. The author says that giving power-of-attorney to someone who can make critical decisions adds needed flexibility. However, the power-of-attorney should go only to someone who knows the patient well and can act in the patient's best interest.

Pear, Robert. "Bush Seeks Big Medicare and Medicaid Saving, but Faces Hard Fight." *New York Times*, February 2, 2007, p. A1. The Republican George W. Bush administration aims to deal with funding problems for Medicare and Medicaid with cuts in spending, but Democrats in Congress call instead for allocating more funds to the programs. The battle raises larger issues concerning government entitlements to health care for the elderly and poor. This article describes some of the controversial proposals being considered.

Preston, Thomas A. "Facing Death on Your Own Terms." *Newsweek*, vol. 2000, no. 21, May 22, 2000, p. 82. This article tells readers what they can do to avoid the possible use of high-tech equipment to prolong their death. Persons should talk over their treatment desires with family members and spell them out in writing with an advance directive. With support of the family and a directive, a patient's wish to withhold treatment of a terminal illness has legal weight. In addition, the directive can stipulate that the patient receive all the pain relief possible.

Quinn, Jane Bryant. "Medicare's in Good Health." *Newsweek*, vol. 143, no. 21, May 24, 2004, p. 41. In criticizing doomsayers, Quinn says that Medicare works well and with modest reforms can continue to provide quality health care for the elderly. She expresses concerns about the trend toward relying on private companies to provide Medicare services but otherwise remains optimistic about this program, even in the face of projected spending deficits.

Schuler, Kate. "Extreme Makeover." *Governing*, June 2005, supp., pp. 18–20. This article makes the case for changing Medicare to emphasize prevention rather than treating diseases after they occur. Opponents point out that patients and providers are comfortable with the traditional ways of doing things and that the reform will raise costs for new tests and screenings. Still, the author believes that the goal of providing quality medical care for the aged requires such changes.

Smith, Wesley J. "'Futile Care' and Its Friends: Hospitals and Legislators Deciding When Life Is Not Worth Living." *Weekly Standard*, vol. 6, no. 42, July 23, 2001, pp. 27–29. By futile care, the author means the justification for denying treatment to patients, usually when physicians or others think the treatment will leave the patient with a poor quality of life. As a critic of this justification, Smith believes that the practice of refusing wanted treatment is really a form of discrimination used primarily against the elderly, disabled, and those most expensive to treat.

Updegrave, Walter. "Can Medicare Be Cured?" *Money*, vol. 32, no. 11, Fall 2003, pp. 72–78. This article presents both sides of the debate over how to run Medicare so that it provides the high-quality medical care for the elderly and keeps costs reasonable. While many want Medicare to remain a government program supported by taxpayers, others want to make Medicare more flexible and reliant on competition. The article discusses the possible future of Medicare as these competing viewpoints vie for dominance.

van Delden, J. J. M., A. M. Vrakking, and A. van der Heide. "Medical Decision Making in Scarcity Situations." *Journal of Medical Ethics*, vol. 30, no. 2, April 2004, pp. 207–211. In interviews with oncologists, cardiologists, and nursing home physicians, the authors find that physicians must make decisions about how to allocate scarce medical resources to patients. However, the physicians say they reject the use of age in making these decisions. Such evidence does not disprove claims that age discrimination affects care but does suggest that physicians oppose age-based rationing of medical care.

Wasik, John F. "The Crisis in Long-Term Care." *Consumers Digest*, vol. 37, no. 3, May/June 1998, pp. 69–76. The crisis described in this article involves not only the high costs of long-term care. In addition, the crisis comes from a two-tiered system of nursing home care that relies on either government Medicaid funding or on private resources. The low payments for Medicaid result in substandard care, while the expensive private payments lead to the treatment of patients as guests. Improving the quality of care and bringing the two tiers of treatment closer together require more resources for Medicaid patients.

Welch, William M. "Medicare: The Next Riddle for the Ages." *USA Today*, March 16, 2005, p. A10. Also available online. URL: http://www.usatoday.com/news/washington/2005-03-16-medicare-riddle_x.htm. Posted on March 16, 2005. The riddle of Medicare comes from two contradictory goals: funding expensive medical care for the elderly and controlling the escalating costs. The story quotes experts who say that solving the funding problem for Medicare will be more difficult than solving the funding problems for Social Security. Although the article raises questions about the ability of Medicare to sustain the services it provides to the elderly, it also highlights the risks to politicians who propose major reforms.

WEB DOCUMENTS

"Advance Directives/Living Wills." University of Michigan Health System. Available online. URL: http://www.med.umich.edu/1libr/aha/umadvdir.htm. Updated in March 2005. Presents basic information on the topic and links to important forms.

"Ageism: How Health Care Fails the Elderly." Alliance for Aging Research. Available online. URL: http://www.agingresearch.org/content/article/detail/694. Downloaded in May 2007. This booklet of less than 20 pages makes a strong case that the elderly do not receive the same quality of medical treatment as younger persons. Although buttressed with citations from scholarly literature, it also presents vivid examples of mistreatment to support its thesis. It recommends more training in geriatrics for health care professionals, greater representation of older persons in clinical studies, more emphasis on screening and prevention at the older ages, and better education of older persons on what they should expect from their health care.

Andre, Claire, and Manuel Velasquez. "Aged-Based Health Care Rationing." Santa Clara University. Available online. URL: http://www.scu. edu/ethics/publications/iie/v3n3/age.html. Downloaded in June 2007. The authors present an even-handed summary of both sides of the debate over rationing. They reach no conclusions—other than to emphasize the importance of the issue—but summarize the main arguments of more impassioned advocates for and against rationing.

Blendon, Robert J., and Catherine Desroches. "Future Health Care Challenges." Issues in Science and Technology Online: Health. Available online. URL: http://www.issues.org/19.4/blendon.html. Downloaded in May 2007. Two Harvard University scholars summarize the problems faced by the health care system in the United States. Among the most serious problems are rising costs, inequality in access, and the growing elderly population. Concerning the elderly, the authors predict increasing shortages of health care services and long-term care facilities.

Board of Trustees. "2006 Annual Report." Federal Hospital Insurance and Federal Supplemental Medical Insurance Trust Funds. Available online. URL: http://www.cms.hhs.gov/ReportsTrustFunds/downloads/tr2006. pdf. Posted on May 1, 2006. The overview chapter in this long and highly technical report clearly states the key conclusion of the board of trustees: The financial outlook of Medicare raises serious concerns and requires timely and effective action. This conclusion has received much publicity, and the document gives the facts to support it.

Caplan, Craig, and Lori Housman. "Redefining Medicare's Long-Term Financial Health: A Closer Look at the 'Medicare Funding Warning' in the Trustees' Report." AARP. Available online. URL: http://www.aarp. org/research/medicare/financing/aresearch-import-874-IB67.html. Posted in June 2004. The warnings from Medicare trustees about the looming deficit in funding lead many to wonder about the financial viability of the program. This report explains the meaning of the warnings and the workings of Medicare finances. It may be too detailed for many readers, but its question-and-answer format explains some puzzling and complex aspects of Medicare.

"Financing Long-Term Care." University of Minnesota Extension Agency. Available online. URL: http://www.financinglongtermcare.umn.edu. Updated in March 2003. The right to quality care for older persons with chronic health and mental problems depends on their ability to pay for long-term care. This web page offers information on financial options, public programs, and needed preparations, all intended to help those approaching old age set up a plan for long-term care.

"Guide to Long-Term Care Planning." National Care Planning Council. Available online. URL: http://www.longtermcarelink.net/eldercare.htm. Downloaded in June 2007. This web page contains the equivalent of a book on topics relating to long-term care. Chapters cover issues such as assisted living, nursing homes, Medicare benefits, and long-term care planning. The material contains a mix of factual information and practical advice.

Hoffman, Earl Dirk, Jr., Clare E. McFarland, and Catherine A. Curtis. "Brief Summaries of Medicare and Medicaid: Title XVIII and Title XIX of the Social Security Act." Centers for Medicare and Medicaid Services. Available online. URL: http://www.cms.hhs.gov/Medicare ProgramRatesStats/downloads/MedicareMedicaidSummaries2006.pdf. Posted on November 1, 2002. Trying to understand the complexities of Medicare and Medicaid will overwhelm most researchers interested in the rights of the elderly, but some attention to the basic workings of the programs is essential. This 21-page document helps toward that end. It describes the historical development of Medicare and Medicaid, the populations they cover, the benefits they pay, and the problems in financing they face. Although some changes have occurred in the program since the 2002 date of the document, most of its information remains current.

Hought, Joy. "Confronting Ageism: The Maturing of Medical School Curricula." Geriatric Times. Available online. URL: http://www.cmellc. com/geriatrictimes/g021205.html. Posted in November/December 2002. This web page describes a study done of 131 medical students to improve their attitude toward and understanding of older patients. The study finds that the students who met several times with a senior mentor had more positive attitudes toward the elderly. The author also discusses the underlying sources of ageism among medical students and the importance of changing negative attitudes.

"Long-Term Care." Medicare: The Official U.S. Government Site for People with Medicare. Available online. URL: http://www.medicare. gov/LongTermCare/Static/Home.asp. Updated on January 22, 2007. This web page answers questions older persons might have about Medicare benefits for long-term care. Although Medicare generally does not pay for custodial, nonskilled care or long-term skilled care, it does (as described on this web page) provide some benefits. The web page also gives advice on choosing and financing long-term care.

"Medicaid Funding." National Conference of State Legislators. Available online. URL: http://www.ncsl.org/programs/health/medfund.htm. Downloaded in June 2007. This web page contains data on Medicaid spending by states, the District of Columbia, and several U.S. territories in fiscal years 2000 and 2001. The data demonstrate large increases in spending, a trend of great concern to the states.

"Medicaid: A Primer." Kaiser Commission on Medicaid and the Uninsured. Available online. URL: http://www.kff.org/medicaid/7334-02.cfm. Posted in July 2005. This 31-page book clearly explains the sometimes complex workings of Medicaid. The Kaiser Foundation, which favors doing more to help those without health insurance, answers some key questions in an informative and understandable format. The questions include: What is Medicaid? Who is covered by Medicaid? What services does Medicaid cover? How much does Medicaid cost? Who pays for Medicaid? The answers demonstrate the value of the program to the elderly and other groups.

"Medicare and You 2007." Centers for Medicare and Medicaid Services. Available online. URL: http://www.medicare.gov/publications/pubs/pdf/10050.pdf. Updated on January 2007. Although long for a government booklet—106 pages—this document clearly explains how Medicare works and what rights its beneficiaries have. A chapter on Medicare basics compares program options for Original Medicare, Medicare Advantage, and Medicare Prescription Drug Coverage. Other chapters on help for people with limited income and private insurance coverage discuss benefits available outside of Medicare. Perhaps most useful, chapter 10 lists the rights of Medicare beneficiaries.

"Medicare Rights: Your Right to Appeal and Other Protections." Humana Medicare. Available online. URL: http://www.humana-medicare.com/medicare-information/medicare-rights.asp. Updated on April 12, 2007. This web page sponsored by a private health care company explains what Medicare patients can do when they believe they wrongly have been denied services. It also has links that can help readers understand how the various components of Medicare work.

"Overview of Medicare Supplemental Insurance." AARP. Available online. URL: http://www.aarp.org/health/medicare/supplemental/a2003-05-02-medicaresupplement.html. Downloaded in May 2007. Also known as Medigap insurance, Medicare Supplemental Insurance helps pay for services not covered by Medicare. Those eligible for Medicare can purchase one of 12 standard Medigap insurance programs from private insurers. This web page describes the advantages of these insurance plans and offers links to particulars on each of the plans. The need for Medigap insurance highlights some of the limitations in government health care available to the elderly.

Annotated Bibliography

"Part D 2007: Addressing Access Problems for Low-Income Persons with Medicare." Medicare Rights Center. Available online. URL: http://www.medicarerights.org/policybrief_autoreenrollment.pdf. Posted in November 2006. This paper written for policy makers by a group representing the rights of Medicare recipients finds that low-income people have not fared well under the new Medicare prescription drug program. It recommends that the Centers for Medicare and Medicaid Services take several steps to meet the prescription drug needs of the poor elderly.

"The Patients' Bill of Rights in Medicare and Medicaid." U.S. Department of Health and Human Services. Available online. URL: http://www.hhs.gov/news/press/1999pres/990412.html. Posted on April 12, 1999. The DHHS regulations on Medicare and Medicaid rights come from a commission appointed by President Bill Clinton in 1997. This press release summarizes the recommendations of the commission and their goal of ensuring patient rights in government health care programs.

"Protect Medicare: Preserve the Fundamental Structure of the Program for the Future." Medicare Rights Center. Available online. URL: http://www.medicarerights.org/protectmedicare.html. Downloaded in June 2007. Making the case for strengthening Medicare in its original form, the Medicare Rights Center opposes efforts to privatize the program. The organization claims that providing subsidies to private health plans in Medicare Advantage and giving responsibility for Medicare prescription drug coverage to private companies represent efforts to dismantle Medicare as a public insurance program.

Vinson, Carey. "HMOs Cure Many of Medicare's Problems." Physician's News Digest. Available online. URL: http://www.physiciansnews.com/commentary/497wp.html. Posted in April 1997. Presenting a more positive view of managed care for Medicare patients than most other commentators, the author argues that HMOs make Medicare services more efficient and less fragmented than the fee-for-service system. He uses the Blue Cross/Blue Shield program to illustrate the strengths of private health care programs. Since the article, Medicare and Medicaid have increasingly relied on managed care.

"Your Medicare Rights." AARP. Available online. URL: http://www.aarp.org/health/medicare/traditional/a2003-04-28-medicarerights.html. Downloaded in June 2007. A brief but helpful listing and discussion of the consumer protections offered by Medicare.

"Your Medicare Rights and Protections." Centers for Medicare and Medicaid Services. Available online. URL: http://www.medicare.gov/Publications/Pubs/pdf/10112.pdf. Updated in August, 2007. The initial listing of Medicare rights here is brief and general (e.g., the right to be protected from discrimination, the right to have your questions answered). However, the remainder of this 44-page booklet details how the rights apply to different Medicare programs. Discussion of how to file a complaint and make an appeal can help beneficiaries act on their rights.

RIGHTS INVOLVING ELDER CARE AND PROTECTION AGAINST ABUSE

BOOKS

Allen, James E. *Nursing Home Federal Requirements: Guidelines to Surveyors and Survey Protocols, 2006.* New York: Springer Publishing, 2007. Federal guidelines set standards for care that nursing homes must meet in order to receive Medicare and Medicaid payments for their older residents. This book explains these regulations and the procedures used by federal surveyors to evaluate nursing homes. The book will most interest those who run nursing homes, but others can use it as a resource on requirements to protect older persons from abuse by nursing home staff.

Biggs, Simon, Chris Phillipson, and Paul Kingston. *Elder Abuse in Perspective.* Philadelphia: Open University Press, 1995. This book differs from most others in its approach to the problem of elder abuse by advancing a historical and social science perspective on the problem. It places elder abuse within the context of wider abuse within families, communities, and institutions and challenges many common beliefs about elder abuse. For example, it disputes that caregiver stress leads to victim abuse, a claim that places older persons in need of care as the source of the problem. Rather, substance abuse, poverty, and crowded living arrangements rather than caregiving tend to create the stress that leads to elder abuse.

Brandl, Bonnie, Carmel Bitondo Dyer, Candace J. Heisler, Joanne Marlatt Otto, Lori A. Stiegel, and Randolph W. Thomas. *Elder Abuse Detection and Intervention: A Collaborative Approach.* New York: Springer Publishing, 2006. The collaborative approach advocated in this volume links multiple agencies—adult protection services, law enforcement, prosecution, health care, and advocacy—in protecting the safety of the elderly. Setting up better reporting systems, evaluating possible interventions, and reviewing policy, legislation, and research should all be part of the collaborative effort to protect elderly victims. Although most valuable to practitioners who deal often with elder abuse, others may be encouraged by the effort to involve multiple partners in the fight against elder abuse.

Cassidy, Thomas M. *Elder Care: What to Look For, What to Look Out For!* 3rd Edition. Falls Hill, N.J.: New Horizon Press, 2004. A medical fraud investigator who once worked for the state of New York, the author gives many examples of abuse of the elderly by corrupt nursing home owners and malicious staff members. He suggests ways to protect older persons from this sort of mistreatment and includes advice from experts on elder law, financial planning, and geriatrics.

Connell, Linda H. *Nursing Homes and Assisted Living Facilities: Your Practical Guide for Making the Right Decision*. Naperville, Ill.: Sphinx Publishing, 2004. The author, a lawyer specializing in the area of domestic relations, makes several recommendations about choosing a nursing home. He also gives tips on evaluating facilities and health care providers, handling the expense of long-term care, asking the right questions to administrators, and finding ways to deal with resistance to a nursing home move.

Gass, Thomas Edward. *Nobody's Home: Candid Reflections of a Nursing Home Aide*. Ithaca, N.Y.: ILR Press, 2004. Motivated by problems caring for his dying mother, the author tells of his experiences while working as a low-paid aide in a nursing home. The description of day-to-day life illustrates the problems even well-intentioned workers and family members have in treating patients in a dignified way. He describes the facility as clean, efficient, and functional but also as sterile and excessively concerned with profit. While the book includes some recommendations for change in the epilogue, its main value comes from the picture it presents of daily life in a nursing home.

Hird, Mary. *Elder Abuse, Neglect, and Maltreatment: What Can Be Done to Stop It*. Pittsburgh: Dorrance Publishing, 2003. Among much else, the author calls for more training and better selection of caregivers for the elderly, higher standards for caregiving, and greater commitment of resources to the problem of elder abuse.

Kane, Robert L., and Joan C. West. *It Shouldn't Be This Way: The Failure of Long-Term Care*. Nashville, Tenn.: Vanderbilt University Press, 2005. Calling long-term care in the United States a failure, the authors recount their experiences when their mother suffered a stroke and spent the last years of her life in a nursing home. Despite many kind and considerate workers, they found inadequate care, low staffing, and poor coordination among caregivers at the nursing home. The book relies on these experiences and knowledge of medical care more generally to make recommendations for improving long-term care.

Kosberg, Jordan I., and Juanita L. Garcia. *Elder Abuse: International and Cross-Cultural Perspectives*. New York: Haworth Press, 1995. The comparisons of elder abuse prevalence and prevention policies across nations such as Australia, Finland, and Ireland demonstrate the diversity of causes and solutions for elder abuse and the seriousness of the problem across the world. Based on these comparisons, the authors suggest ideas for policy changes in the United States.

Mellor, M. Joanna, and Patricia J. Brownell, eds. *Elder Abuse and Mistreatment: Policy, Practice, and Research*. New York: Haworth Press, 2006. The chapters of this edited volume will most interest scholars and students in the fields of gerontology and geriatrics but also may appeal to a broader audience. Topics such as identifying elder mistreatment, building elder abuse shelters, and setting up support groups touch on practical issues of protecting the elderly.

Mezey, Mathy D., ed. *The Encyclopedia of Elder Care*. Amherst, N.Y.: Prometheus Books, 2004. The encyclopedia includes nearly 300 entries on providing top-quality care for the elderly. The alphabetic listing of entries and cross references between entries make it easy to access information from the encyclopedia on topics such as home care, nursing home care, rehabilitation, case management, and assisted living.

National Research Council. *Elder Mistreatment: Abuse, Neglect, and Exploitation in an Aging America*. Washington, D.C.: National Academy Press, January 2003. Also available online. URL: http://www.nap.edu/books/0309084342/html. Downloaded in May 2007. Like other reports from the National Research Council, this one presents an in-depth review of scholarly studies on a major problem and makes recommendations based on the literature for how to address it. This volume on elder abuse states that the topic has not received the attention it deserves and aims to move a research agenda forward by summarizing existing information. It does less to give practical advice for protecting the elderly than to make a strong case for the importance of the topic.

Payne, Brian K. *Crime and Elder Abuse: An Integrated Perspective*. Springfield, Ill.: Charles C. Thomas, 2005. Viewing elder abuse as not only a social problem but also a crime, this book's perspective differs from most others. For example, it discusses how elder victimization compares to younger victimization and how the criminal justice system responds to incidents of elder abuse. It also considers the motives of offenders as well as the consequences for victims.

Pillemer, Karl, Diane A. Menio, and Beth Hudson Keller. *Abuse-Proofing Your Facility: A Practical Guide for Preventing Abuse in Long-Term Care Facilities*. Somerville, Mass.: Frontline Publishing, 2001. Written for administrators, this book offers practical advice to correct problems in long-term care facilities that give rise to elder abuse. Chapters cover topics such as hiring practices, staffing shortages, effective supervision, staff training, stress management, and conflict resolution.

Sandell, Diane S., and Lois Hudson. *Ending Elder Abuse: A Family Guide*. Fort Bragg, Calif.: QED Press, 2000. Diane Sandell's 91-year-old mother died from a beating she received while living in a California nursing home. With her coauthor, she advises family members, caregivers, and legislators on how to prevent and stop the problem of elder abuse. The authors acknowledge that caregivers feel frustration with elderly patients and suggest ways to deal with such feelings before they lead to abuse. They also suggest ways to pick safe care facilities for loved ones.

Annotated Bibliography

Somers, Marion. *Elder Care Made Easier: Doctor Marion's 10 Steps to Help You Care for an Aging Loved One*. Omaha, Neb.: Addicus Books, 2006. Books on caring for the elderly can help family members do their best to protect the well-being and rights of older relatives. This book by a manager of a geriatric care practice gives advice on how to communicate openly with an older relative in need of care and to protect his or her safety. It also contains guidance on legal and financial matters.

Summers, Randal W., and Allan M. Hoffman, eds. *Elder Abuse: A Public Health Perspective*. Washington, D.C.: American Public Health Association, 2006. The public health perspective presented in this edited volume attempts to shift the common view of elder abuse as a criminal problem of individuals and their family members to a view of elder abuse as a public health problem for health care professionals. As a first step toward dealing more effectively with the problem, better data and reporting are necessary. Other steps include developing national policies, educating people about the importance of the problem, and providing more funds for research and intervention.

Tatara, Toshio, ed. *Understanding Elder Abuse in Minority Populations*. Philadelphia: Brunner/Mazel, 1999. The editor lauds the progress made in understanding elder abuse among Caucasian populations but criticizes the lack of research on how the problem affects minority populations. Part I includes chapters on African Americans, part II on Hispanics, part III on American Indians, and part IV on Asian Americans. Part V identifies similarities and differences in elder abuse across race and ethnic groups.

ARTICLES

Buri, Hilary, Jeanette M. Daly, and Arthur J. Hartz. "Factors Associated with Self-Reported Elder Mistreatment in Iowa's Frailest Elders." *Research on Aging*, vol. 28, no. 5, September 2006, pp. 562–581. Based on survey responses given by a sample of older persons in the Iowa Medicaid Waiver program, this study finds associations between abuse and old age, living alone, low income, and depression. The article discusses the clinical implications of these findings.

Coyne, Andrew C., Mildred Potenza, and Lisa J. Berbig. "Abuse in Families Coping with Dementia." *Aging*, no. 367, 1996, pp. 92–95. As described in this article, dementia increases the risk for elder abuse, especially in families with a history of violence. Caregivers of persons with dementia need support and services to cope nonviolently with the difficult tasks they face. Other articles in the same issue cover related topics on elder abuse.

"The Everything Guide to Elder Care." *New York*, vol. 39, no. 44, December 11, 2006, pp. 62–69, 116–117. Although focused on New York City, a special section of this issue offers guidance on finding quality elder care that people living most anywhere can use. It also discusses financing options and the varied forms that elder care can take.

"Forecasting Elder Care Trends for the 21st Century." *USA Today*, vol. 129, no. 2663, August 2000, pp. 6–7. The predictions offered in this article include: Medicaid will be gutted before federal and state government can create public programs to cover the costs of long-term care; workers will ask for long-term care benefits in lieu of pay raises; and a shortage of care workers will hamper employers trying to provide care for the elderly. These provocative claims follow from projections made by a study of the increasing longevity and size of the elderly population.

France, David. "'And Then He Hit Me': Domestic Violence among Older People." *AARP The Magazine*, vol. 49, no. 1C, January/February 2006, pp. 60–63, 76–77, 81–82. Domestic violence most often occurs early in life but can continue into old age and contribute to the prevalence of elder abuse. The article cites figures that 4–6 percent of older people claim to be in physically abusive relationships. The article discusses programs designed to reduce such violence and gives advice for older persons currently affected by domestic violence.

Fulmer, Terry, Lisa Guadagno, and Carmel Bitondo Dyer. "Progress in Elder Abuse Screening and Assessment Instruments." *Journal of the American Geriatrics Society*, vol. 52, no. 2, February 2004, pp. 297–304. This article concludes that health care personnel can use a brief set of screening questions to identify victims of elder abuse. It discusses some of the questions used in the screening and the benefits of routine use of the questions in treating older patients.

Gutner, Toddi. "License to Steal." *Business Week*, no. 3987, June 5, 2006, pp. 124–125. Along with citing statistics on the seriousness of financial fraud committed against the elderly, this article discusses some proposals in Congress to address the problem. A key to prevention is training for law and elder care professionals on how to detect and report elder fraud.

Menio, Diane A. "Advocating for the Rights of Vulnerable Nursing Home Residents: Creative Strategies." *Journal of Elder Abuse & Neglect*, vol. 8, no. 3, 1996, pp. 59–72. This article describes how advocates of the elderly have worked to change nursing home practices that can lead to abuse.

Mouton, Charles P. "Intimate Partner Violence and Health Status among Older Women." *Violence Against Women*, vol. 9, no. 12, December 2003, pp. 1465–1477. This study of women ages 50–79 finds that intimate partner violence persists into old age. About 5 percent of the women reported physical abuse and 23 percent reported verbal abuse. These results highlight the special vulnerability of older women to abuse by spouses and partners.

Payne, Brian K., and Laura Burke Fletcher. "Elder Abuse in Nursing Homes: Prevention and Resolution Strategies and Barriers." *Journal of*

Criminal Justice, vol. 33, no. 2, March/April 2005, pp. 119–125. This article reports the results of a survey of 76 nursing home administrators on elder abuse and strategies used to prevent it. It differs from other articles on prevention of abuse by reporting the views of those responsible for ensuring the safety of older persons in nursing homes rather than the views of victims and family members.

Rogers, Patrick. "Full Exposure: G. O'Donnell Uncovers Elder Abuse at Cheshire Convalescent Center Resulting in Arrests of D. Kolenda and P. Rzewnicki." *People Weekly*, vol. 54, no. 26, December 18, 2000, pp. 117–118. Upset by the poor conditions of his father's nursing home, Gerry O'Donnell videotaped the conditions there. When the state health department did little in response to the tape, he brought it to a New Haven television station. After the station aired the tape, police arrested the administrator and director of nursing, charging them with criminal cruelty and neglect. The article describes the case and the use of criminal charges to prevent abuse in nursing homes.

Stedman, Nancy. "A Father's Death, a Daughter's Legacy." *Health*, vol. 16, no. 4, May 2002, pp. 130–133, 154–156. This article describes a suit brought by the children of a recently deceased parent against a physician for elder abuse. The children claim that the failure to adequately manage pain during the last week of their father's life represented a form of elder abuse. The suit succeeded and has encouraged physicians to learn more about pain management of dying patients.

Tatge, Mark. "The Old Folks Home." *Forbes*, vol. 176, no. 12, December 12, 2005, pp. 156, 158. This article discusses the use of assisted living as an alternative to nursing home care for older persons in need of help. However, problems in giving medication, maintaining sufficient staffing, and adequately training employees can occur in assisted living arrangements. The article offers tips for finding quality assisted living for the elderly.

Ward, Vicky. "In Mrs. Astor's Shadow." *Vanity Fair*, vol. 48, no. 12, December 2006, pp. 228, 230, 235–236, 238, 240–243. This story about the mistreatment of 104-year-old Brooke Astor, a rich former socialite living in New York City, highlights the facts of the case and the people involved. More generally, it demonstrates that elder abuse can occur among the privileged as well as the poor and emphasizes the vulnerability of the elderly in all social classes.

Wasik, John F. "The Fleecing of America's Elderly." *Consumers Digest*, vol. 39, no. 2, March/April 2000, pp. 77–83. This article cites a conservative estimate that 3 million elderly persons are being abused financially. Most often the victim knows the abuser well. Law enforcement agencies across the country have set up task forces to catch and prosecute abusers, but the article tells what older persons themselves can do to prevent financial abuse.

Wood, Stacey, and Mary Stephens. "Vulnerability to Elder Abuse and Neglect in Assisted Living Facilities." *The Gerontologist*, vol. 43, no. 5, October 2003, pp. 753–757. This in-depth study of 27 residents of assisted living facilities found that they are poorly informed about the services available to victims of elder abuse and the actions to take if victimized.

WEB DOCUMENTS

"Elder Abuse and Neglect: In Search of Solutions." American Psychological Association Online. Available online. URL: http://www.apa.org/pi/aging/eldabuse.html. Downloaded in June 2007. This web page sponsored by professional psychologists introduces readers to the problem of elder abuse. It defines key terms, gives several real life examples, discusses causes, and offers solutions to the problem. Solidly referenced and clearly written, the web page offers a good starting place for research on elder abuse.

"Elder Rights: LTC Ombudsman. Legislation and Regulations." Administration on Aging. Available online. URL: http://www.aoa.gov/prof/aoaprog/elder_rights/LTCombudsman/Legislation_Reg/legislation_reg.asp. Updated on September 9, 2004. The Older Americans Act requires that each state have a long-term care ombudsman program. The state ombudsmen advocate for residents of nursing homes, board and care homes, and other assisted living facilities. This web page describes the laws and regulations that guide the program and includes links to related documents.

"Elder Rights and Resources: Elder Abuse." Administration on Aging. Available online. URL: http://www.aoa.gov/eldfam/Elder_Rights/Elder_Abuse/Elder_Abuse.asp. Updated on June 6, 2006. The federal government agency that sponsors state and community services for elderly persons has created a web page with basic information on elder abuse. The web page highlights the seriousness of the problem, gives information on reporting elder abuse, and describes programs of the Administration on Aging to combat the problem.

"Fact Sheet: Elder Abuse Prevalence and Incidence." National Center on Elder Abuse. Available online. URL: http://www.elderabusecenter.org/pdf/publication/FinalStatistics050331.pdf. Posted in March 2005. This two-page fact sheet is filled with useful statistics on elder abuse, a behavior too often left unreported. With a full listing of its sources, the National Center on Elder Abuse summarizes the most reliable information. For example, it cites figures that 1 to 2 million Americans age 65 and over have been injured, mistreated, or otherwise exploited. Other cited figures suggest an even more widespread problem.

"Guide to Choosing a Nursing Home." Centers for Medicare and Medicaid Services. Available online. URL: http://www.feddesk.com/freehand

books/1216-4.pdf. Downloaded in June 2007. This detailed yet easy to understand booklet encourages older persons to think about nursing home care before the need arises. Aiming to help older persons and their family members make good decisions, it explains how to find and compare nursing homes, lists the rights of nursing home residents, and includes a checklist to evaluate nursing homes.

Hawes, Catherine. "Elder Abuse in Residential Long-Term Care Facilities: What Is Known About Prevalence, Causes, and Prevention." Testimony before the U.S. Senate Committee on Finance. Available online. URL: http://finance.senate.gov/hearings/testimony/061802chtest.pdf. Posted on June 18, 2002. In her testimony, Professor Hawes of Texas A&M University highlights the vulnerability of nursing home patients to abuse, a problem created in large part by inadequate staffing. She notes that the federal government can help by passing stronger regulations and funding training programs to reduce elder abuse.

"Information about Laws Related to Elder Abuse." National Center on Elder Abuse. Available online. URL: http://www.elderabusecenter.org/ pdf/publication/InformationAboutLawsRelatedtoElderAbuse.pdf. Downloaded in June 2007. This document identifies the major federal laws, state laws for adult protective services, institutional abuse laws, criminal laws, and laws relating to the long-term care ombudsman program. It also gives guidance on how to obtain copies of the laws from libraries or the Internet.

Klauber, Martin, and Bernadette Wright. "Legislation: The 1987 Nursing Home Reform Act Fact Sheet." AARP. Available online. URL: http:// www.aarp.org/research/legis-polit/legislation/aresearch-import-687- FS84.html. Posted in February 2001. The Nursing Home Reform Act of 1987 was a landmark in protecting the rights of nursing home residents. This web page describes the concerns that led to the legislation, the rights it guarantees to nursing home patients, and some concerns that have arisen since 1987.

Nerenberg, Lisa. "Abuse in Nursing Homes." National Center on Elder Abuse. Available online. URL: http://www.elderabusecenter.org/default. cfm?p=abuseinnursinghomes.cfm. Updated on May 17, 2003. Along with highlighting the seriousness of elder abuse, the author lists 10 recommendations to reduce its prevalence in nursing homes. The recommendations call for fostering better communication between nursing home and law enforcement agencies, forming support groups for nursing home staff, and publicizing clear definitions of elder abuse and the need to report it.

"Prevention of Elder Abuse, Neglect, and Exploitation." Cornell University Law School, U.S. Code Collection. Available online. URL: http://www4. law.cornell.edu/uscode/html/uscode42/usc_sec_42_00003058—i000-.

html. Downloaded in June 2007. This page reproduces U.S. federal law on elderly abuse. The law allocates funds for state agencies to develop prevention programs and sets standards for coordinating action of varied agencies.

"Residents' Rights." National Citizens' Coalition for Nursing Home Reform. Available online. URL: http://www.nccnhr.org/public/50_156_449. cfm. Downloaded in June 2007. This fact sheet lays out a long list of rights of nursing home residents. They include the right to be fully informed, participate in health care decisions, make independent decisions, receive visitors, and enjoy privacy, dignity, and security of possessions.

"Rights of Older Persons." Preventing Abuse of Older People by Family or Friends. Available online. URL: http://www.agedrights.asn.au/prevent/ rights.html. Downloaded in June 2001. In 1991, the United Nations adopted a set of principles on treatment of older persons and encouraged all member nations to incorporate the principles into their programs and policies. The rights aim to assure that older persons have independence, participate in social life, receive quality care, pursue self-fulfillment, and are treated with dignity. This web page lists the rights in more detail but says little about the ability of nations to reach the broad and ambitious goals.

"Statistics Related to Elder Abuse by Family or Friends." Preventing Abuse of Older People by Family or Friends. Available online. URL: http:// www.agedrights.asn.au/prevent/statistics.html. Downloaded in June 2007. The Australian organization that sponsors this web page presents interesting statistics on elder abuse. Psychological and financial abuse are most common, while physical abuse affects 12 percent and neglect affects 11 percent of victims. Further, most family abuse comes from children of the elderly victim.

Stiegel, Lori. "The Changing Role of the Courts in Elder Abuse Cases." American Bar Association. Available online. URL: http://www.utahbar. org/sites/noecomm/html/the_changing_role_of_the_court.html. Downloaded in June 2007. According to this document, case law has been changing to view elder abuse as a legal problem for the courts rather than a problem left to social workers. Increased civil and criminal action against nursing home abuses are one example of this trend. However, the document notes that the states vary widely in their enforcement of elder abuse laws.

CHAPTER 8

ORGANIZATIONS AND AGENCIES

The organizations and agencies listed in this chapter fall into five categories:

- federal government organizations,
- international organizations,
- advocacy organizations,
- service and charitable organizations, and
- professional and research organizations.

Each state also has its own organizations on aging services, health care, Medicaid, and adult protective services that are too numerous to list, but a federal government web page can help in locating these state organizations (http://www.usa.gov/Topics/Seniors/FederalState.shtml).

For each organization, the listing includes the web site and e-mail. Rather than list their e-mail address, many organizations include a web-based form for submitting questions and comments via the Internet. In these cases, the text notes that e-mail is available via a web form. Each listing also includes phone numbers, postal addresses, and brief descriptions of the organizations.

FEDERAL GOVERNMENT ORGANIZATIONS

Administration on Aging (AOA)
URL: http://www.aoa.gov
E-mail: aoainfo@aoa.hhs.gov
Phone: (202) 619-0724
One Massachusetts Avenue
Washington, DC 20201
Sponsors home and community services such as home-delivered meals, congregate meals, transportation, adult day care, legal assistance, and health promotion through funding from the Older Americans Act.

Centers for Medicare and
  Medicaid Services (CMS)
URL: http://www.cms.hhs.gov
E-mail: web form
Phone: (877) 267-2323

7500 Security Boulevard
Baltimore, MD 21244
Has the mission of ensuring effective, up-to-date health care coverage and quality care for Medicare and Medicaid beneficiaries.

Civil Rights Center (CRC)
URL: http://www.dol.gov/
oasam/programs/crc
E-mail: CivilRightsCenter@dol.gov
Phone: (202) 693-6500
200 Constitution Avenue, NW
Washington, DC 20210
A unit within the Department of Labor that has responsibility for administering and enforcing the Age Discrimination Act of 1975.

Employee Benefit Security
Administration (EBSA)
URL: http://www.dol.gov/ebsa
E-mail: web form
Phone: (866) 444-3272
200 Constitution Avenue, NW
Suite S-2524
Washington, DC 20210
Protects the pensions, health care plans, and other benefits of workers by providing information on worker rights, encouraging the growth of benefit programs, and enforcing violations of benefit laws.

Health Care Financing
Administration (HCFA)
URL: http://www.os.dhhs.gov/
about/opdivs/hcfa.html
Phone: (410) 966-3000
200 Independence Avenue, SW
Washington, DC 20201
An agency within the Department of Health and Human Services

that oversees Medicare, the federal portion of Medicaid, and quality assurance for federal health care programs.

National Institute on Aging
(NIA)
URL: http://www.nia.nih.gov
E-mail: web form
Phone: (301) 496-1752
Building 31
Room 5C27
31 Center Drive, MSC 2292
Bethesda, MD 20892
A unit of the National Institutes of Health (NIH) that sponsors scientific research, training, and health information dissemination on the nature of aging and has the goal of extending the years of healthy, active life during old age.

Pension Benefit Guaranty
Corporation (PBGC)
URL: http://www.pbgc.gov
E-mail: mypension@pbgc.gov
Phone: (800) 400-7242
P.O. Box 151750
Alexandria, VA 22315-1750
Protects the retirement incomes of workers with private-sector defined-benefit pension plans by collecting insurance premiums from employers and paying retirement benefits to retirees in pension plans that have ended.

Railroad Retirement Board (RRB)
URL: http://www.rrb.gov
E-Mail: web form
Phone: (312) 751-7139
844 North Rush Street
Chicago, IL 60611-2092

An independent agency in the federal government that administers retirement-survivor benefit programs for railroad workers and their families and is closely related to, but still separate from, Social Security.

**U.S. Department of Health and
Human Services (HHS)**
URL: http://www.hhs.gov
E-mail: web form
Phone: (877) 696-6775
200 Independence Avenue, SW
Washington, DC 20201
The cabinet department most concerned with issues of aging, it contains key agencies such as the Social Security Administration, the Administration on Aging, and the National Institute on Aging.

**U.S. Department of Housing and
Urban Development (HUD)**
URL: http://www.hud.gov
E-mail: hud@custhelp.com
Phone: (202) 708-1112
451 7th Street, SW
Washington, DC 20410
Has the mission to increase home ownership, support community development, increase access to affordable housing, and eliminate discrimination in housing choices, and has several programs for older persons such as reverse mortgages and loans.

U.S. Department of Labor (DOL)
URL: http://www.dol.gov
E-mail: web form
Phone: (866) 487-2365
200 Constitution Avenue, NW
Washington, DC 20210

A cabinet-level agency that promotes the welfare of workers, job seekers, and retirees by administering employment laws and improving working conditions, job opportunities, and retirement and health care benefits.

**U.S. Equal Employment
Opportunity Commission
(EEOC)**
URL: http://www.eeoc.gov
E-mail: info@ask.eeoc.gov
Phone: (800) 669-4000
1801 L Street, NW
Washington, DC 20507
Enforces the ADEA, provides oversight and coordination of federal equal employment opportunity regulations and policies, and investigates charges of age discrimination submitted by workers and job applicants.

**U.S. Senate Special Committee
on Aging**
URL: http://aging.senate.gov
Phone: (202) 224-5364
G31 Dirksen Senate Office
Building
Washington, DC 20510
Investigates, debates, and submits recommendations for legislation on matters relating to older Americans and publishes materials for those interested in public policies affecting the elderly.

**U.S. Social Security
Administration (SSA)**
URL: http://www.ssa.gov
E-mail: web form

Phone: (800) 772-1213
Windsor Park Building
6401 Security Boulevard
Baltimore, MD 21235

Manages Social Security and pays retirement, disability, and survivors benefits to workers and their families.

INTERNATIONAL ORGANIZATIONS

Global Action on Aging
URL: http://www.globalaging.org
E-mail: globalaging@globalaging. org
Phone: (212) 557-3163
777 UN Plaza
Suite 6J
New York, NY 10017
A part of the United Nations Programme on Ageing that reports on the needs of older persons within the global economy and advocates on their behalf to improve income support, health care access, and human rights.

HelpAge International
URL: http://www.helpage.org
E-mail: web form
Phone: +44 20 7278 7778
P.O. Box 32832
London N1 9ZN
United Kingdom
A global network of nonprofit organizations with a mission to improve the lives of disadvantaged older people by supporting local service programs and influencing national policies.

International Association of Gerontology and Geriatrics (IAGG)
URL: http://www.iagg.com.br
E-mail: iagg@iagg.com.br
Phone: +55 21 22351510

Rua Hilário de Gouveia 66
1102 Copacabana
Rio de Janeiro
Brazil RJ 22040-020
Promotes worldwide gerontological research and training, the advancement of geriatrics as a medical specialty focused on the elderly, and a better quality of life for aging people.

International Association of Homes and Services for the Ageing (IAHSA)
URL: http://www.iahsa.net
E-mail: iahsa@aahsa.org
Phone: (202) 508-9468
2519 Connecticut Avenue, NW
Washington, DC 20008
Represents the interests of service providers to the aged worldwide and creates a platform for those interested in serving the elderly to share their knowledge and best practices.

International Federation on Ageing (IFA)
URL: http://www.ifa-fiv.org/en/accueil.aspx
Phone: (514) 396-3358
4398 Boulevard Saint-Laurent
Suite 302
Montreal QC H2W 1Z5
Canada

Seeks to inform, educate, and promote policies and practices that improve the quality of life of older persons and strengthen the ties between nongovernmental organizations and governments in dealing with aging issues.

International Longevity Center (ILC)
URL: http://www.ilcusa.org
E-mail: info@ilcusa.org
Phone: (212) 288-1468
60 East 86th Street
New York, NY 10028
A research, policy, and educational organization with the mission of helping societies address the issues of population aging and longevity in positive and constructive ways and highlighting older people's productivity and contributions.

United Nations Programme on Ageing
URL: http://www.un.org/esa/socdev/ageing
E-mail: web form

Phone: (703) 276-1914
Department of Economic and Social Affairs
United Nations, DC2-1320
New York, NY 10017
A part of the United Nations Department of Economic and Social Affairs that advocates a "society for all ages," promotes integration of the elderly with other generations, and fosters equity and activity across all age groups.

World Health Organization (WHO)
URL: http://www.who.int/en
E-mail: info@who.org
Phone: (+ 41 22) 791 21 11
Avenue Appia 20
1211 Geneva 27
Switzerland
An agency of the United Nations that deals with health issues and has several projects relating to aging and the life course such as prevention of falls in old age, age-friendly cities, and prevention of elder abuse.

ADVOCACY ORGANIZATIONS

AARP
URL: http://www.aarp.org
E-mail: web form
Phone: (888) 687-2277
601 E Street, NW
Washington, DC 20049
A leading organization for people age 50 and over that provides services and products for members and advocates on legislative, consumer, and legal issues.

Alliance for Retired Americans
URL: http://www.retiredamericans.org
E-mail: web form
Phone: (202) 637-5399
815 16th Street, NW
Fourth Floor
Washington, DC 20006
Enrolls and mobilizes retired union members and other senior and community activists into a move-

ment that aims to preserve health and economic security programs for older Americans.

Gray Panthers
URL: http://www.graypanthers. org
E-mail: info@graypanthers.org
Phone: (800) 280-5362
1612 K Street, NW
Suite 300
Washington, DC 20006
An intergenerational organization that seeks to honor maturity and unite generations through working for social and economic justice, participatory democracy, and peace.

National Asian Pacific Center on Aging (NAPCA)
http://www.napca.org
E-mail: website@napca.org
Phone: (800) 336-2722
1511 Third Avenue
Suite 914
Seattle, WA 98101
Advocates on behalf of the Asian Pacific American aging community at the local, state, and national levels, and educates seniors and the general public on the unique needs of this community.

National Center on Elder Abuse
URL: http://www. elderabusecenter.org
E-mail: web form
Phone: (202) 898-2586
1201 15th Street, NW
Suite 350
Washington, DC 20005
A resource center on elder rights for law enforcement and legal pro-

fessionals, public policy leaders, researchers, and the public that aims to promote understanding, knowledge, and action on elder abuse, neglect, and exploitation.

National Citizens' Coalition for Nursing Home Reform (NCCNHR)
URL: http://www.nccnhr.org
Phone: (202) 332-2276
1828 L Street, NW
Suite 801
Washington, DC 20036
Provides information and leadership on federal and state regulatory and legislative policies, and develops strategies and models to improve care and life for residents of nursing homes and other long-term care facilities.

National Committee for the Prevention of Elder Abuse (NCPEA)
URL: http://www. preventelderabuse.org
E-mail: ncpea@verizon.net
Phone: (202) 682-4140
1612 K Street, NW
Washington, DC 20006
An association of researchers, practitioners, educators, and advocates with the mission of preventing abuse, neglect, and exploitation of older persons and adults with disabilities.

National Committee to Preserve Social Security and Medicare (NCPSSM)
URL: http://www.ncpssm.org
Phone: (800) 966-1935
10 G Street, NE

Suite 600
Washington, DC 20002
Serves as an advocate for the federal programs of Social Security and Medicare and for a healthy, productive, and secure retirement.

**National Indian Council on
   Aging (NICOA)**
URL: http://www.nicoa.org
Phone: (505) 292-2001
10501 Montgomery Boulevard,
   NE
Suite 210
Albuquerque, NM 87111-3846
Advocates improved comprehensive health and social services for American Indian and Alaska Native elders.

**National Senior Citizens Law
   Center (NSCLC)**
URL: http://www.nsclc.org

E-mail: nsclc@nsclc.org
Phone: (202) 289-6976
1101 14th Street, NW
Suite 400
Washington, DC 20005
Advocates for elderly and disabled poor people in federal policymaking on income support and health care, and litigates on issues that have broad impact on seniors.

Older Women's League (OWL)
URL: http://www.owl-national.org
E-mail: owlinfo@owl-national.org
Phone: (800) 825-3695
3300 North Fairfax Drive
Suite 218
Arlington, VA 22201
Strives to improve the status and quality of life of midlife and older women through research, education, and advocacy activities.

SERVICE AND CHARITABLE
ORGANIZATIONS

**Association of Jewish Aging
   Services (AJAS)**
URL: http://www.ajas.org
E-mail: info@ajas.org
Phone: (202) 543-7500
316 Pennsylvania Avenue, SE
Suite 402
Washington, DC 20003-1172
Coordinates homes and residential facilities for Jewish elderly, including residential health care, assisted living, group homes, independent housing, and congregate housing.

Generations United (GU)
URL: http://www.gu.org

E-mail: gu@gu.org
Phone: (202) 289-3979
1333 H Street, NW
Suite 500W
Washington, DC 20005
Focuses on improving the lives of children, youth, and older people through intergenerational strategies, programs, and public policies.

Medicare Rights Center (MRC)
URL: http://www.
   medicarerights.org
E-mail: web form
Phone: (212) 869-3850
520 Eighth Avenue

North Wing
3rd Floor
New York, NY 10018
Provides free counseling and information to people with Medicare questions and problems, and works for the goal of helping older and disabled people get good, affordable health care.

National Caucus and Center for the Black Aged (NCBA)
URL: **http://www.ncba-aged.org**
E-mail: **info@ncba-aged.org**
Phone: **(202) 637-8400**
1220 L Street, NW
Suite 800
Washington, DC 20005
Supports elders in communities of color with programs for senior employment, health and wellness, and housing management.

National Council on Aging (NCOA)
URL: **http://www.ncoa.org**
E-mail: **web form**
Phone: **(202) 479-1200**
1901 L Street, NW
4th Floor
Washington, DC 20036
Organizes individuals and agencies such as senior centers, adult day service centers, faith-based service organizations, and senior housing

facilities, and has the goal of helping older people remain healthy and independent, find jobs, and gain access to benefits programs.

Pension Rights Center (PRC)
URL: **http://www.pensionrights. org**
E-mail: **web form**
Phone: **(202) 296-3776**
1350 Connecticut Avenue, NW
Suite 206
Washington, DC 20036-1739
Protects and promotes the retirement security of American workers, retirees, and their families by providing counseling, policy analysis, and information on pension rights.

Women's Institute for a Secure Retirement (WISER)
URL: **http://www.wiser.heinz.org**
E-mail: **info@wiserwomen.org**
Phone: **(202) 393-5452**
1725 K Street, NW
Suite 201
Washington, DC 20006
Provides low and moderate income women (ages 18 to 65) with basic financial information that helps them take financial control over their lives, and works to increase awareness of the barriers that prevent women's adequate participation in the nation's retirement systems.

PROFESSIONAL AND RESEARCH ORGANIZATIONS

Alliance for Aging Research (AAR)
URL: **http://www.agingresearch. org**

Phone: **(202) 293-2856**
2021 K Street, NW
Suite 305

Washington, DC 20006

Dedicated to accelerating the pace of medical discoveries, advancing science, and improving the experience of aging through behavioral and medical research.

American Association of Homes and Services for the Aging (AAHSA)
URL: http://www.aahsa.org
E-mail: info@aahsa.org
Phone: (202) 783-2242
2519 Connecticut Avenue, NW
Washington, DC 20008-1520

An association of community organizations that provides adult day services, home health care, community services, senior housing, assisted living residences, continuing care retirement living, and nursing home care.

American Federation of Teachers (AFT)
URL: http://www.aft.org
E-mail: web form
Phone: (202) 879-4400
555 New Jersey Avenue, NW
Washington, DC 20001

Provides information on retirement issues such as preserving Social Security and Medicare to its union members and retirees.

American Geriatrics Society (AGS)
URL: http://www.
americangeriatrics.org
E-mail: info@americangeriatrics.
org
Phone: (212) 308-1414
350 Fifth Avenue

Suite 801
New York, NY 10118

Organizes health professionals devoted to improving the health, independence, and quality of life of all older people, and provides leadership for programs in patient care, research, education, and public policy.

American Society on Aging (ASA)
URL: http://www.asaging.org
E-mail: info@asaging.org
Phone: (800) 537-9728
833 Market Street
Suite 511
San Francisco, CA 94103

An organization of practitioners, educators, administrators, policymakers, business people, researchers, and students who work with the physical, emotional, social, economic, and spiritual aspects of aging and want to improve their knowledge and skills.

Employee Benefits Research Institute (EBRI)
URL: http://www.ebri.org
E-mail: info@ebri.org
Phone: (202) 659-0670
2121 K Street, NW
Suite 600
Washington, DC 20037-1896

Uses research and education to enhance the development of sound employee benefit plans for retirement and health care and supports sound public policy to regulate and promote these plans.

Gerontological Society of America (GSA)
URL: http://www.geron.org

E-mail: geron@geron.org
Phone: (202) 842-1275
1030 15th Street, NW
Suite 250
Washington, DC 20005
An organization of researchers, educators, practitioners, and policy makers that has the goal of advancing, integrating, and using basic and applied research on aging to improve the quality of life of aging people.

Meals on Wheels Association of America (MOWAA)
URL: http://www.mowaa.org
E-mail: mowaa@mowaa.org
Phone: (703) 548-5558
203 S. Union Street
Alexandria, VA 22314
Represents those who provide meal services to people in need and offers tools, information, cash grants, and leadership to program members.

National Academy of Elder Law Attorneys (NAELA)
URL: http://www.naela.org
E-mail: web form
Phone: (520) 881-4005
1604 North Country Club Road
Tucson, AZ 85716
Consists of attorneys in the private and public sectors (also some judges, professors of law, and students) who deal with legal issues affecting the elderly and disabled such as public benefits, estate planning, and health and long-term care.

National Association for Home Care and Hospice (NAHC)
URL: http://www.nahc.org

E-mail: pr@nahc.org
Phone: (202) 547-7424
228 Seventh Street, SE
Washington, DC 20003
A trade association representing the interests and concerns of home care agencies, hospices, home care aide organizations, and medical equipment suppliers.

National Association of Area Agencies on Aging (N4A)
URL: http://www.n4a.org
Phone: (202) 872-0888
1730 Rhode Island Avenue, NW
Suite 1200
Washington, DC 20036
An umbrella organization for area agencies on aging and Native American aging programs that advocates on behalf of the local aging agencies and helps older Americans get needed resources and support services.

National Association of State Units on Aging (NASUA)
URL: http://www.nasua.org
E-mail: info@nasua.org
Phone: (202) 898-2578
1201 15th Street, NW
Suite 350
Washington, DC 20005
Represents the nation's state and territorial agencies on aging, advances policies that meet the needs of a diverse aging population, and promotes the rights, independence, and opportunities of older persons.

National Center for Assisted Living (NCAL)
URL: http://www.ncal.org

Phone: (202) 842-4444
1201 L Street, NW
Washington, DC 20005
An organization of assisted living providers that informs the public about assisted living, fosters professional development of its members, and contributes to developing and changing government policies on assisted living.

PART III

APPENDICES

APPENDIX A

THE AGE DISCRIMINATION IN EMPLOYMENT ACT OF 1967

This document reproduces the text of the Age Discrimination in Employment Act of 1967 (Pub. L. 90-202) (ADEA), as amended and listed in volume 29 of the U.S. Code, beginning at section 621. The Older Workers Benefit Protection Act (Pub. L. 101-433) amends several sections of the ADEA. In addition, section 115 of the Civil Rights Act of 1991 (Pub. L. 102-166) amends section 7(e) of the ADEA (29 U.S.C. 626(e)). Italicized notes of explanation come from the source of the document, the Equal Employment Opportunity Commission, which was last updated on January 17, 1997 (http://www.eeoc.gov/policy/adea.html).

An Act
To prohibit age discrimination in employment.

Be it enacted by the Senate and House of Representatives of the United States of America in Congress assembled, that this Act may be cited as the "Age Discrimination in Employment Act of 1967".

* * *

STATEMENT OF FINDINGS AND PURPOSE
SEC. 621.
    (a) The Congress hereby finds and declares that—
        (1) in the face of rising productivity and affluence, older workers find themselves disadvantaged in their efforts to retain employment, and especially to regain employment when displaced from jobs;
        (2) the setting of arbitrary age limits regardless of potential for job performance has become a common practice, and certain otherwise desirable practices may work to the disadvantage of older persons;
        (3) the incidence of unemployment, especially longterm unemployment with resultant deterioration of skill, morale, and employer acceptability is,

217

relative to the younger ages, high among older workers; their numbers are great and growing; and their employment problems grave;

(4) the existence in industries affecting commerce, of arbitrary discrimination in employment because of age, burdens commerce and the free flow of goods in commerce.

(b) It is therefore the purpose of this chapter to promote employment of older persons based on their ability rather than age; to prohibit arbitrary age discrimination in employment; to help employers and workers find ways of meeting problems arising from the impact of age on employment.

EDUCATION AND RESEARCH PROGRAM
SEC. 622.

(a) The Secretary of Labor *[EEOC]* shall undertake studies and provide information to labor unions, management, and the general public concerning the needs and abilities of older workers, and their potentials for continued employment and contribution to the economy. In order to achieve the purposes of this chapter, the Secretary of Labor *[EEOC]* shall carry on a continuing program of education and information, under which he may, among other measures—

(1) undertake research, and promote research, with a view to reducing barriers to the employment of older persons, and the promotion of measures for utilizing their skills;

(2) publish and otherwise make available to employers, professional societies, the various media of communication, and other interested persons the findings of studies and other materials for the promotion of employment;

(3) foster through the public employment service system and through cooperative effort the development of facilities of public and private agencies for expanding the opportunities and potentials of older persons;

(4) sponsor and assist State and community informational and educational programs.

(b) Not later than six months after the effective date of this chapter, the Secretary shall recommend to the Congress any measures he may deem desirable to change the lower or upper age limits set forth in section 631 of this title.

PROHIBITION OF AGE DISCRIMINATION
SEC. 623.

(a) It shall be unlawful for an employer—

(1) to fail or refuse to hire or to discharge any individual or otherwise discriminate against any individual with respect to his compensation, terms, conditions, or privileges of employment, because of such individual's age;

(2) to limit, segregate, or classify his employees in any way which would deprive or tend to deprive any individual of employment opportunities or otherwise adversely affect his status as an employee, because of such individual's age; or

(3) to reduce the wage rate of any employee in order to comply with this chapter.

(b) It shall be unlawful for an employment agency to fail or refuse to refer for employment, or otherwise to discriminate against, any individual because of such individual's age, or to classify or refer for employment any individual on the basis of such individual's age.

(c) It shall be unlawful for a labor organization—

(1) to exclude or to expel from its membership, or otherwise to discriminate against, any individual because of his age;

(2) to limit, segregate, or classify its membership, or to classify or fail or refuse to refer for employment any individual, in any way which would deprive or tend to deprive any individual of employment opportunities, or would limit such employment opportunities or otherwise adversely affect his status as an employee or as an applicant for employment, because of such individual's age;

(3) to cause or attempt to cause an employer to discriminate against an individual in violation of this section.

(d) It shall be unlawful for an employer to discriminate against any of his employees or applicants for employment, for an employment agency to discriminate against any individual, or for a labor organization to discriminate against any member thereof or applicant for membership, because such individual, member or applicant for membership has opposed any practice made unlawful by this section, or because such individual, member or applicant for membership has made a charge, testified, assisted, or participated in any manner in an investigation, proceeding, or litigation under this chapter.

(e) It shall be unlawful for an employer, labor organization, or employment agency to print or publish, or cause to be printed or published, any notice or advertisement relating to employment by such an employer or membership in or any classification or referral for employment by such a labor organization, or relating to any classification or referral for employment by such an employment agency, indicating any preference, limitation, specification, or discrimination, based on age.

(f) It shall not be unlawful for an employer, employment agency, or labor organization—

(1) to take any action otherwise prohibited under subsections (a), (b), (c), or (e) of this section where age is a bona fide occupational qualification reasonably necessary to the normal operation of the particular business, or where the differentiation is based on reasonable factors other

than age, or where such practices involve an employee in a workplace in a foreign country, and compliance with such subsections would cause such employer, or a corporation controlled by such employer, to violate the laws of the country in which such workplace is located;

(2) to take any action otherwise prohibited under subsection (a), (b), (c), or (e) of this section—

(A) to observe the terms of a bona fide seniority system that is not intended to evade the purposes of this chapter, except that no such seniority system shall require or permit the involuntary retirement of any individual specified by section 631(a) of this title because of the age of such individual; or

(B) to observe the terms of a bona fide employee benefit plan—

(i) where, for each benefit or benefit package, the actual amount of payment made or cost incurred on behalf of an older worker is no less than that made or incurred on behalf of a younger worker, as permissible under section 1625.10, title 29, Code of Federal Regulations (as in effect on June 22, 1989); or

(ii) that is a voluntary early retirement incentive plan consistent with the relevant purpose or purposes of this chapter. Notwithstanding clause (i) or (ii) of subparagraph (B), no such employee benefit plan or voluntary early retirement incentive plan shall excuse the failure to hire any individual, and no such employee benefit plan shall require or permit the involuntary retirement of any individual specified by section 631(a) of this title, because of the age of such individual. An employer, employment agency, or labor organization acting under subparagraph (A), or under clause (i) or (ii) of subparagraph (B), shall have the burden of proving that such actions are lawful in any civil enforcement proceeding brought under this chapter; or

(3) to discharge or otherwise discipline an individual for good cause.

(g) *[Repealed]*

(h) (1) If an employer controls a corporation whose place of incorporation is in a foreign country, any practice by such corporation prohibited under this section shall be presumed to be such practice by such employer.

(2) The prohibitions of this section shall not apply where the employer is a foreign person not controlled by an American employer.

(3) For the purpose of this subsection the determination of whether an employer controls a corporation shall be based upon the—

(A) interrelation of operations,

(B) common management,

(C) centralized control of labor relations, and

(D) common ownership or financial control, of the employer and the corporation.

Appendix A

(i) It shall not be unlawful for an employer which is a State, a political subdivision of a State, an agency or instrumentality of a State or a political subdivision of a State, or an interstate agency to fail or refuse to hire or to discharge any individual because of such individual's age if such action is taken—

(1) with respect to the employment of an individual as a firefighter or as a law enforcement officer and the individual has attained the age of hiring or retirement in effect under applicable State or local law on March 3, 1983, and

(2) pursuant to a bona fide hiring or retirement plan that is not a subterfuge to evade the purposes of this chapter.

(j) (1) Except as otherwise provided in this subsection, it shall be unlawful for an employer, an employment agency, a labor organization, or any combination thereof to establish or maintain an employee pension benefit plan which requires or permits—

(A) in the case of a defined benefit plan, the cessation of an employee's benefit accrual, or the reduction of the rate of an employee's benefit accrual, because of age, or

(B) in the case of a defined contribution plan, the cessation of allocations to an employee's account, or the reduction of the rate at which amounts are allocated to an employee's account, because of age.

(2) Nothing in this section shall be construed to prohibit an employer, employment agency, or labor organization from observing any provision of an employee pension benefit plan to the extent that such provision imposes (without regard to age) a limitation on the amount of benefits that the plan provides or a limitation on the number of years of service or years of participation which are taken into account for purposes of determining benefit accrual under the plan.

(3) In the case of any employee who, as of the end of any plan year under a defined benefit plan, has attained normal retirement age under such plan—

(A) if distribution of benefits under such plan with respect to such employee has commenced as of the end of such plan year, then any requirement of this subsection for continued accrual of benefits under such plan with respect to such employee during such plan year shall be treated as satisfied to the extent of the actuarial equivalent of in-service distribution of benefits, and

(B) if distribution of benefits under such plan with respect to such employee has not commenced as of the end of such year in accordance with section 1056(a)(3) of this title *[section 206(a)(3) of the Employee Retirement Income Security Act of 1974]* and section 401(a)(14)(C) of title 26 *[the Internal Revenue Code of 1986]*, and the payment of benefits under such plan with respect to such employee is not suspended during such plan year pursuant to section 1053(a)(3)(B) of this title *[section 203(a)(3)(B) of the Employee Retirement Income Security Act of 1974]* or section 411(a)(3)(B) of title 26 *[the Internal Revenue Code of 1986]*, then any requirement of this subsection for continued accrual of benefits under such plan with respect to such employee during such plan year shall be treated as satisfied to the extent of any adjustment in the benefit payable under the plan during such plan year attributable to the delay in the distribution of benefits after the attainment of normal retirement age. The provisions of this paragraph shall apply in accordance with regulations of the Secretary of the Treasury. Such regulations shall provide for the application of the preceding provisions of this paragraph to all employee pension benefit plans subject to this subsection and may provide for the application of such provisions, in the case of any such employee, with respect to any period of time within a plan year.

(4) Compliance with the requirements of this subsection with respect to an employee pension benefit plan shall constitute compliance with the requirements of this section relating to benefit accrual under such plan.

(5) Paragraph (1) shall not apply with respect to any employee who is a highly compensated employee (within the meaning of section 414(q) of title 26 *[the Internal Revenue Code of 1986]*) to the extent provided in regulations prescribed by the Secretary of the Treasury for purposes of precluding discrimination in favor of highly compensated employees within the meaning of subchapter D of chapter 1 of title 26 *[the Internal Revenue Code of 1986]*.

(6) A plan shall not be treated as failing to meet the requirements of paragraph (1) solely because the subsidized portion of any early retirement benefit is disregarded in determining benefit accruals.

(7) Any regulations prescribed by the Secretary of the Treasury pursuant to clause (v) of section 411(b)(1)(H) of title 26 *[the Internal Revenue Code of 1986]* and subparagraphs (C) and (D) of section 411(b)(2) of title 26 *[the Internal Revenue Code of 1986]* shall apply with respect to the requirements of this subsection in the same manner and to the same extent as such regulations apply with respect to the requirements of such sections 411(b)(1)(H) and 411(b)(2).

(8) A plan shall not be treated as failing to meet the requirements of this section solely because such plan provides a normal retirement age described in section 1002(24)(B) of this title *[section 3(24)(B) of the Employee Retirement Income Security Act of 1974]* and section 411(a)(8)(B) of title 26 *[the Internal Revenue Code of 1986]*.

(9) For purposes of this subsection—

(A) The terms "employee pension benefit plan", "defined benefit plan", "defined contribution plan", and "normal retirement age" have the meanings provided such terms in section 1002 of this title *[section 3 of the Employee Retirement Income Security Act of 1974]*.

(B) The term "compensation" has the meaning provided by section 414(s) of title 26 *[the Internal Revenue Code of 1986]*.

(k) A seniority system or employee benefit plan shall comply with this chapter regardless of the date of adoption of such system or plan.

(l) Notwithstanding clause (i) or (ii) of subsection (f)(2)(B) of this section—

(1) It shall not be a violation of subsection (a), (b), (c), or (e) of this section solely because—

(A) an employee pension benefit plan (as defined in section 1002(2) of this title *[section 3(2) of the Employee Retirement Income Security Act of 1974]*) provides for the attainment of a minimum age as a condition of eligibility for normal or early retirement benefits; or

(B) a defined benefit plan (as defined in section 1002(35) of this title *[section 3(35) of such Act]*) provides for—

(i) payments that constitute the subsidized portion of an early retirement benefit; or

(ii) social security supplements for plan participants that commence before the age and terminate at the age (specified by the plan) when participants are eligible to receive reduced or unreduced old age insurance benefits under title II of the Social Security Act (42 U.S.C. 401 et seq.), and that do not exceed such old age insurance benefits.

(2) (A) It shall not be a violation of subsection (a), (b), (c), or (e) of this section solely because following a contingent event unrelated to age

(i) the value of any retiree health benefits received by an individual eligible for an immediate pension;

(ii) the value of any additional pension benefits that are made available solely as a result of the contingent event unrelated to age and following which the individual is eligible for not less than an immediate and unreduced pension; or

(iii) the values described in both clauses (i) and (ii); are deducted from severance pay made available as a result of the contingent event unrelated to age.

(B) For an individual who receives immediate pension benefits that are actuarially reduced under subparagraph (A)(i), the amount of the deduction available pursuant to subparagraph (A)(i) shall be reduced by the same percentage as the reduction in the pension benefits.

(C) For purposes of this paragraph, severance pay shall include that portion of supplemental unemployment compensation benefits (as described in section 501(c)(17) of title 26 *[the Internal Revenue Code of 1986]*) that—

(i) constitutes additional benefits of up to 52 weeks;

(ii) has the primary purpose and effect of continuing benefits until an individual becomes eligible for an immediate and unreduced pension; and

(iii) is discontinued once the individual becomes eligible for an immediate and unreduced pension.

(D) For purposes of this paragraph and solely in order to make the deduction authorized under this paragraph, the term "retiree health benefits" means benefits provided pursuant to a group health plan covering retirees, for which (determined as of the contingent event unrelated to age)—

(i) the package of benefits provided by the employer for the retirees who are below age 65 is at least comparable to benefits provided under title XVIII of the Social Security Act (42 U.S.C. 1395 et seq.);

(ii) the package of benefits provided by the employer for the retirees who are age 65 and above is at least comparable to that offered under a plan that provides a benefit package with one fourth the value of benefits provided under title XVIII of such Act; or

(iii) the package of benefits provided by the employer is as described in clauses (i) and (ii).

(E) (i) If the obligation of the employer to provide retiree health benefits is of limited duration, the value for each individual shall be calculated at a rate of $3,000 per year for benefit years before age 65, and $750 per year for benefit years beginning at age 65 and above.

(ii) If the obligation of the employer to provide retiree health benefits is of unlimited duration, the value for each individual shall be calculated at a rate of $48,000 for individuals below age 65, and $24,000 for individuals age 65 and above.

(iii) The values described in clauses (i) and (ii) shall be calculated based on the age of the individual as of the date of the contingent event unrelated to age. The values are effective on October 16, 1990, and shall be adjusted on an annual basis, with respect to a contingent event that occurs subsequent to the first year after October 16, 1990, based on the medical component of the Consumer Price Index for all urban consumers published by the Department of Labor.

(iv) If an individual is required to pay a premium for retiree health benefits, the value calculated pursuant to this subparagraph shall be reduced by whatever percentage of the overall premium the individual is required to pay.

(F) If an employer that has implemented a deduction pursuant to subparagraph (A) fails to fulfill the obligation described in subparagraph (E), any aggrieved individual may bring an action for specific performance of the obligation described in subparagraph (E). The relief shall be in addition to any other remedies provided under Federal or State law.

(3) It shall not be a violation of subsection (a), (b), (c), or (e) of this section solely because an employer provides a bona fide employee benefit plan or plans under which longterm disability benefits received by an individual are reduced by any pension benefits (other than those attributable to employee contributions)—

(A) paid to the individual that the individual voluntarily elects to receive; or

(B) for which an individual who has attained the later of age 62 or normal retirement age is eligible.

STUDY BY SECRETARY OF LABOR
SEC. 624.

(a) (1) The Secretary of Labor *[EEOC]* is directed to undertake an appropriate study of institutional and other arrangements giving rise to involuntary retirement, and report his findings and any appropriate legislative recommendations to the President and to the Congress. Such study shall include—

(A) an examination of the effect of the amendment made by section 3(a) of the Age Discrimination in Employment Act Amendments of 1978 in raising the upper age limitation established by section 631(a) of this title *[section 12(a)]* to 70 years of age;

(B) a determination of the feasibility of eliminating such limitation;

(C) a determination of the feasibility of raising such limitation above 70 years of age; and

(D) an examination of the effect of the exemption contained in section 631(c) of this title, relating to certain executive employees, and the exemption contained in section 631(d) of this title, relating to tenured teaching personnel.

(2) The Secretary *[EEOC]* may undertake the study required by paragraph (1) of this subsection directly or by contract or other arrangement.

(b) The report required by subsection (a) of this section shall be transmitted to the President and to the Congress as an interim report not later than January 1, 1981, and in final form not later than January 1, 1982.

TRANSFER OF FUNCTIONS
[All functions relating to age discrimination administration and enforcement vested by Section 6 in the Secretary of Labor or the Civil Service Commission were transferred to the Equal Employment Opportunity Commission effective January 1, 1979 under the President's Reorganization Plan No. 1.]

Rights of the Elderly

ADMINISTRATION
SEC. 625.

The Secretary *[EEOC]* shall have the power—

(a) to make delegations, to appoint such agents and employees, and to pay for technical assistance on a fee for service basis, as he deems necessary to assist him in the performance of his functions under this chapter;

(b) to cooperate with regional, State, local, and other agencies, and to cooperate with and furnish technical assistance to employers, labor organizations, and employment agencies to aid in effectuating the purposes of this chapter.

RECORDKEEPING, INVESTIGATION, AND ENFORCEMENT
SEC. 626.

(a) The Equal Employment Opportunity Commission shall have the power to make investigations and require the keeping of records necessary or appropriate for the administration of this chapter in accordance with the powers and procedures provided in sections 209 and 211 of this title *[sections 9 and 11 of the Fair Labor Standards Act of 1938, as amended]*.

(b) The provisions of this chapter shall be enforced in accordance with the powers, remedies, and procedures provided in sections 211(b), 216 (except for subsection (a) thereof), and 217 of this title *[sections 11(b), 16 (except for subsection (a) thereof), and 17 of the Fair Labor Standards Act of 1938, as amended]*, and subsection (c) of this section. Any act prohibited under section 623 of this title *[section 4]* shall be deemed to be a prohibited act under section 215 of this title *[section 15 of the Fair Labor Standards Act of 1938, as amended]*. Amounts owing to a person as a result of a violation of this chapter shall be deemed to be unpaid minimum wages or unpaid overtime compensation for purposes of sections 216 and 217 of this title *[sections 16 and 17 of the Fair Labor Standards Act of 1938, as amended]*: Provided, That liquidated damages shall be payable only in cases of willful violations of this chapter. In any action brought to enforce this chapter the court shall have jurisdiction to grant such legal or equitable relief as may be appropriate to effectuate the purposes of this chapter, including without limitation judgments compelling employment, reinstatement or promotion, or enforcing the liability for amounts deemed to be unpaid minimum wages or unpaid overtime compensation under this section. Before instituting any action under this section, the Equal Employment Opportunity Commission shall attempt to eliminate the discriminatory practice or practices alleged, and to effect voluntary compliance with the requirements of this chapter through informal methods of conciliation, conference, and persuasion.

(c) (1) Any person aggrieved may bring a civil action in any court of competent jurisdiction for such legal or equitable relief as will effectuate the purposes of this chapter: Provided, That the right of any person to bring such action shall terminate upon the commencement of an action by the Equal Employment Opportunity Commission to enforce the right of such employee under this chapter.

(2) In an action brought under paragraph (1), a person shall be entitled to a trial by jury of any issue of fact in any such action for recovery of amounts owing as a result of a violation of this chapter, regardless of whether equitable relief is sought by any party in such action.

(d) No civil action may be commenced by an individual under this section until 60 days after a charge alleging unlawful discrimination has been filed with the Equal Employment Opportunity Commission. Such a charge shall be filed—

(1) within 180 days after the alleged unlawful practice occurred; or

(2) in a case to which section 633(b) of this title applies, within 300 days after the alleged unlawful practice occurred, or within 30 days after receipt by the individual of notice of termination of proceedings under State law, whichever is earlier.

Upon receiving such a charge, the Commission shall promptly notify all persons named in such charge as prospective defendants in the action and shall promptly seek to eliminate any alleged unlawful practice by informal methods of conciliation, conference, and persuasion.

(e) Section 259 of this title *[section 10 of the Portal-to-Portal Act of 1947]* shall apply to actions under this chapter. If a charge filed with the Commission under this chapter is dismissed or the proceedings of the Commission are otherwise terminated by the Commission, the Commission shall notify the person aggrieved. A civil action may be brought under this section by a person defined in section 630(a) of this title *[section 11(a)]* against the respondent named in the charge within 90 days after the date of the receipt of such notice.

(f) (1) An individual may not waive any right or claim under this chapter unless the waiver is knowing and voluntary. Except as provided in paragraph (2), a waiver may not be considered knowing and voluntary unless at a minimum—

(A) the waiver is part of an agreement between the individual and the employer that is written in a manner calculated to be understood by such individual, or by the average individual eligible to participate;

(B) the waiver specifically refers to rights or claims arising under this chapter;

(C) the individual does not waive rights or claims that may arise after the date the waiver is executed;

(D) the individual waives rights or claims only in exchange for consideration in addition to anything of value to which the individual already is entitled;

(E) the individual is advised in writing to consult with an attorney prior to executing the agreement;

(F) (i) the individual is given a period of at least 21 days within which to consider the agreement; or

(ii) if a waiver is requested in connection with an exit incentive or other employment termination program offered to a group or class of employees, the individual is given a period of at least 45 days within which to consider the agreement;

(G) the agreement provides that for a period of at least 7 days following the execution of such agreement, the individual may revoke the agreement, and the agreement shall not become effective or enforceable until the revocation period has expired;

(H) if a waiver is requested in connection with an exit incentive or other employment termination program offered to a group or class of employees, the employer (at the commencement of the period specified in subparagraph (F)) informs the individual in writing in a manner calculated to be understood by the average individual eligible to participate, as to—

(i) any class, unit, or group of individuals covered by such program, any eligibility factors for such program, and any time limits applicable to such program; and

(ii) the job titles and ages of all individuals eligible or selected for the program, and the ages of all individuals in the same job classification or organizational unit who are not eligible or selected for the program.

(2) A waiver in settlement of a charge filed with the Equal Employment Opportunity Commission, or an action filed in court by the individual or the individual's representative, alleging age discrimination of a kind prohibited under section 623 or 633a of this title *[section 4 or 15]* may not be considered knowing and voluntary unless at a minimum—

(A) subparagraphs (A) through (E) of paragraph (1) have been met; and

(B) the individual is given a reasonable period of time within which to consider the settlement agreement.

(3) In any dispute that may arise over whether any of the requirements, conditions, and circumstances set forth in subparagraph (A), (B), (C), (D), (E), (F), (G), or (H) of paragraph (1), or subparagraph (A) or (B) of paragraph (2), have been met, the party asserting the validity of a waiver shall have the burden of proving in a court of competent jurisdiction that a waiver was knowing and voluntary pursuant to paragraph (1) or (2).

(4) No waiver agreement may affect the Commission's rights and responsibilities to enforce this chapter. No waiver may be used to justify

interfering with the protected right of an employee to file a charge or participate in an investigation or proceeding conducted by the Commission.

NOTICE TO BE POSTED
SEC. 627.
Every employer, employment agency, and labor organization shall post and keep posted in conspicuous places upon its premises a notice to be prepared or approved by the Equal Employment Opportunity Commission setting forth information as the Commission deems appropriate to effectuate the purposes of this chapter.

RULES AND REGULATIONS
SEC. 628.
In accordance with the provisions of subchapter II of chapter 5 of title 5 *[United States Code]*, the Equal Employment Opportunity Commission may issue such rules and regulations as it may consider necessary or appropriate for carrying out this chapter, and may establish such reasonable exemptions to and from any or all provisions of this chapter as it may find necessary and proper in the public interest.

CRIMINAL PENALTIES
SEC. 629.
Whoever shall forcibly resist, oppose, impede, intimidate or interfere with a duly authorized representative of the Equal Employment Opportunity Commission while it is engaged in the performance of duties under this chapter shall be punished by a fine of not more than $500 or by imprisonment for not more than one year, or by both: Provided, however, That no person shall be imprisoned under this section except when there has been a prior conviction hereunder.

DEFINITIONS
SEC. 630.
For the purposes of this chapter—
(a) The term "person" means one or more individuals, partnerships, associations, labor organizations, corporations, business trust, legal representatives, or any organized groups of persons.
(b) The term "employer" means a person engaged in an industry affecting commerce who has twenty or more employees for each working day in each of twenty or more calendar weeks in the current or preceding calendar year:
Provided, That prior to June 30, 1968, employers having fewer than fifty employees shall not be considered employers. The term also means (1) any

agent of such a person, and (2) a State or political subdivision of a State and any agency or instrumentality of a State or a political subdivision of a State, and any interstate agency, but such term does not include the United States, or a corporation wholly owned by the Government of the United States.

(c) The term "employment agency" means any person regularly undertaking with or without compensation to procure employees for an employer and includes an agent of such a person; but shall not include an agency of the United States.

(d) The term "labor organization" means a labor organization engaged in an industry affecting commerce, and any agent of such an organization, and includes any organization of any kind, any agency, or employee representation committee, group, association, or plan so engaged in which employees participate and which exists for the purpose, in whole or in part, of dealing with employers concerning grievances, labor disputes, wages, rates of pay, hours, or other terms or conditions of employment, and any conference, general committee, joint or system board, or joint council so engaged which is subordinate to a national or international labor organization.

(e) A labor organization shall be deemed to be engaged in an industry affecting commerce if (1) it maintains or operates a hiring hall or hiring office which procures employees for an employer or procures for employees opportunities to work for an employer, or (2) the number of its members (or, where it is a labor organization composed of other labor organizations or their representatives, if the aggregate number of the members of such other labor organization) is fifty or more prior to July 1, 1968, or twentyfive or more on or after July 1, 1968, and such labor organization—

(1) is the certified representative of employees under the provisions of the National Labor Relations Act, as amended *[29 U.S.C. 151 et seq.]*, or the Railway Labor Act, as amended *[45 U.S.C. 151 et seq.]*; or

(2) although not certified, is a national or international labor organization or a local labor organization recognized or acting as the representative of employees of an employer or employers engaged in an industry affecting commerce; or

(3) has chartered a local labor organization or subsidiary body which is representing or actively seeking to represent employees of employers within the meaning of paragraph (1) or (2); or

(4) has been chartered by a labor organization representing or actively seeking to represent employees within the meaning of paragraph (1) or (2) as the local or subordinate body through which such employees may enjoy membership or become affiliated with such labor organization; or

(5) is a conference, general committee, joint or system board, or joint council subordinate to a national or international labor organization, which includes a labor organization engaged in an industry affecting

commerce within the meaning of any of the preceding paragraphs of this subsection.

(f) The term "employee" means an individual employed by any employer except that the term "employee" shall not include any person elected to public office in any State or political subdivision of any State by the qualified voters thereof, or any person chosen by such officer to be on such officer's personal staff, or an appointee on the policymaking level or an immediate adviser with respect to the exercise of the constitutional or legal powers of the office. The exemption set forth in the preceding sentence shall not include employees subject to the civil service laws of a State government, governmental agency, or political subdivision. The term "employee" includes any individual who is a citizen of the United States employed by an employer in a workplace in a foreign country.

[The exclusion from the term "employee" of any person chosen by an elected official "to be on such official's personal staff, or an appointee on the policymaking level or an immediate advisor with respect to the exercise of the constitutional or legal powers of the office" remains in section 11(f). However, the Civil Rights Act of 1991 now provides special procedures for such persons who feel they are victims of age and other types of discrimination prohibited by EEOC enforced statutes. See section 321 of the Civil Rights Act of 1991.]

(g) The term "commerce" means trade, traffic, commerce, transportation, transmission, or communication among the several States; or between a State and any place outside thereof; or within the District of Columbia, or a possession of the United States; or between points in the same State but through a point outside thereof.

(h) The term "industry affecting commerce" means any activity, business, or industry in commerce or in which a labor dispute would hinder or obstruct commerce or the free flow of commerce and includes any activity or industry "affecting commerce" within the meaning of the Labor Management Reporting and Disclosure Act of 1959 *[29 U.S.C. 401 et seq.]*.

(i) The term "State" includes a State of the United States, the District of Columbia, Puerto Rico, the Virgin Islands, American Samoa, Guam, Wake Island, the Canal Zone, and Outer Continental Shelf lands defined in the Outer Continental Shelf Lands Act *[43 U.S.C. 1331 et seq.]*.

(j) The term "firefighter" means an employee, the duties of whose position are primarily to perform work directly connected with the control and extinguishment of fires or the maintenance and use of firefighting apparatus and equipment, including an employee engaged in this activity who is transferred to a supervisory or administrative position.

(k) The term "law enforcement officer" means an employee, the duties of whose position are primarily the investigation, apprehension, or detention of individuals suspected or convicted of offenses against the criminal laws of a State, including an employee engaged in this activity who is transferred to a supervisory or administrative position. For the purpose of this subsection, "detention" includes the duties of employees assigned to guard individuals incarcerated in any penal institution.

(l) The term "compensation, terms, conditions, or privileges of employment" encompasses all employee benefits, including such benefits provided pursuant to a bona fide employee benefit plan.

AGE LIMITATION
SEC. 631.

(a) The prohibitions in this chapter *[except the provisions of section 4(g)]* shall be limited to individuals who are at least 40 years of age.

(b) In the case of any personnel action affecting employees or applicants for employment which is subject to the provisions of section 633a of this title *[section 15]*, the prohibitions established in section 633a of this title *[section 15]* shall be limited to individuals who are at least 40 years of age.

(c) (1) Nothing in this chapter shall be construed to prohibit compulsory retirement of any employee who has attained 65 years of age and who, for the 2-year period immediately before retirement, is employed in a bona fide executive or a high policymaking position, if such employee is entitled to an immediate nonforfeitable annual retirement benefit from a pension, profit-sharing, savings, or deferred compensation plan, or any combination of such plans, of the employer of such employee, which equals, in the aggregate, at least $44,000.

(2) In applying the retirement benefit test of paragraph (1) of this subsection, if any such retirement benefit is in a form other than a straight life annuity (with no ancillary benefits), or if employees contribute to any such plan or make rollover contributions, such benefit shall be adjusted in accordance with regulations prescribed by the Equal Employment Opportunity Commission, after consultation with the Secretary of the Treasury, so that the benefit is the equivalent of a straight life annuity (with no ancillary benefits) under a plan to which employees do not contribute and under which no rollover contributions are made.

(d) Nothing in this chapter shall be construed to prohibit compulsory retirement of any employee who has attained 70 years of age, and who is serving under a contract of unlimited tenure (or similar arrangement providing for unlimited tenure) at an institution of higher education (as defined by section 1141(a) of title 20 *[section 1201(a) of the Higher Education Act of 1965]*).

ANNUAL REPORT
SEC. 632.

The Equal Employment Opportunity Commission shall submit annually in January a report to the Congress covering its activities for the preceding year and including such information, data and recommendations for further legislation in connection with the matters covered by this chapter as it may find advisable. Such report shall contain an evaluation and appraisal by the Commission of the effect of the minimum and maximum ages established by this chapter, together with its recommendations to the Congress. In making such evaluation and appraisal, the Commission shall take into consideration any changes which may have occurred in the general age level of the population, the effect of the chapter upon workers not covered by its provisions, and such other factors as it may deem pertinent.

FEDERAL-STATE RELATIONSHIP
SEC. 633.

(a) Nothing in this chapter shall affect the jurisdiction of any agency of any State performing like functions with regard to discriminatory employment practices on account of age except that upon commencement of action under this chapter such action shall supersede any State action.

(b) In the case of an alleged unlawful practice occurring in a State which has a law prohibiting discrimination in employment because of age and establishing or authorizing a State authority to grant or seek relief from such discriminatory practice, no suit may be brought under section 626 of this title *[section 7]* before the expiration of sixty days after proceedings have been commenced under the State law, unless such proceedings have been earlier terminated: Provided, That such sixty day period shall be extended to one hundred and twenty days during the first year after the effective date of such State law. If any requirement for the commencement of such proceedings is imposed by a State authority other than a requirement of the filing of a written and signed statement of the facts upon which the proceeding is based, the proceeding shall be deemed to have been commenced for the purposes of this subsection at the time such statement is sent by registered mail to the appropriate State authority.

NONDISCRIMINATION ON ACCOUNT OF AGE IN FEDERAL GOVERNMENT EMPLOYMENT
SEC. 633a.

(a) All personnel actions affecting employees or applicants for employment who are at least 40 years of age (except personnel actions with regard to aliens employed outside the limits of the United States) in military departments as defined in section 102 of title 5 *[United States Code]*, in executive agencies as defined in section 105 of title 5 *[United States Code]* (including employees and applicants for employment who are paid from nonappropriated funds), in the United States Postal Service and the Postal Rate Commission, in those units in the government of the District of Columbia having positions in the competitive service, and in those units of the legislative and judicial branches of the Federal Government having positions in the competitive service, and in the Library of Congress shall be made free from any discrimination based on age.

(b) Except as otherwise provided in this subsection, the Equal Employment Opportunity Commission is authorized to enforce the provisions of subsection (a) of this section through appropriate remedies, including reinstatement or hiring of employees with or without backpay, as will effectuate the policies of this section. The Equal Employment Opportunity Commission shall issue such rules, regulations, orders, and instructions as it deems necessary and appropriate to carry out its responsibilities under this section. The Equal Employment Opportunity Commission shall—

(1) be responsible for the review and evaluation of the operation of all agency programs designed to carry out the policy of this section, periodically obtaining and publishing (on at least a semiannual basis) progress reports from each department, agency, or unit referred to in subsection (a) of this section;

(2) consult with and solicit the recommendations of interested individuals, groups, and organizations relating to nondiscrimination in employment on account of age; and

(3) provide for the acceptance and processing of complaints of discrimination in Federal employment on account of age.

The head of each such department, agency, or unit shall comply with such rules, regulations, orders, and instructions of the Equal Employment Opportunity Commission which shall include a provision that an employee or applicant for employment shall be notified of any final action taken on any complaint of discrimination filed by him thereunder. Reasonable exemptions to the provisions of this section may be established by the Commission but only when the Commission has established a maximum age requirement on the basis of a determination that age is a bona fide occupational qualification necessary to the performance of the duties of the position. With respect to employment in the Library of Congress, authorities granted in this subsection to the Equal Employment Opportunity Commission shall be exercised by the Librarian of Congress.

(c) Any person aggrieved may bring a civil action in any Federal district court of competent jurisdiction for such legal or equitable relief as will effectuate the purposes of this chapter.

(d) When the individual has not filed a complaint concerning age discrimination with the Commission, no civil action may be commenced by any individual under this section until the individual has given the Commission not less than thirty days' notice of an intent to file such action. Such notice shall be filed within one hundred and eighty days after the alleged unlawful practice occurred. Upon receiving a notice of intent to sue, the Commission shall promptly notify all persons named therein as prospective defendants in the action and take any appropriate action to assure the elimination of any unlawful practice.

(e) Nothing contained in this section shall relieve any Government agency or official of the responsibility to assure nondiscrimination on account of age in employment as required under any provision of Federal law.

(f) Any personnel action of any department, agency, or other entity referred to in subsection (a) of this section shall not be subject to, or affected by, any provision of this chapter, other than the provisions of section 631(b) of this title *[section 12(b)]* and the provisions of this section.

(g) (1) The Equal Employment Opportunity Commission shall undertake a study relating to the effects of the amendments made to this section by the Age Discrimination in Employment Act Amendments of 1978, and the effects of section 631(b) of this title *[section 12(b)]*, as added by the Age Discrimination in Employment Act Amendments of 1978.

(2) The Equal Employment Opportunity Commission shall transmit a report to the President and to the Congress containing the findings of the Commission resulting from the study of the Commission under paragraph (1) of this subsection. Such report shall be transmitted no later than January 1, 1980.

EFFECTIVE DATE
[Section 16 of the ADEA (not reproduced in the U.S. Code)]
[This Act shall become effective one hundred and eighty days after enactment, except (a) that the Secretary of Labor may extend the delay in effective date of any provision of this Act up to an additional ninety days thereafter if he finds that such time is necessary in permitting adjustments to the provisions hereof, and (b) that on or after the date of enactment the Secretary of Labor [EEOC] is authorized to issue such rules and regulations as may be necessary to carry out its provisions.]

APPROPRIATIONS
SEC. 634.
There are hereby authorized to be appropriated such sums as may be necessary to carry out this chapter.

APPENDIX B

MODEL STATEMENT OF ERISA RIGHTS, 2004

In its HR Document Center, the federal government provides a statement that clearly summarizes the pension rights of workers and retirees under the Employment Retirement Income Security Act (ERISA). With specific information filled in, employers can use the statement to inform their own workers and retirees of these rights. This last document was updated on January 1, 2004 (URL: http://service.govdelivery.com/service/document.html?code=HRDOC_367).

Note: A summary plan description will be deemed to comply with the requirements to provide participants with a statement of their rights if it includes the following information. You should delete items of information which are not applicable to your particular plan.

YOUR RIGHTS

As a participant in (Name of Plan) you are entitled to certain rights and protections under the Employee Retirement Income Security Act of 1974 (ERISA). ERISA provides that all plan participants shall be entitled to the following.

You can examine, without charge, at the plan administrator's (Name) office and at other specified locations, such as worksites and union halls, all documents governing the plan, including insurance contracts and collective bargaining agreements, and a copy of the latest annual report (Form 5500 Series) filed by the plan with the U.S. Department of Labor and available at the Employee Benefits Security Administration.

You can obtain, upon written request to the plan administrator, copies of documents governing the operation of the plan, including insurance contracts and collective bargaining agreements, and copies of the latest annual report (Form 5500 Series) and updated summary plan description. The administrator may make a reasonable charge for the copies.

The plan administrator is required by law to furnish each participant with a copy of the summary of his/her annual financial report.

You may also obtain a statement telling you whether you have a right to receive a pension at normal retirement age and if so, what your benefits would be at normal retirement age if you stop working under the plan now. If you do not have a right to a pension, the statement will tell you how many more years you have to work to be eligible for a pension. This statement must be requested in writing and is not required to be given more than once every 12 months. The plan must provide the statement free of charge.

CONTINUE GROUP HEALTH PLAN COVERAGE

You can continue health care coverage for yourself, spouse, or dependents if there is a loss of coverage under the plan as a result of a qualifying event. You or your dependents may have to pay for such coverage. Review this summary plan description and the documents governing the plan on the rules governing your COBRA continuation coverage rights.

There is a reduction or elimination of exclusionary periods of coverage for preexisting conditions under your group health plan, if you have creditable coverage from another plan. You should be provided a certificate of creditable coverage, free of charge, from your group health plan or health insurance issuer when you lose coverage under the plan, when you become entitled to elect COBRA continuation coverage, when your COBRA continuation coverage ceases, if you request it before losing coverage, or if you request it up to 24 months after losing coverage. Without evidence of creditable coverage, you may be subject to a preexisting condition exclusion for 12 months (18 months for late enrollees) after your enrollment date in your coverage.

PRUDENT ACTIONS BY PLAN FIDUCIARIES

In addition to creating rights for plan participants, ERISA imposes duties upon the people who are responsible for the operation of the employee benefit plan. The people who operate your plan, called "fiduciaries" of the plan, have a duty to do so prudently and in the interest of you and other plan participants and beneficiaries. No one, including your employer, your union, or any other person, may fire you or otherwise discriminate against you in any way to prevent you from obtaining a (pension, welfare) benefit or exercising your rights under ERISA.

ENFORCE YOUR RIGHTS

If your claim for a (pension, welfare) benefit is denied or ignored, in whole or in part, you have a right to know why this was done, to obtain copies of documents relating to the decision without charge, and to appeal any denial, all within certain time schedules.

Under ERISA, there are steps you can take to enforce the above rights. For instance, if you request a copy of plan documents or the latest annual report from the plan and do not receive it within 30 days, you may file suit in a federal court. In such a case, the court may require the plan administrator to provide the materials and pay you up to $110 a day until you receive the materials, unless the materials were not sent because of reasons beyond the control of the administrator.

If you have a claim for benefits that is denied or ignored, in whole or in part, you may file suit in a state or federal court. In addition, if you disagree with the plan's decision or lack thereof concerning the qualified status of a domestic relations order or a medical child support order, you may file suit in federal court.

If it should happen that plan fiduciaries misuse the plan's money, or if you are discriminated against for asserting your rights, you may seek assistance from the U.S. Department of Labor, or you may file suit in a federal court. The court will decide who should pay court costs and legal fees. If you are successful, the court may order the person you have sued to pay these costs and fees. If you lose, the court may order you to pay these costs and fees if, for example, it finds your claim is frivolous.

ASSISTANCE WITH YOUR QUESTIONS

If you have any questions about your plan, you should contact (Name of Plan). If you have any questions about this statement or about your rights under ERISA, or if you need assistance in obtaining documents from the plan administrator, you should contact the nearest office of the Employee Benefits Security Administration, U.S. Department of Labor, listed in your telephone directory or 200 Constitution Avenue N.W., Washington, D.C. 20210. You may also obtain certain publications about your rights and responsibilities under ERISA by calling the publications hotline of the Employee Benefits Security Administration.

APPENDIX C

YOUR MEDICARE RIGHTS AND PROTECTIONS, 2006

Selections from this federal government booklet contain information for Medicare beneficiaries on their right to file a complaint, right to get health care, right to privacy, and where to get help with questions. It was last revised in April 2006 (http://www.medicare.gov/Publications/Pubs/pdf/10112.pdf).

SECTION 2. YOUR MEDICARE RIGHTS

If you have Medicare, you have certain guaranteed rights and protections. You have these rights whether you have the Original Medicare Plan (with or without a Medigap policy) or a Medicare Health Plan. You have the right to the following:

1. Be treated with dignity and respect at all times

2. Be protected from discrimination
Discrimination is against the law. Every company or agency that works with Medicare must obey the law. You can't be treated differently because of your

- race,
- color,
- national origin,
- disability,
- age,
- religion, or
- sex (under certain conditions).

Also, your rights to health information privacy are protected. If you think that you haven't been treated fairly for any of these reasons, call the Office for Civil Rights in your state. Call toll-free 1-800-368-1019. TTY users should call 1-800-537-7697. You can also visit www.hhs.gov/ocr on the web for more information.

3. Get information about Medicare that you can understand to help you make health care decisions
This information includes

- what is covered,
- what costs are paid,
- how much you have to pay, and
- what to do if you want to file a complaint.

You can have someone help you make decisions when you need it.

4. Have your questions about the Medicare Program answered
You can call 1-800-MEDICARE (1-800-633-4227) to get your questions answered or get the telephone number of your State Health Insurance Assistance Program. TTY users should call 1-877-486-2048. If you enrolled in a Medicare Health Plan, you can also call your plan.

5. Culturally competent services
You have the right to get health care services in a language you can understand and in a culturally sensitive way. For more information about getting health care services in languages other than English, call the Office for Civil Rights in your state or call toll-free 1-800-368-1019. TTY users should call 1-800-537-7697. You can also visit www.hhs.gov/ocr on the web for more information.

6. Get emergency care when and where you need it
A medical emergency is when you think your health is in serious danger—when every second counts. If you think your health is in danger because you have a bad injury, sudden illness, or an illness quickly getting much worse, you can get emergency care anywhere in the United States.

If you are enrolled in a Medicare Health Plan, your plan materials describe your emergency care costs. You don't need to get permission from your primary care doctor before you get emergency care. Your primary care doctor is the doctor you see first for health problems. If you are admitted to the hospital, you, a family member, or your primary care doctor should contact your Medicare Health Plan as soon as possible so the plan can manage your care. If you get emergency care, you will have to pay your regular share of the cost (copayment). Then, your plan will pay its share. If your plan doesn't pay its share for your emergency care, you have the right to appeal.

7. Learn about all of your treatment choices in clear language that you can understand

You have the right to fully participate in all your health care decisions. If you can't fully participate, you can ask family members, friends, or anyone you trust to help you make a decision about what treatment is right for you. Medicare Health Plans can't have rules that stop your doctor from telling you what you need to know about your treatment choices.

8. File a complaint

You can file a complaint about payment, services you received, other concerns or problems you have in getting health care, and the quality of the health care you received.

Your Medicare Quality of Care Concerns

You have a right to file a complaint if you think you aren't getting quality services or you have quality of care issues. This type of complaint is called a "grievance" if you are enrolled in a Medicare Health Plan or a Medicare drug plan. If you are enrolled in the Original Medicare Plan or a Medicare Health Plan and if you want to file a complaint about the quality of health care you have received, you can call your plan or call the Quality Improvement Organization in your state. To get this telephone number, call 1-800-MEDICARE (1-800-633-4227). TTY users should call 1-877-486-2048.

9. Your Medicare Appeal Rights

You have the right to appeal decisions relating to your claims for benefits. For more information on appeals, see Sections 3–5 in this booklet or call the State Health Insurance Assistance Program in your state. To get this telephone number call 1-800-MEDICARE (1-800-633-4227). TTY users should call 1-877-486-2048.

Important: If you need help with filing an appeal, you can have someone else help you. This process is called an "Appointment of Representative." You can name a family member, friend, advocate, attorney, doctor, or someone else to act on your behalf. Medicare has a form you and your representative can fill out to complete this process. This form is available at www.medicare.gov/basics/forms/default.asp on the web (CMS Form Number 1696). You can also appoint a representative with a letter signed and dated by you and the person helping you. The form or letter must be sent with your appeal request. If you have questions about appointing a representative, you can call 1-800-MEDICARE (1-800-633-4227). TTY users should call 1-877-486-2048.

10. Have your health information that Medicare collects about you kept private

Medicare may collect information about you as part of its regular business, such as paying your health care bills and making sure you get quality health care. Medicare keeps the information it collects about you private. When Medicare asks for your health information, they must tell you the following:

- Why it is needed
- Whether it is required or optional
- What happens if you don't give the information
- How it will be used

If you want to know more about how Medicare uses your personal information, call 1-800-MEDICARE (1-800-633-4227). TTY users should call 1-877-486-2048.

Your state may have additional privacy laws that protect your personal information. If you want to know about the laws in your state, call your State Health Insurance Assistance Program. To get this telephone number, call 1-800-MEDICARE (1-800-633-4227). TTY users should call 1-877-486-2048.

11. Know your health information privacy rights

You have privacy rights under a Federal law that protects your health information. Your health care provider or health plan must follow this law to protect your privacy rights. These rights are important for you to know. You can exercise these rights, ask questions about them, and file a complaint if you think your rights are being denied or your health information isn't being protected. If you are enrolled in the Original Medicare Plan, see the "Notice of Privacy Practices for the Original Medicare Plan" on pages 22–24. If you are enrolled in a Medicare Health Plan or a Medicare drug plan, your plan materials describe your privacy rights.

SECTION 3. YOUR RIGHTS AND PROTECTIONS IN THE ORIGINAL MEDICARE PLAN

In addition to the rights listed in Section 2, if you are in the Original Medicare Plan, you have the following rights and protections:

1. Access to doctors, specialists (including women's health specialists), and hospitals

You can see any doctor or specialist, or go to Medicare-certified hospitals that participate in Medicare.

2. Timely information on Medicare payment, and fair and efficient appeal processes

If you have the Original Medicare Plan, you can get certain information, notices and appeal rights that help you resolve issues when Medicare doesn't pay for health care including

- Advance Beneficiary Notices (ABNs)—You are given this notice by your doctor, health care provider, or supplier before you get an item or service that Medicare may not pay for (see below and pages 12–15).

- Important Message from Medicare—You are given this notice about your rights once you are admitted to a hospital.

- Fast Appeals—You are given a notice of non-coverage that will explain your appeal rights before you are discharged from care or before Medicare stops paying for certain types of care (see pages 16–17).

- Billing Information—You can ask for this information after you get an item or service (see page 18).

- General Appeal Rights—You have these rights if you disagree with the coverage or payment decision Medicare makes on your claim . . .

3. General Appeal Rights

After Medicare makes a decision on a claim, you have the right to a fair, efficient, and timely process for appealing health care payment decisions or initial determinations on items or services you received. Reasons you may appeal include the following:

- A service or item you received isn't covered, and you think it should be

- A service or item is denied, and you think it should be paid

The Medicare Summary Notice is mailed to you by the company that handles claims for Medicare. This notice indicates if your claim is approved or denied. If the claim is denied, the reason for the denial will be included on the notice. The notice will also include information about how to file an appeal. You can file an appeal if you disagree with Medicare's decision on payment or coverage for the items or services you received. If you appeal, ask your doctor, health care provider, or supplier for any information that might help your case. You should keep a copy of everything you send to Medicare as part of your appeal. . . .

4. Your rights to buy a Medigap policy

In some situations, you have the right to buy a Medigap policy outside of your Medigap open enrollment period. These rights are called "Medigap Protections." They are also called guaranteed issue rights because the law says that insurance companies must issue you a Medigap policy. There are a few situations involving health coverage changes where you may have a guaranteed issue right to buy a Medigap policy. In these situations, an insurance company

- must sell you a Medigap policy,
- must cover all your pre-existing conditions, and
- can't charge you more for a Medigap policy because of your health problems.

To learn about the situations where you have a guaranteed issue right to buy a Medigap policy because you lost certain kinds of health coverage, you can

- visit www.medicare.gov on the web and view the booklet "Choosing a Medigap Policy: A Guide to Health Insurance for People With Medicare" (CMS Pub. No. 02110).
- call 1-800-MEDICARE (1-800-633-4227). TTY users should call 1-877-486-2048.

For more detailed Medigap information

- visit www.medicare.gov on the web. Select "Search Tools" at the top of the page.
- call 1-800-MEDICARE (1-800-633-4227). TTY users should call 1-877-486-2048. A customer service representative will help you.
- call the State Health Insurance Assistance Program in your state. Ask if they have a Medigap rate comparison shopping guide for your state. To get this telephone number, call 1-800-MEDICARE (1-800-633-4227). TTY users should call 1-877-486-2048.

If you think any of your Medigap rights have been violated, call your State Health Insurance Assistance Program. . . .

SECTION 4. YOUR RIGHTS AND PROTECTIONS IN A MEDICARE HEALTH PLAN

In addition to the rights and protections listed in Section 2, if you are in a Medicare Health Plan, you have the following rights and protections. If you are in one of these plans and want to know more about your rights and protections, including rights and protections you may have in addition to those discussed in this booklet, read your plan's membership materials or call your plan.

Note about PACE (Programs of All-inclusive Care for the Elderly): To get a detailed list of your PACE rights and protections, visit www.cms.hhs.gov/pace/downloads/prtemp.pdf on the web. Or, you can call 1-800-MEDICARE (1-800-633-4227). TTY users should call 1-877-486-2048.

Note about Medicare Cost Plans: If you have a Medicare Cost Plan and you want to appeal services that were provided outside the plan's network (without the plan's involvement), you will need to follow the Original Medicare Plan appeal process as described in Section 3.

1. Choice of health care providers

You may have the right to choose health care providers within the plan so you can get the health care you need.

2. Access to health care providers

If you have a complex or serious medical condition, you have the right to get a treatment plan from your doctor. This treatment plan lets you directly see a specialist within the plan as many times as you and your doctor think you need. Women have the right to go directly to a women's health care specialist without a referral within the plan for routine and preventive health care services.

3. Know how your doctors are paid

You have the right to know how your health plan pays its doctors. When you ask your health plan how it pays its doctors, the health plan must tell you. Medicare doesn't allow a health plan to pay doctors in a way that wouldn't let you get the care you need.

4. A fair, efficient, and timely appeals process

You have the right to a fair, efficient, and timely process to resolve differences with your health plan. This process includes the initial decision made by the health plan, an internal review and an independent external review. You have the right to ask your plan to provide or pay for a service you think should be covered, provided, or continued. If you think your health could be seriously harmed by waiting for a decision about a service, ask the plan for a fast decision. The plan must answer you within 72 hours if

- it determines your life or health could be seriously harmed if the plan took the normal 14 days to respond, or
- a doctor supports your request and certifies you would be harmed.

If the plan denies what you asked for, the plan must tell you, in writing, why they won't pay for a service, and how to appeal this decision. After you file your appeal, the plan will review its decision.

You also have the right to ask your plan for a copy of the file that contains your medical and other information about your appeal. You may want to call or write your plan and ask for a copy of your file. The plan may charge you a fee for copying this information and sending it to you. Then, if the plan doesn't decide in your favor, your appeal is automatically sent to an independent organization that works for Medicare, not for the plan. This independent organization will review your appeal. You have a right to get a copy of the case file that the plan sends to the independent organization, if you ask for it.

Note: If you have drug coverage through a Medicare Health Plan, see Section 5 for the appeal timeframes.

5. Fast appeals in Skilled Nursing Facilities, Home Health Agencies, and Comprehensive Outpatient Rehabilitation Facilities

You also have the right to a fast appeals process. This option is available whenever you are getting services from a skilled nursing facility, home health agency, or comprehensive outpatient rehabilitation facility.

You will get a notice from your provider that will tell you how to ask for an appeal if you think your health plan is ending coverage of these services too soon. You will be able to get a quick review of this decision, with independent doctors looking at your case and deciding if your services need to continue.

See your plan's membership materials or call your plan for details about your appeal rights.

6. File a grievance about other concerns or problems

You have a right to file a grievance if you have concerns or problems with your Medicare Health Plan. For example, if you believe your plan's hours of operation should be different, or there aren't enough specialists in the plan to meet your needs, you can file a grievance. Check your plan's membership materials or call your plan to find out how to file a grievance.

7. Fast appeals in Hospitals

If you are admitted to a hospital that participates in Medicare, you should be given a copy of the "Important Message From Medicare" notice. It explains your rights as a hospital patient. If you aren't given a copy, ask for it. The "Important Message From Medicare" notice tells you

- that you have the right to get all of the hospital care you need, and any follow-up care that is covered by your Medicare Health Plan after you leave the hospital,
- what to do if you think the hospital is making you leave too soon,

- what your appeal rights are, and
- what you may have to pay.

When your health plan thinks you no longer need inpatient hospital care, they will give you another notice about your discharge and appeal rights **if** you think your hospital care should continue. You have to tell someone in the hospital (like a doctor or nurse) if you think your hospital care should continue. If you aren't given a notice, ask for it. This notice explains

- why you are being discharged,
- how to get a fast appeal,
- when to ask for a fast appeal, and
- what you may have to pay.

When you get this notice, if you still think the hospital is making you leave too soon, you can call or write the Quality Improvement Organization in your state to get a fast appeal. If you file timely, you will be able to stay in the hospital at no charge while the Quality Improvement Organization reviews your case. The hospital can't force you to leave before the Quality Improvement Organization makes a decision. To get this telephone number, call 1-800-MEDICARE (1-800-633-4227). TTY users should call 1-877-486-2048.

Important: Before you are discharged from the hospital, the hospital must give you a notice about your discharge and appeal rights if you tell someone in the hospital that you think your hospital care should continue. If the hospital doesn't provide you with a notice explaining your discharge and appeal rights, and you decide to stay in the hospital after your discharge date, you can't be charged for the costs of your care.

If you have questions about your rights as a hospital patient, call your Medicare Health Plan or the Quality Improvement Organization in your state. Their telephone number is on the notice of discharge and appeal rights the hospital gives you. Or, you can call 1-800-MEDICARE (1-800-633-4227). TTY users should call 1-877-486-2048.

8. Call your Medicare Health Plan

- before you get a service or supply to find out if it will be covered. Your plan must tell you if you ask.
- to get information about skilled nursing facility coverage.
- if you have questions about home health care rights and protections.

9. Privacy of Personal Health Information

You have the right to have the privacy of your health information protected. For more information about your rights to privacy, look in your plan materials or call your plan.

SECTION 5. YOUR RIGHTS AND APPEALS IN A MEDICARE DRUG PLAN

If your pharmacist tells you that your Medicare drug plan won't cover a drug you believe should be covered, or that you will have to pay more for the drug than you think is required, you have the right to request a coverage determination by your plan. You may also pay for the prescription and request that the plan pay you back by requesting a coverage determination.

You, your doctor, or your appointed representative can call your plan or write them a letter to request that the plan cover the prescription you need. Once your plan has received the request, it generally has 72 hours (for a standard request for coverage or to pay you back) or 24 hours (for an expedited request for coverage) to notify you of its decision.

Note: For some types of coverage determinations called exceptions, you will need a supporting statement from your doctor explaining why you need a particular drug. Check with your plan to find out if the supporting statement is required. Once your plan gets the statement, its decision-making time period begins.

Tip: Any person you appoint, such as a family member or your doctor, may help you request a coverage determination or an appeal. If you have questions about appointing a representative, you can call 1-800-MEDI-CARE (1-800-633-4227). TTY users should call 1-877-486-2048. You can also get a copy of the "Appointment of Representative" form at www.medi-care.gov/basics/forms/default.asp on the web (CMS Form Number 1696).

If the plan decides not to cover the drug, you can appeal the decision . . .

What can I do if I have a complaint about my Medicare drug plan?

If you have a complaint about your Medicare drug plan, you have the right to file a complaint (called a "grievance") with the plan. You should file your complaint within 60 days of the event that led to your complaint. Some examples of why you might file a complaint include the following:

- You believe your plan's customer service hours of operation should be different.
- You have to wait too long for your prescription.
- The company offering your plan is sending you materials not related to the drug plan that you didn't ask to get.

APPENDIX D

What You Need to Know When You Get Retirement or Survivors Benefits, 2007

The selections presented from an electronic booklet from the Social Security Administration list the rights (and responsibilities) of those eligible for Social Security. This text was posted in January 2007 (URL: http://www.ssa.gov/pubs/10077. html).

ABOUT YOUR BENEFITS

WHEN AND HOW YOUR BENEFITS ARE PAID

Social Security benefits are paid each month in the month following the month for which they are due; for example, you would receive your July benefit in August. Generally, the day of the month you receive your benefit payment depends on the birth date of the person on whose earnings record you receive benefits. For example, if you get benefits as a retired worker, your benefit will be determined by your birth date. If you receive benefits based on your spouse's work, your benefit payment date will be determined by your spouse's birth date.

Date of birth	Benefits paid each month on
1st–10th	Second Wednesday
11th–20th	Third Wednesday
21st–31st	Fourth Wednesday

If you receive both Social Security and SSI benefits, your Social Security payment will arrive on the third of the month and your SSI payment will arrive on the first of the month.

DIRECT DEPOSIT

If you did not sign up for direct deposit when you applied for benefits, we strongly urge you to do it now.

Direct deposit is a simple, safe, and secure way to receive your benefits. Contact your bank to help you sign up. Or you can sign up for direct deposit by contacting us.

If you do not have an account, you may want to consider an Electronic Transfer Account. This low-cost federally insured account lets you enjoy the safety, security, and convenience of automatic payments. You can contact us or visit the website at *www.eta-find.gov* to get information about this program, or to find a bank, savings and loan or credit union near you offering this account.

IF YOU GET YOUR CHECKS BY MAIL

To be safe, you should cash or deposit your check soon after you receive it. You should not sign your check until you are at the place where you will cash it. If you sign the check ahead of time and lose it, the person who finds it could cash it.

A government check must be cashed within 12 months after the date of the check or it will be void. After a year, if you are still entitled to the payment, we will replace the voided check.

IF YOUR CHECK IS LATE OR MISSING

If your check is not delivered on its due date, wait three workdays before reporting the missing check to us. The most common reason checks are late is because a change of address was not reported.

If your check is ever lost or stolen, contact us immediately. Your check can be replaced, but it takes time.

RETURNING BENEFITS NOT DUE

If you receive a check that you know is not due you, take it to any Social Security office or return it to the U.S. Treasury Department at the address on the check envelope. You should write VOID on the front of the check and enclose a note telling why you are sending the check back. If you knowingly accept payments that are not due you, you may face criminal charges.

Appendix D

PAYING TAXES ON YOUR BENEFITS

About one-third of all people receiving Social Security benefits have to pay taxes on their benefits. You will have to pay taxes on your benefits if you file a federal tax return as an "individual," and your total income is more than $25,000. If you file a joint return, you will have to pay taxes if you and your spouse have a total income that is more than $32,000. If you are married and file a separate return, you probably will pay taxes on your benefits.

To have federal taxes withheld, you can get a Form W-4V from the Internal Revenue Service by calling the toll-free telephone number, 1-800-829-3676, or by visiting our website. After completing and signing the form, return it to your local Social Security office by mail or in person.

For more information, call the Internal Revenue Service's toll-free number, 1-800-829-3676, to ask for Publication 554, *Tax Information for Older Americans*, and Publication 915, *Social Security Benefits and Equivalent Railroad Retirement Benefits*.

SERVICES WE OFFER

FREE SOCIAL SECURITY SERVICE

Some businesses advertise that they can provide name changes or Social Security cards for a fee. These services are provided free by Social Security, so do not pay for something that is free. Call us or visit our website first. Social Security is the best place to get information about Social Security.

INFORMATION UPDATES

Every so often, we will send you important information about your Social Security benefits, such as:

- **Cost-of-living adjustments**

  Each January, your benefits will increase automatically if the cost of living has increased. If you receive your benefits by direct deposit, we will notify you of your new amount in advance. If you receive your benefits by check, we will include a notice explaining the cost-of-living adjustment with your check.

- **Annual earnings limit**

  If you are younger than full retirement age, there is a limit to how much you can earn and still receive all your Social Security benefits. This amount increases each year. We will notify you of the new amount in advance. For more information, including the year 2007 limits, see "How earnings affect your benefits."

How We Will Contact You

We generally mail you a letter or notice when we want to contact you, but sometimes a Social Security representative may come to your home. Our representative will show you identification before talking about your benefits. If you ever doubt someone who says he or she is from Social Security, call the Social Security office to ask if someone was sent to see you. And remember, Social Security employees will never ask you for money to have something done.

WHAT YOU NEED TO REPORT TO US

Your Responsibilities

It is important to let us know as soon as possible whenever one of the changes listed below occurs.

NOTE: Failure to report a change may result in an overpayment. If you are overpaid, we will recover any payments not due you. Also, if you fail to report changes in a timely way or you intentionally make a false statement, your benefits may be stopped. For the first violation, your benefits will stop for six months; for the second violation, 12 months; and for the third, 24 months.

You can call, write or visit us to make a report. Have your claim number handy. If you receive benefits based on your work, your claim number is the same as your Social Security number. If you receive benefits on someone else's work record, your claim number will be shown on any letter we send you about your benefits.

Information you give to another government agency may be provided to Social Security by the other agency, but you also must report the change to us.

If Your Estimated Earnings Change

If you are working, we usually ask you to estimate your earnings for the year. If later you realize your earnings will be higher or lower than you estimated, let us know as soon as possible so we can adjust your benefits. See "Working and getting Social Security at the same time" for help in making accurate estimates.

Appendix D

If You Move

When you plan to move, tell us your new address and phone number as soon as you know them. Even if you receive your benefits by direct deposit, Social Security must have your correct address so we can send letters and other important information to you. Your benefits will be stopped if we are unable to contact you. You can change your address at *Online Claims & Services*. Or you can call 1-800-772-1213 and use our automated system.

If any family members who are getting benefits are moving with you, please tell us their names. Be sure you also file a change of address with your post office.

If You Change Direct Deposit Accounts

If you change financial institutions or open a new account, you can change your direct deposit online if you have a personal identification number and a password. Or, we can change your direct deposit information over the telephone after we verify your identity. Have your new and old bank account numbers handy when you call us. They will be printed on your personal checks or account statements. It takes about 30–60 days to change this information. Do not close your old account until after you make sure your Social Security benefits are being deposited into the new account.

If a Person Is Not Able to Manage Funds

Sometimes a person is unable to manage his or her own money. If this happens, someone should let us know. We can arrange to send benefits to a relative or other person who agrees to use the money for the well-being of the person getting benefits. We call this person a "representative payee." For more information, ask for *A Guide For Representative Payees* (Publication No. 05-10076).

NOTE: People who have "power of attorney" for someone do not automatically qualify to be a representative payee.

If You Get a Pension from Non-covered Work

If you start receiving a pension from a job for which you did not pay Social Security taxes—for example, from the federal Civil Service Retirement System or some state or local pension systems—your Social Security benefits may need to be recalculated, and they may be reduced. Also, tell us if the amount of your pension changes.

IF YOU GET MARRIED OR DIVORCED

If you get married or divorced, your Social Security benefits may be affected, depending on the kind of benefits you receive.

If your benefits are stopped because of marriage or remarriage, they may be started again if the marriage ends.

If you get:	Then:
Your own retirement benefits	Your benefits will continue
Spouse's benefits	Your benefits will continue if you get divorced and you are age 62 or older unless you were married less than 10 years.
Widow's or widower's benefits	Your benefits will continue if you remarry when you are age 60 or older.
Any other kind of benefits	Generally, your benefits will stop when you get married. Your benefits may be started again if the marriage ends.

IF YOU CHANGE YOUR NAME

If you change your name—by marriage, divorce, or court order—you need to tell us right away. If you do not give us this information, your benefits will be issued under your old name and, if you have direct deposit, payments may not reach your account. If you receive checks, you may not be able to cash them if your identification is different than the name on your check.

IF YOU GET BENEFITS BECAUSE YOU ARE CARING FOR A CHILD

If you receive benefits because you are caring for a child who is younger than age 16 or disabled, you should notify us right away if the child is no longer in your care or changes address. Give us the name and address of the person with whom the child is living.

A temporary separation may not affect your benefits if you continue to exercise parental control over the child, but your benefits will stop if you no longer have responsibility for the child. If the child returns to your care, we can start sending benefits to you again.

Your benefits will end when the youngest unmarried child in your care reaches age 16 unless the child is disabled. Your child's benefits can continue as explained in "Benefits for children."

Appendix D

IF SOMEONE ADOPTS A CHILD WHO IS RECEIVING BENEFITS

When a child who is receiving benefits is adopted, let us know the child's new name, the date of the adoption decree, and the adopting parent's name and address. The adoption will not cause benefits to end.

IF YOU BECOME A PARENT AFTER YOU BEGIN TO RECEIVE BENEFITS

If you become the parent of a child (including an adopted child) after you begin receiving benefits, let us know so we can decide whether the child is eligible for benefits.

IF YOU HAVE AN OUTSTANDING WARRANT FOR YOUR ARREST

You must tell us if you have an outstanding arrest warrant for:

- A crime that is a felony under the laws of the state in which you live; or
- A crime punishable by death or imprisonment for more than one year in states that do not classify crimes as felonies.

You cannot receive Social Security benefits for any months in which there is an outstanding arrest warrant for a crime that is a felony (or a crime that is punishable by death or imprisonment for more than one year).

IF YOU ARE CONVICTED OF A CRIMINAL OFFENSE

If you get Social Security benefits and are convicted of a crime, Social Security should be notified immediately. Benefits generally are not paid for the months a person is confined, but any family members who are eligible may continue to receive benefits.

IF YOU HAVE COMMITTED A CRIME AND ARE CONFINED TO AN INSTITUTION

Benefits usually are not paid to persons who commit a crime and are confined to an institution by court order and at public expense. This applies if the person has been found:

- Not guilty by reason of insanity or similar factors (such as mental disease, mental defect, or mental incompetence); or
- Incompetent to stand trial.

IF YOU VIOLATE A CONDITION OF PAROLE OR PROBATION

You must tell us if you are violating a condition of your probation or parole imposed under federal or state law. You cannot receive Social Security benefits for any month in which you violate a condition of your probation or parole.

IF YOU LEAVE THE UNITED STATES

If you are a U.S. citizen, you can travel to or live in most foreign countries without affecting your Social Security benefits. There are, however, a few countries where we cannot send Social Security payments. These countries are Cambodia, Cuba, North Korea, Vietnam, and areas that were in the former Soviet Union (other than Armenia, Estonia, Latvia, Lithuania, and Russia). However, exceptions can be made for certain eligible beneficiaries in countries other than Cuba and North Korea. For more information about these exceptions, please contact your local Social Security office.

Let us know if you plan to go outside the United States for a trip that lasts 30 days or more. Tell us the name of the country or countries you plan to visit and the date you expect to leave the United States. We will send you special reporting instructions and tell you how to arrange for your benefits while you are away. Be sure to notify us when you return to the United States.

If you are not a U.S. citizen and you return to live in the United States, you must provide evidence of your noncitizen status in order to continue receiving benefits. If you work outside the United States, different rules apply in determining whether you can get your benefits.

For more information, ask for *Your Payments While You Are Outside The United States* (Publication No. 05-10137).

IF YOUR CITIZEN STATUS CHANGES

If you are not a citizen, let us know if you become a U.S. citizen or your noncitizen status changes. If your immigration status expires, you must give us new evidence that shows you continue to be in the United States lawfully.

IF A BENEFICIARY DIES

Let us know if a person receiving Social Security benefits dies. Benefits are not payable for the month of death. That means if the person died any time in July, for example, the check received in August (which is payment for

July) must be returned. If direct deposit is used, also notify the financial institution of the death as soon as possible so it can return any payments received after death. Family members may be eligible for Social Security survivors benefits when a person getting benefits dies.

IF YOU ARE RECEIVING SOCIAL SECURITY AND RAILROAD RETIREMENT BENEFITS

If you are receiving both Social Security and Railroad Retirement benefits based on your spouse's work and your spouse dies, you must tell us immediately. You will no longer be eligible to receive both benefits. You will be notified which survivor benefit you will receive.

WORKING AND GETTING SOCIAL SECURITY AT THE SAME TIME

HOW EARNINGS AFFECT YOUR BENEFITS

You can continue to work and still get Social Security retirement benefits. Your earnings in (and after) the month you reach your full retirement age will not affect your Social Security benefits. However, your benefits will be reduced if your earnings exceed certain limits for the months before you reach your full retirement age. (The full retirement age is 65 and 10 months for people born in 1942 and will gradually increase to 67 for persons born in 1960 or later.)

- If you are younger than full retirement age, $1 in benefits will be deducted for each $2 in earnings you have above the annual limit ($12,960 in 2007).

- In the year you reach your full retirement age, your benefits will be reduced $1 for every $3 you earn over a different limit ($34,440 in 2007) until the month you reach full retirement age. Then you get your full Social Security benefit payments, no matter how much you earn.

If you are younger than full retirement age and some of your benefits are withheld because your earnings are more than $12,960, there is some good news. When you reach full retirement age, your benefits will be increased to take into account those months in which you received no benefit or reduced benefits.

Also, any wages you earn after signing up for Social Security may increase your overall average earnings, and your benefit probably will increase.

For more information, ask for *How Work Affects Your Benefits* (Publication No. 05-10069).

A SPECIAL MONTHLY RULE

Sometimes people who retire in mid-year already have earned more than the yearly earnings limit. That is why there is a special monthly rule that applies to earnings for one year, usually the first year of retirement. Under this rule, you can get full Social Security benefits for any whole month you earn under a certain limit, regardless of your yearly earnings.

In 2007, a person younger than full retirement age (age 65 and 10 months for people born in 1942) is considered retired if monthly earnings are $1,080 or less. For example, John Smith retires at age 62 on August 30, 2007. He will make $45,000 through August. He takes a part-time job beginning in September, earning $500 per month. Although his earnings for the year substantially exceed the 2007 limit ($12,960), he will receive a Social Security payment for September through December. This is because his earnings in those months are less than $1,080, the special "first year of retirement" monthly limit for people younger than full retirement age. If Mr. Smith earns more than $1,080 in any of those months (September through December), he will not receive a benefit for that month.

Beginning in 2008, only the yearly limits will apply to him because he will be beyond his first year of retirement and have already used the special monthly rule during that year.

If you are self-employed, the monthly limit is based on whether you perform substantial services in your business. In general, if you work more than 45 hours a month in self-employment, you will not be able to get benefits for that month.

For detailed information about whether your work is substantial, ask for *When You Retire From Your Own Business: What You Need To Know* (Publication No. 05-10038).

IF YOU WORKED FOR WAGES

Wages count toward the earnings limit when they are earned, not when they are paid. If you have income that you earned in one year, but the payment was deferred to a following year, these earnings will not be counted for the year you receive them. Some examples of deferred income include accumulated sick or vacation pay, bonuses, stock options and other deferred compensation. If you are paid wages in one year for work you did in previous years, you should contact us.

We have arrangements with the Internal Revenue Service to have employers report some types of deferred compensation directly on the Form W-2. These amounts are shown in a box labeled, "Nonqualified Plan." We will subtract the amount shown in the box from your total earnings to determine which earnings we count for that year.

Appendix D

IF YOU ARE SELF-EMPLOYED

If you are self-employed, income counts when you receive it—not when you earn it—except if it is paid in a year after you become entitled to Social Security and was earned before you became entitled to Social Security. For example, if you started getting Social Security in June 2006 and you receive some money in February 2007 for work you did before June 2006, it will not count against your 2007 earnings limit. However, if the money you receive in February 2007 was for work you did after June 2006, it will count against your 2007 earnings limit.

REPORTING YOUR EARNINGS

Because your earnings may affect your Social Security benefits, we need to know how much you earn during the year. Usually, we get that information from:

- The earnings your employer reports on your W-2; and
- Your self-employment earnings reported on your income tax return.
- You need to report your earnings to us after the end of the year only if:
  - You are eligible for the special monthly rule and you earned less than the monthly limit (if so, let us know so we can pay you benefits for that month);
  - Some or all of the earnings shown on your W-2 were not earned in the year reported;
  - Your wages were over the limit and you also had a net loss in self-employment;
  - Your W-2 shows employer-reported wages that you will include on a self-employment tax return (ministers, for example);
  - You filed a self-employment tax return, but you did not perform any services in your business or you file your tax return on a fiscal year basis;
  - You are a farmer and you get federal agricultural program payments or you have income from carryover crops; or
  - We withheld some benefits, but you had no earnings for the year or your earnings were less than you told us.

If we have to adjust the amount of your benefits, based on your report, we will tell you. It is important for you to review the information. About mid-year, we may send you a letter asking you to estimate your current and next year's earnings. Your estimates will help us avoid paying you too much or too little in benefits.

NOTE: If you also are receiving Supplemental Security Income (SSI) payments in addition to your Social Security benefits, you must report all of your earnings to Social Security.

YOUR EARNINGS ESTIMATE AND YOUR BENEFITS

We adjusted your benefits this year based on the earnings you told us you expected to receive this year.

If other family members get benefits based on your work, your earnings may affect the total family benefits. But, if you get benefits as a family member, your earnings affect only your benefits.

REVISING YOUR ESTIMATE

When you work, you should save your pay stubs. At any time during the year, if you see that your earnings will be different from what you estimated, you should call us to revise the estimate. This will help us keep the amount of your Social Security benefits correct.

OTHER IMPORTANT INFORMATION

RETIREMENT BENEFITS FOR WIDOWS OR WIDOWERS

You can switch to retirement benefits based on your own work if they are higher than those you receive as a result of your deceased spouse's work. These benefits may be higher as early as age 62 or possibly as late as age 70. The rules are complex and vary depending on your situation. If you have not talked with a Social Security representative about retirement benefits (or your circumstances have changed), contact your local Social Security office to discuss the options available to you. . . .

CAN YOU GET SSI?

If you have limited income and resources, SSI may be able to help. SSI is a federal program that we manage. It is financed from general revenues, not from Social Security taxes.

SSI pays monthly checks to people who are age 65 or older, or who are blind or disabled. If you get SSI, you may get other benefits, too, such as Medicaid, food stamps, and other social services.

We do not count some income and some resources when we decide whether you are eligible for SSI. Your house and your car, for example, usually are not counted as resources. Call us for more information or to apply for SSI.

A Message about Food Stamps

You can get a food stamp application and information at any Social Security office. Or call our toll-free number. Ask for *Food Stamps And Other Nutrition Programs* (Publication No. 05-10100) or *Food Stamp Facts* (Publication No. 05-10101).

If You Disagree with a Decision We Make

If you have any questions about your payment amount or about information we send you, contact us.

If you disagree with a decision we make, you have the right to ask that it be reconsidered. Your request must be in writing and filed with any Social Security office within 60 days of the date you receive the letter you are questioning.

If you still are not satisfied, there are further steps you can take. Ask for *Your Right To Question The Decision Made On Your Claim* (Publication No. 05-10058).

Your Right to Be Represented

You have the right to be represented by an attorney or other qualified person of your choice in any business with us. This does not mean you have to have an attorney or other representative, but we will be glad to work with one if you wish.

For more information about getting a representative, ask for *Your Right To Representation* (Publication No. 05-10075).

Protection of Your Personal Information

You should keep your Social Security card in a safe place with your other important papers. Do not carry it with you unless you need to show it to an employer or service provider.

Social Security keeps personal and confidential information—names, Social Security numbers, earnings records, ages and beneficiary addresses—for millions of people. Generally, we will discuss your information only with you. When you call or visit us, we will ask you several questions to help us verify your identity. If you want someone else to help with your Social Security business, we need your permission to discuss your information with that person.

We urge you to be careful with your Social Security number and to protect its confidentiality whenever possible.

We are committed to protecting the privacy of your records. When we are required by law to give information to other government agencies that administer health or welfare programs, such as Medicaid and food stamps, those agencies are not allowed to share that information with anyone else. . . .

APPENDIX E

NURSING HOME RESIDENTS' RIGHTS, 2007

This short document provided by Seniors-Site.com lists the rights of nursing home residents under federal law. This version of the document was downloaded in July 2007 (URL: http://seniors-site.com/nursingm/rights.html).

The federal government has passed laws that establish the rights of nursing home residents. Most states have also passed laws that provide additional protection. You can obtain a copy of the **"Nursing Home Residents' Rights,"** by contacting your area ombudsman. The phone number is located in your phone directory.

Each person admitted to a nursing home has the following rights among others:

- To be fully informed, as evidenced by the patient's **written acknowledgment** prior to or at the time of admission and during the stay, of these rights and all rules and regulations governing patient conduct and responsibilities.
- To be fully informed prior to or at the time of admission and during the stay of services available in the facility, and **of related charges** of these services including any charges not paid by Medicaid or not included in the basic rate per day.
- To be fully informed by a physician of his/her medical condition, unless the physician decides that informing the patient is contraindicated, and to be given the opportunity **to participate in planning his/her medical treatment and to refuse to participate in experimental research.**
- To **refuse treatment** to the extent permitted by law and to be informed of the medical consequences of such refusal.
- To be transferred or discharged **only** for medical reasons or for his/her welfare or that of other patients or for nonpayment for his/her stay

(except as prohibited by the Medicaid program); to be given reasonable advance notice to ensure orderly transfer or discharge.

- To be **encouraged and assisted** throughout his/her stay to exercise his/her rights as a patient and as a citizen, and to this end **to voice grievances and recommend changes** in policies and services to facility staff and/or outside representatives of his/her choice, free from restraint, interference, coercion, discrimination, or reprisal.

- **To manage his/her personal financial affairs** or to be given at least a quarterly accounting of financial transactions made on his/her behalf, should the facility accept his/her written delegation of this responsibility subject to specific record keeping requirements.

- **To be free from mental and physical abuse, and to be free from chemical and (except in emergencies) physical restraints,** except as authorized in writing by a physician for a specified and limited period of time, or when necessary to protect the patient from injury to himself or herself or to others. The use is authorized by a professional staff member identified in the written policies and procedures of the facility as having the authority to do so and promptly reported to the resident's physician by the staff member.

- To be assured **confidential treatment** of his/her personal and medical records, and to approve or refuse to release them to any individual outside the facility except in the case of his/her transfer to another facility or as required by law.

- To be **treated with consideration, respect, and full recognition of his/her dignity** and individuality, including privacy in treatment and care for his/her personal needs.

- **Not to be required** to perform services for the facility that are not included for therapeutic purposes in his/her plan of care.

- **To associate and communicate privately** with persons of his/her choice and to send and receive his/her personal mail unopened unless medically contraindicated.

- To **meet with and participate** in the activities of social, religious, and community groups at his/her discretion unless medically contraindicated.

- To **retain and use his/her personal clothing and possessions** as space permits unless to do so would infringe upon the rights of other patients and unless medically contraindicated.

- If married, **to be assured of privacy** for visits by his/her spouse, and, if both are patients in the facility, to be permitted to share a room unless medically contraindicated.

- To have daily visiting hours established.
- To have the **right to visitation by an ombudsman and the individual's physician at any time,** and (with consent of the resident) family, individuals that provide health, social, legal, or other services and others who may wish to visit.

INDEX

Locators in **boldface** indicate main topics. Locators followed by *c* indicate chronology
entries. Locators followed by *b* indicate biographical entries.
Locators followed by *g* indicate glossary entries.

A

AAR. *See* Alliance for
Aging Research
AARP 207
eligibility age for
membership 4
and future of elderly
rights 64
and gray lobby 16
and Medicare claims
appeals 47
Bill Novelli and 125
and Nursing Home
Reform Act 58, 82
AARP Public Policy
Institute 33
abandonment 57
abuse by inaction 101
abuse of elders. *See* elder
abuse
abuse of pension funds
39–40
accrued benefit 98–99
Achenbaum, Andrew 120*b*
addiction 54
ADEA. *See* Age
Discrimination in
Employment Act of 1967
Administration on Aging
(AOA) 76, 108*c*, 121, 203
administrator 34, 74–75,
80, 108*c*, 127
adult children 11

Adult Protective Services
62, 88, 115*c*, 116*c*
advance directive 55–56,
83, 112*c*
affirmative action 32,
128*g*
AFT (American
Federation of Teachers)
211
age-based programs 81,
115*c*–116*c*
age-based rationing 52–54
age discrimination
and ADEA 31, 79–80
American Ballet
Company suit 118*c*
bibliography 160–168
British regulations
117*c*
Capital One Financial
case 114*c*
civil service reform
107*c*
Cooper v. IBM 98–99
defined 128*g*
early legal history
20–21
EEOC enforcement
of ADEA regulations
122
elimination of private
health benefits for
retirees 119*c*

establishing proof of
26–30
Raymond Gregory's
writings 123
*Hazen Paper Company
v. Biggins* 91–93
in hiring/firing **19–26**
and IBM cash-balance
plan 38, 113*c*
impact of laws/lawsuits
29–30
Lyndon B. Johnson's
speech 109*c*
*Kimel v. Florida Board of
Regents* 93–95
*Massachusetts Board of
Retirement v. Murgia*
88–91, 110*c*
New York State
legislature report
107*c*
Older Workers Benefit
Protection Act 83,
112*c*
online research
resources 140
Richard Posner's views
of laws opposing 125
print research resources
143
reasons to allow 30–32
recommendations for
change in laws 32–33

Index

Dan Seligman on
counterproductive-
ness of laws against
126
Smith v. City of Jackson
95–97, 116*c*
state laws 86, 87, 108*c*
Age Discrimination Act
(1975) 22, **81,** 110*c*
Age Discrimination in
Employment Act of 1967
(ADEA) **21–24, 79–80,**
109*c*, **217–235**
amendments (1978)
110*c*
amendments (1986)
111*c*
criticism of 30
EEOC enforcement
of regulations 26,
27, 122
end of mandatory
retirement
restrictions 112*c*
and *Hazen Paper
Company v. Biggins*
91–93
Jacob Javits's
cosponsorship of 123
Lyndon Johnson's
support for 123
and *Kimel v. Florida
Board of Regents* 93,
94
and *Massachusetts
Board of Retirement v.
Murgia* 90
need for stronger
enforcement of 32
and Older Workers
Benefit Protection
Act 24, 82–83, 112*c*
Claude Pepper's work
on amendments 125
and *Smith v. City of
Jackson* 95–97
and state laws 87

*Age Discrimination in the
American Workplace*
(Gregory) 123, 143
ageism **16–19**
Robert N. Butler's
coining of term 109*c*,
121
defined 16–17, 128*g*
and discrimination in
medical screenings
114*c*
and elder abuse 60
and Gray Panther
movement 124
and older workers
25–26
Erdman Palmore's
writings on 125
and rationing 53, 54
age of retirement. *See*
retirement age
Age Wave 122
aging 4–5, 8–9
Aging and Old Age (Posner)
125
agricultural (preindustrial)
societies. *See*
preindustrial societies
AGS (American Geriatrics
Society) 211
airline pilots. *See* pilots
airlines 23, 38, 124
AJAS (Association of Jewish
Aging Services) 209
Alabama 22, 88, 93
alcohol dependency 54
Alliance for Aging
Research (AAR) 54, 55,
210–211
Alliance for Retired
Americans 207–208
Alzheimer's Association
118*c*
Alzheimer's disease 12, 60,
117*c*, 118*c*, 120, 128*g*
AMA. *See* American
Medical Association

American Airlines 23
American Association of
Homes and Services
for the Aging (AAHSA)
211
American Association of
Retired Persons (AARP)
21, 108*c*. *See also* AARP
American Ballet Theatre
Company 118*c*
American Federation of
Teachers (AFT) 211
American Geriatrics
Society (AGS) 211
American Health Care
Association 61, 113*c*
American Medical
Association (AMA) 50,
77, 107*c*, 116*c*, 126
American Psychological
Association (APA) 57,
141
American Revolution 7,
13, 71
American Society on
Aging (ASA) 211
Andrus, Ethel Percy 108*c*
annuity 37, 128*g*
antibiotics 8
AOA. *See* Administration
on Aging
APA. *See* American
Psychological
Association
appeals 47
Aristotle 17, 120*b*
Arkansas 43, 87
artificial life support 55
ASA (American Society on
Aging) 211
assets, Medicaid eligibility
and 48, 79, 87, 111*c*
assisted living 12, 56,
128*g*
Association of Jewish
Aging Services (AJAS)
209

Astor, Brooke 60, 117c, 118c, 120b
Astrue, Michael J. 120b
AT&T 38
awards, in age discrimination cases 27

B

baby boomer 3–4, 14–15, 122, 128g–129g
balance, in research resources 137–138
bankruptcies 34, 36
beauty, worship of 17–18
Belt, Bradley 37, 121b
benefit accrual 98–99
benefit levels
    and ERISA 35
    and long-term solvency of Social Security 44
    and Older Workers Benefit Protection Act 82–83
    and Senior Citizens Freedom to Work Act 84
    and Social Security Act 73, 74
Bernanke, Ben S. 118c
Bethlehem Steel 36, 113c
Better Business Bureau 63
Beverly Enterprises 113c
bias
    in hiring 22–23
    in research materials on elderly 136
    and workplace discrimination 19
bibliography 146–202
    elder care/elder abuse issues 194–202
    general aging/ageism topics 146–160
    medical care, Medicare, and Medicaid 181–194

pensions, income, and Social Security 168–181
work and age discrimination 160–168
Biggins, Walter F. 91, 92
birth rates. *See* fertility rates
Blank, Robert 53
Bond, Christopher 57, 59, 121b
bookstore catalogs 141–142
Briarcliff Manor, New York 60, 118c, 120
budget, federal. *See* graying of the federal budget
Buffett, Warren 4
burden of proof 97
Bureau of Labor Statistics 24
Bush, George H. W. 112c
Bush, George W. and administration 121b
    Herb Kohl's criticism of elderly program cuts 124
    Medicare cut proposal 49, 118c
    Medicare Prescription Drug Improvement and Modernization Act 114c–115c
    Pension Protection Act 38, 117c
    retirement age for commercial pilots 21, 119c
    Social Security reform 44
    State of the Union Address (2004) 115c
Butler, Robert N. 16–18, 109c, 121b

C

California 60, 88
Callahan, Daniel 53, 111c, 121b
Canada 45
cancer 54
Capital One Financial 26, 114c
Carbonell, Josefina G. 121b
care. *See* elder care
caregiver 62, 113c
caregiver neglect
    and elder abuse laws 58
    as form of elder abuse 57
    Heitzman, People v. 100–102
    in nursing homes 61
    Senior Care and Protection Act 114c
    Sienarecki v. Florida 102–103
cash-balance conversion
    Cooper v. IBM 98, 99
    defined 129g
    effect on older workers 38
    at IBM 98, 99, 113c, 118c
    Pension Protection Act 39, 86
    Jane Bryant Quinn on 125
    and shift to defined-contribution pension 37
    at Xerox Corporation 114c
Catastrophic Health Care Act (1988) 50, 51, 79, 111c, 112c
Cazzola, Olga 24
CBS News 60–61
Census Bureau, U.S. 8
Centers for Disease Control (CDC) 54, 114c

Centers for Medicare
and Medicaid Services
(CMS) 46–47, 85, 127,
203–204
certified nurse assistants
61
Chamber of Commerce,
U.S. 49
changes, in elderly
population **4–18**
aging and longevity
8–9
aging in 20th/21st
centuries 7–12
family and care 11–12
government policies
12–16
graying of the
federal budget
14–16
Medicare 14
Social Security
13–14
negative images/
treatment of elderly
16–19
preindustrial societies
5–7
retirement 9–11
chemical restraints 61, 82
children 11, 12, 41, 48
Choices for Independence
76–77, 117*c*
chronic disease 9
church elders 6
civil rights, age
discrimination and 32
Civil Rights Act (1964)
95, 96
Civil Rights Center (CRC)
204
Civil War 13, 71–72, 105*c*
Clinton, William J. 84,
112*c*, 113*c*, 121*b*–122*b*
CMS. *See* Centers for
Medicare and Medicaid
Services

coinsurance 46
COLA. *See* cost-of-living
allowance
college faculty 21, 112*c*
colonial America 5–7, 123
Colorado 20, 87, 124
commercial pilots. *See*
pilots
Committee on the Cost of
Medical Care 77, 106*c*
competition, economic
31, 51
compulsory retirement. *See*
mandatory retirement
computerization 28
computer programmers
25–26
Confederacy 72
Congress, U.S.
ADEA 79
Age Discrimination Act
110*c*
airline pilot retirement
age 119*c*
Catastrophic Health
Care Act 112*c*
Elder Justice Act 62,
116*c*, 122–124
Rahm Emanuel and
122
ERISA 35
Orrin Hatch and 123
*Kimel v. Florida Board of
Regents* 94
Peter King and 124
Medicaid eligibility 48
Medicare reform 49,
51, 110*c*
naval officer retirement
age 105*c*
Older Americans Act
2004 amendments
117*c*
Pension Protection
Act 38
Retirement Protection
Act 84

and Roosevelt's
universal health
coverage proposal
106*c*
Senate Special
Committee on Aging
114*c*
Smith v. City of Jackson
96
Social Security Act
amendments 109*c*
Social Security COLA
adjustment 107*c*
Social Security reform/
privatization 115*c*
and Truman's national
health insurance
proposal 77
veterans' pension
legislation 106*c*
Constitution of the
United States of
America 22. *See also*
specific amendments, e.g.:
Fourteenth Amendment
consumer fraud 62–63
Consumer Price Index 42,
74, 109*c*
Coolidge, Calvin 77,
106*c*
Cooper, Kathi v. IBM
98–99
copayment 14, 50, 78, 85,
129*g*
Cornell Law School
research web page 144
corporations 9, 20
cosmetic surgery 17
cost control
and future of elderly
rights 65
*Marks v. Loral
Corporation* 30
Medicare **49–52**, 110*c*
and use of age as
criterion for hiring/
firing 31

cost-of-living allowance
(COLA) 42, 74, 107*c*,
125, 129*g*
cost sharing 78, 84
counseling, on health
issues 54
court cases **88–103**
  and ADEA violations
  27
  Cooper v. IBM **98–99**
  Federal Appeals Court
  decisions **98–99**
  *Griggs v. Duke Power
  Company* 95, 96
  *Hazen Paper Company v.
  Biggins* 35, **91–93**
  Heitzman, People v.
  100–102
  *Kimel v. Florida Board of
  Regents* 22, 79, **93–95**
  *Marks v. Loral
  Corporation* 30
  *Massachusetts Board of
  Retirement v. Murgia*
  22, **88–91**, 110*c*
  *Oubre v. Entersy
  Operations* 82
  Sienarecki v. Florida
  102–103
  Smith v. City of Jackson
  29–30, 93, **95–97**,
  116*c*
  state court decisions
  100–103
  Supreme Court
  decisions **88–97**
  *United States v. Florida
  Board of Regents*
  93–95
Court of Appeals, U.S.
125
CRC (Civil Rights Center)
204
culpable negligence 103
custodial care 56
custodial nursing home 56
Cutrone, Larry 38

D
deductible 46, 50, 78, 85,
129*g*
deficit spending 127
defined-benefit pension
33–34
  Cooper v. IBM 98, 99
  defined 129*g*
  defined-contribution
  pension v. 37–38
  and ERISA 80
  and Pension Protection
  Act 39
  Jane Bryant Quinn on
  125–126
  shift to defined-
  contribution pension
  37, 39
defined-contribution
pension **34–35**
  corporations' prefer-
  ence for 37–38
  defined 129*g*
  and Pension Protection
  Act 38–39, 86
  Jane Bryant Quinn on
  125
  and Social Security
  reform 44
Delaware 88
dementia 129*g*
Democratic Party 44, 64,
77
demographics 63–64
Dependent Pension Act
(1890) 72, 105*c*–106*c*
dependents 74
desertion 57
direct caregiver 101
disability
  Medicare 78
  Social Security 43
  veterans' benefits
  71–72, 105*c*
discounts 18, 85
discrimination. *See also* age
  discrimination; ageism
  and ADEA 79–80

and beliefs about older
  workers **25–26**
  defined 129*g*
  as informal rationing
  54
  and Medicare/Medicaid
  rights 46
  online research
  resources 140
  and Retirement Equity
  Act 81
  against women 18
discrimination by disparate
  impact. *See* disparate
  impact
disparate impact **29–30**
  and ADEA 79–80
  defined 129*g*
  *Hazen Paper Company
  v. Biggins* 92
  Smith v. City of Jackson
  29–30, 95–97, 116*c*
disparate treatment 92,
95, 129*g*
District Court of
  Massachusetts 91
District of Columbia 87,
88
divorce
  and benefit distribution
  to surviving spouse 40
  and changes in elder
  care 11
  and Retirement Equity
  Act 81, 111*c*
  and Social Security
  benefits 42
  and workplace
  discrimination 26
DOL. *See* Labor, U.S.
  Department of
do not resuscitate order
56
downsizing 24
drug dependency 54
Duke University 125
Dychtwald, Ken 122*b*

Index

E

early retirement
  as age discrimination 24
  defined 129*g*
  and future of elderly rights 64
  and Senior Citizens Freedom to Work Act 84
  and Social Security 42, 44, 74, 108*c*
earnings cap 44
earnings test 42, 84, 113*c*. *See also* means-test
Earp, Naomi C. 122*b*
EBRI (Employee Benefits Research Institute) 211
EBSA (Employee Benefit Security Administration) 204
education 22, 76
EEOC. *See* Equal Employment Opportunity Commission, U.S.
Eisenhower, Dwight D. 75, 122*b*
elder abuse **57–61**. *See also* caregiver neglect
  Brooke Astor case 60, 117*c*, 118*c*, 120
  Beverly Enterprises case 113*c*
  bibliography 194–202
  Christopher Bond's work in Senate 121
  defined 57–59, 129*g*
  and elder care 56
  Elder Justice Act 116*c*
  extent of 59–61
  and family's role in elder care 12
  Heitzman, People v. 100–102
  House Committee on Aging

recommendations 110*c*
  during Hurricane Katrina aftermath 116*c*, 117*c*
  National Clearinghouse on Abuse in Later Life shelter program 116*c*
  Nursing Home Reform Act 81–82
  Older Americans Act amendments 112*c*
  online research resources 141
  Orange County Elder Abuse Forensic Center 117*c*
  prevention 61–63
  research resources 144
  Senate Special Committee on Aging 114*c*
  Senior Care and Protection Act 114*c*
  Sienarecki v. Florida 102–103
  Social Security Protection Act 86
  state laws 86, 88
Elder Abuse Forensic Center (Orange County, California) 117*c*
elder care **56–63**
  and aging population 9
  bibliography 194–202
  and elder abuse **57–63**
  family and **11–12**
  online research resources 141
Elder Justice Act (2005-2007 proposals) 62, 114*c*, 116*c*, 121–124
elderly
  difficulty of defining 4
  as group 5
  as proportion of population 8–9

elders (church) 6
election of 1948 77
election of 1964 77
Eleventh Amendment 93, 94
eligibility requirements
  early veterans' benefits 72
  Medicaid 45, 47–48, 79
  Medicare 45, 52
Emanuel, Rahm 122*b*
emergency shelters, for abused elders 110*c*, 116*c*
emotional abuse 57
Employee Benefit Research Institution 40
Employee Benefit Security Administration (EBSA) 204
Employee Benefits Research Institute (EBRI) 211
Employee Retirement Income Security Act of 1974 (ERISA) **35–37**, **80–81**
  Bradley Belt's view of 121
  Cooper v. IBM 98, 99
  Hazen Paper Company v. Biggins 91, 93
  Model Statement of Rights **236–238**
  online research resources 144
  passage of 35, 109*c*
  provisions for pension fund abuse suits 40
  Retirement Equity Act 81, 111*c*
employee stock ownership 36, 113*c*
employer matching 35
employer-sponsored pension plans 40

employment rights. *See*
  age discrimination
Enron Corporation 36,
  113*c*
entitlements 65, 127
Equal Employment
  Opportunity
  Commission, U.S.
  (EEOC) 205
  and ADEA compliance
    32
  age discrimination
    cases 23, 26–27
  American Ballet
    Theatre Company
    suit 118*c*
  Naomi C. Earp's
    leadership of 122
  and *Massachusetts
    Board of Retirement v.
    Murgia* 90
  Medicare regulations
    for employers 119*c*
  Sidley Austin Brown
    & Wood case 115*c*–
    116*c*
equal protection clause
  90
equal treatment, right to
  54–55
ERISA. *See* Employee
  Retirement Income
  Security Act of 1974
Europe 10, 13, 45, 77
euthanasia 129*g*
evaluation, of research
  resources 137
"exaltation," of old age 6,
  122
executives 23, 79
extraordinary measures
  55, 111*c*, 121

F

factory work 9, 20
False Claims Act 59

family
  and elder abuse 59,
    61–62
  and elder care **11–12**
federal budget. *See* graying
  of the federal budget
federal legislation **71–86**.
  See also specific laws, e.g.:
  Social Security Act
Federal Reserve 118*c*, 123
fee-for-service plan 45,
  47, 50, 129*g*
Ferguson, Karen 122*b*
fertility rates 8, 11
fiduciaries 34, 80, 130*g*
financial exploitation 57,
  86
FindLaw web page 144
Fischer, David Hackett
  5–7, 122*b*
flight attendants 23
Florida 103, 125
Florida Board of Regents
  93, 94
food stamps 43
forced retirement. *See*
  mandatory retirement
Ford, Gerald 109*c*
Ford Motor Company
  36–37, 113*c*–114*c*
formulary 85
Fortune magazine 126
401(k)
  benefit distribution to
    surviving spouse 40
  Cooper v. IBM 99
  defined 128*g*
  defined-contribution
    pension 35
  Enron Corporation
    bankruptcy 36, 113*c*
  Pension Protection Act
    38–39, 86
Fourteenth Amendment
  89, 90, 94
Franklin, Benjamin 7,
  123*b*

fraud
  and elder abuse 58,
    62–63
  and Nursing Home
    Reform Act 59
  and Social Security
    Protection Act 86
  and Welfare and
    Pension Plans
    Disclosure Act 75
French Revolution 7
Fuller, Ida 73–74, 107*c*
funding
  and Catastrophic
    Health Care Act
    repeal 112*c*
  of defined-benefit
    pension 34
  and future of elderly
    rights 65
  of Medicare/Medicaid
    49–54, 126
  of PBGC 124
  and Pension Protection
    Act 86, 117*c*
  of private pensions
    37–41
  of Social Security **43–
    44**, 73, 118*c*, 126
  and state laws 87
future issues **63–65**

G

Gallo, Carol 28
the Gap 28–29
gender inequality 81, 111*c*
General Accounting
  Office (Government
  Accountability Office;
  GAO) 60, 127
General Motors 37
Generations United (GU)
  209
Georgia 43, 87, 88
geriatricians 54–55
Germany 13, 105*c*

Index

Gerontological Society of America (GSA) 211–212
gerontology 5, 120, 121, 125, 130*g*
Global Action on Aging 206
Government Accountability Office. *See* General Accounting Office
graduate schools 22
grants 76
graying of the federal budget **14–16,** 130*g*
gray lobby 15–16, 125
Gray Panthers 16, 124, 208
Great Britain 6, 117*c*
Great Depression 13, 72–73
Greenspan, Alan 123*b*
Gregory, Raymond 25, 32, 123*b*
grievances 47
Griggs v. Duke Power Company 95, 96
Growing Old in America (Fischer) 5–7, 122, 142
GSA (Gerontological Society of America) 211–212
GU (Generations United) 209
guaranteed minimum income 44

H
Harper, Sarah 10
Harrington, Michael 10, 108*c*, 123*b*
Hastings Center 121
Hatch, Orrin 116*c*, 123*b*
Hazen, Robert and Thomas 91
Hazen Paper Company v. Walter F. Biggins 35, **91–93**

Health, Education, and Welfare, U.S. Department of (HEW) 76
Health and Human Services, U.S. Department of (HHS) 62, 115*c*, 116*c*, 121, 205
Health Care Financing Administration (HCFA) 204
health insurance, national 77
health insurance, private 83, 115*c*
Health Insurance for the Aged and Disabled 77. *See also* Medicare
Health Maintenance Organization (HMO) 45, 50, 85, 130*g*
heart disease 54
Heitzman, Jerry 100
Heitzman, Robert, Jr. 100
Heitzman, Robert, Sr. 100
Heitzman, Susan Valerie, People v. **100–102**
HelpAge International 206
Henry J. Kaiser Foundation 115*c*
Hertz, Ann 28–29
HEW (Health, Education, and Welfare, U.S. Department of) 76
HHS. *See* Health and Human Services, U.S. Department of
high-income elderly Catastrophic Health Care Act 111*c*
future of elderly rights 64
Medicare Part B premium 118*c*, 119*c*
Medicare reform 50
Social Security 43, 123

high-income workers 44
high-tech industry 25–26
hiring/firing 31. *See also* age discrimination
HMO. *See* Health Maintenance Organization
home health care 51
Hospital Insurance (Medicare) 109*c*. *See also* Medicare Part A
hotlines 62
House Committee on Aging 110*c*
House of Representatives, U.S. 124, 125
Housing and Urban Development, U.S. Department of (HUD) 205
Hurricane Katrina 116*c*, 117*c*
hybrid pension 37, 39, 86

I
IAGG (International Association of Gerontology and Geriatrics) 206
IAHSA (International Association of Homes and Services for the Ageing) 206
IBM 37, 38, 98–99, 113*c*, 118*c*
IFA (International Federation on Ageing) 206–207
ILC (International Longevity Center) 207
immunity, state. *See* state immunity from federal lawsuits
Improving the Quality of Care in Nursing Homes (Institute of Medicine report) 81–82, 111*c*

income. *See also* pension
bibliography 168–181
and future of elderly
rights 64
and Medicaid eligibility
48
online research
resources 140
print research resources
143
income redistribution 41
independent living 8, 12,
117*c*
Indiana 88
indirect evidence 28–29.
See also disparate impact
Individual Retirement
Account (IRA) 35, 40,
44, 86, 130*g*
industrialization 9, 11,
17, 20
infant mortality 6
inflation 42, 74. *See also*
cost-of-living allowance
informal discrimination
92
informed consent 55
Institute of Medicine
81–82, 111*c*
insurance, Social Security
as 41, 73–74
insurance companies 52
intelligence, aging and
30–31
intentional discrimination
79, 116*c*
Internal Revenue Code 86
International Association
of Gerontology and
Geriatrics (IAGG) 206
International Association
of Homes and Services
for the Ageing (IAHSA)
206
International Federation
on Ageing (IFA) 206–
207

International Longevity
Center (ILC) 207
Internet, elder abuse via
63
involuntary manslaughter
100
involuntary retirement
83. *See also* mandatory
retirement
Iowa 88
IRA. *See* Individual
Retirement Account
isolation 59–60, 120

J

Jackson, Mississippi 95–97
Javits, Jacob K. 123*b*
job experience 22–23
Johnson, Lyndon B. 123*b*
and ADEA 109*c*
on age discrimination
21, 109*c*
and John F. Kennedy
124
and Medicare Act 77,
109*c*
and Older Americans
Act 75, 108*c*
and Harry S. Truman
126
Jury Verdict Research 27
justice, rationing and 53
Justice, U.S. Department
of 63

K

Kaiser/Commonwealth
Fund 49
Kaiser Family Foundation
47, 48
Kansas 87
Kennedy, Anthony 97
Kennedy, John F. 77,
123*b*–124*b*
Kimel, J. Daniel 93, 94

*Kimel, J. Daniel, Jr. v.
Florida Board of Regents*
22, 79, **93–95**
King, Peter 124*b*
K-Mart 28
Kohl, Herb 124*b*
Kuhn, Maggie 16, 124*b*

L

labor. *See* workplace
issues/rights
Labor, U.S. Department
of (DOL) 39–40, 75,
108*c*, 205
labor force, elderly in
(2004) 11
labor shortages 61
labor unions 77
Lamm, Richard 53, 110*c*–
111*c*, 124*b*
law firms, mandatory
retirement at 115*c*–117*c*
lawsuits 27, 28, 31, 38,
125. *See also* court cases
legal issues **71–103**
basis for elderly rights
3
court cases **88–103**
Federal Appeals
Court decisions
98–99
state court decisions
100–103
Supreme Court
decisions 88–97
laws and regulations
71–88
federal legislation
71–86
state laws/
regulations
86–88
research resources
144–145
and right to refuse
treatment 56

Index

Senior Care and
Protection Act 57–58
state elder abuse laws
57–58
legislation **71–86**. *See also*
specific laws, e.g. Social
Security Act
leisure 10, 64
libraries, as research
resource 142
library catalogs 141
Library of Congress
catalog 141
life expectancy
in 1900 7–8, 106*c*
in 2005 (U.S.) 115*c*
defined 130*g*
female v. male 9
improvement in **8–9**,
63–64
in preindustrial
societies 6
life support 55
Lincoln, Blanche 123,
124*b*
living will 56, 83
lobbying 15–16
longevity. *See* life
expectancy
long-term care 45, 48, 79,
87, 111*c*. *See also* nursing
homes
Long-Term Care
Ombudsman Program
59, 62, 76, 110*c*, 112*c*
long-term solvency
of Medicare/Medicaid
49–54
of Social Security
43–44
Loral Corporation 30
Louisiana 88, 116*c*, 117*c*
Love, Helen 60–61
low-income elderly. *See*
also poverty
and Choices for
Independence 117*c*

and Medicaid 47–48,
78–79
and Older Americans
Act 77
and Older Americans
Act amendments
112*c*
and Social Security
Act 74
and Social Security
reform 44
and SSI 43
lump-sum payment 37,
130*g*

M

Magruder, Thelma 61
managed plans 50. *See*
also Health Maintenance
Organization
mandatory retirement
in 1800s–1900s 20,
105*c*
in 1950s 20–21
in 1960s 21
and ADEA 21, 79
and ADEA
amendments 111*c*,
125
age discrimination
23–24
defined 130*g*
Massachusetts Board of
Retirement v. Murgia
22, 88–91
as means of promoting
economic efficiency
31
New York Bar
Association report
117*c*
and Older Workers
Benefit Protection
Act 83
and Social Security 10
market competition 50

Marks v. Loral Corporation
30
Marshall, Anthony 60,
117*c*, 118*c*, 120
Marshall, Philip 60
Massachusetts 20, 28, 110*c*
Massachusetts Board of
Retirement v. Murgia 22,
88–91, 110*c*
McCain, John 4
Meals on Wheels
Association of America
(MOWAA) 212
means-test 33, 43, 130*g*.
See also assets, Medicaid
eligibility and; earnings
test
mediation, in age
discrimination cases 27
Medicaid 130*g*
asset requirement
reform (1988) 48,
111*c*
bibliography 181–194
creation of program
109*c*
eligibility requirements
45
funding problems
49–54
and future of elderly
rights 65
and home care 51
and Medicare 14,
78–79
and nursing home
certification 62
and Nursing Home
Reform Act 58, 59,
81, 111*c*
online research
resources 140
and Patient Self-
Determination Act
83, 112*c*
print research resources
143–144

Medicaid *(continued)*
rights involving **47–48**
and SSI 43
and state laws 86, 87
Kelly M. Weems's
administration of
127
Medicaid fraud 58
medical care. *See also*
Medicaid; Medicare
bibliography 181–194
online research
resources 140
print research resources
143–144
rationing debate
52–54
rights **45–56**
medical schools 22
Medicare
and Age Discrimination
Act 110*c*
and ageism 18
AMA poll on
reimbursement cuts
50, 116*c*
and baby boomer
retirement 3, 4
Ben Bernanke's
warnings on deficits
118*c*
bibliography 181–194
George W. Bush's
proposed cuts 118*c*
and Catastrophic
Health Care Act
111*c*
changes since inception
14
cost control **49–52,**
110*c*
defined 130*g*
differing viewpoints/
bias in research
resources 136
eligibility requirements
45

and elimination of
private health benefits
for retirees 119*c*
funding problems
49–54
and future of elderly
rights 65
and Gray Panthers 16
growth in spending 15
and home care 51
and long-term care 48
and Medicaid 48
New York Times report
on benefit denial
by private insurers
118*c*–119*c*
and nursing home
certification 62
and Nursing Home
Reform Act 58, 59,
81, 111*c*
online research
resources 140
and Patient Self-
Determination Act
83, 112*c*
prescription drug
coverage 84, 114*c*–
115*c*
print research resources
143–144
privatization problems
118*c*–119*c*
rationing debate
52–54
rights and protections
45–47, **239–248**
Robert Samuelson's
concerns for future
of 126
taxes to fund 3–4
Harry S. Truman and
126
trust fund crisis report
117*c*
Kelly M. Weems's
administration of 127

Medicare Act (1965) 14,
77–79, 109*c*, 123
Medicare Advantage
defined 130*g*
funding of 52
grievance procedure
47
market-based reform
50
Medicare/Medicaid
rights 47
prescription drug
coverage 46, 85
private plans 118*c*
Medicare Advantage (Part
C) 45
Medicare fraud 58
Medicare Part A 45,
77–78
Medicare Part B
George W. Bush's
proposed changes
118*c*
changes for wealthy
elderly 50
funding of 52
and Medicare Act 77,
78
as part of original
Medicare plan 45
premium increases
115*c*, 119*c*
Medicare Prescription
Drug benefit (Part D)
deadline problems 117*c*
funding of 52
grievance procedure 47
introduction of 46,
116*c*
and market
competition 50
and Medicare
Modernization Act
85
as response to public
demand 51
satisfaction levels 49

Medicare Prescription
Drug Improvement and
Modernization Act 14,
84–85, 114*c*–115*c*, 121,
144
Medicare Rights Center
(MRC) 112*c*, 209–210
Medicare Supplemental
Insurance (Medigap) 45
medication, nursing home
abuse and 61
Medigap 78, 130*g*
men
and ageism 18
elderly in workforce
(2004) 11
life expectancy (U.S.,
2004-2005) 9, 115*c*
and retirement plan
participation 40
mental retardation 62
Merrill Lynch 36
Michigan 87, 88
Millard, Charles E. F.
124*b*
Miller, Bob 23–24
Minnesota 88
minority rights 63
Mississippi 87
Missouri 57–58, 88, 114*c*,
121
mistreatment. *See* elder
abuse
Misuraca, Katie 61
Model Statement of
ERISA Rights (2004)
236–238
Montana 87
moral basis for elderly
rights 3
mortality rate 7, 8, 11
MOWAA (Meals on
Wheels Association of
America) 212
MRC. *See* Medicare
Rights Center
Murgia, Robert 88, 89

N
NAELA (National
Academy of Elder Law
Attorneys) 212
NAHC (National
Association for Home
Care and Hospice) 212
NAPCA (National Asian
Pacific Center on Aging)
208
NASUA (National
Association of State
Units on Aging) 212
National Academy of
Elder Law Attorneys
(NAELA) 212
National Asian Pacific
Center on Aging
(NAPCA) 208
National Association for
Home Care and Hospice
(NAHC) 212
National Association of
Area Agencies on Aging
(N4A) 212
National Association of
State Units on Aging
(NASUA) 212
National Caucus and
Center for the Black
Aged (NCBA) 210
National Center for
Assisted Living (NCAL)
212–213
National Center on Elder
Abuse 208
National Citizens'
Coalition for Nursing
Home Reform
(NCCNHR) 208
National Clearinghouse
on Abuse in Later Life
116*c*
National Commission
on Social Security
Reform (Greenspan
Commission) 123, 126

National Committee for
the Prevention of Elder
Abuse (NCPEA) 208
National Committee
to Preserve Social
Security and Medicare
(NCPSSM) 208–209
National Council on
Aging (NCOA) 210
National Do Not Call
Registry 63
National Family Caregiver
Program 76, 113*c*
National Fraud
Information Center 63
national health insurance
77, 106*c*, 107*c*, 126
National Indian Council
on Aging (NICOA) 209
National Institute on
Aging (NIA) 16, 121,
204
National Pension
Assistance Resource
Center 39
National Retired Teachers
Association (NRTA) 21
National Senior Citizens
Law Center (NSCLC)
209
Native Americans 113*c*
NCAL (National Center
for Assisted Living)
212–213
NCBA (National Caucus
and Center for the Black
Aged) 210
NCCNHR (National
Citizens' Coalition for
Nursing Home Reform)
208
NCOA (National Council
on Aging) 210
NCPEA (National
Committee for the
Prevention of Elder
Abuse) 208

NCPSSM (National Committee to Preserve Social Security and Medicare) 208–209
need-based programs 13, 16, 74, 78–79
negative images/treatment of elderly **16–19, 25–26,** 120
neglect. *See* caregiver neglect
negligence 103
Nevada 87, 88
New Jersey 87
New Mexico 88
New Orleans, Louisiana 116*c*, 117*c*
Newsweek 125, 126
New York Bar Association 117*c*
New York Daily News, The 60, 117*c*, 120
New York State 20, 87, 107*c*
New York Times, The 118*c*–119*c*
NIA. *See* National Institute on Aging
NICOA (National Indian Council on Aging) 209
Nixon, Richard M. 124*b*–125*b*
North Carolina 88
North Dakota 87
Northwest Airlines 36, 84
Novelli, Bill 125*b*
Nowack, Henry 118*c*
NRTA (National Retired Teachers Association) 21
NSCLC (National Senior Citizens Law Center) 209
nurse assistants 61
Nursing Home Ombudsman Program 76, 110*c*

nursing home reform 124
Nursing Home Reform Act (1987) 58–59, **81–82,** 111*c*
Nursing Home Residents' Rights (2007) **263–265**
nursing homes
  Beverly Enterprises case 113*c*
  changes in elder care 12
  defined 130*g*
  elder abuse in 60–61
  elder care rights 56
  geographical variation in costs 48
  home care v. 51
  Hurricane Katrina negligent homicide case 116*c*
  Improving the Quality of Care in Nursing Homes 111*c*
  Medicaid payments 48
  Older Americans Act 76, 112*c*
  percentage of elderly in 56
  residents' rights under federal law **263–265**
  worker shortages 113*c*

O

OASDI. *See* Old Age, Survivors, and Disability Insurance
O'Connor, Sandra Day 92, 97
Office of Administrator of the Centers for Medicare and Medicaid Services 127
old age 4, 10, 130*g*–131*g*
Old Age, Survivors, and Disability Insurance (OASDI) 74, 107*c*

Old Age and Survivors Insurance 14–15
Older Americans Act (1965) **75–77,** 108*c*
  1978 amendments 110*c*
  1992 amendments 112*c*
  2000 amendments 113*c*
  2004 amendments 117*c*
  Lyndon B. Johnson and 123
  Long-Term Care Ombudsman Program 110*c*
  National Family Caregiver Program 113*c*
  Nursing Home Ombudsman Program 110*c*
Older Americans Act reauthorization (1992) 59
Older Women's League (OWL) 209
Older Workers Benefit Protection Act (1990) 24, **82–83,** 112*c*
oldest old 131*g*
ombudsman 62, 76, 112*c*, 131*g*
Omnibus Budget Reconciliation Act (1987) 81, 111*c*
Orange County, California 117*c*
Oregon 87
Original Medicare 47
Other America: Poverty in the United States, The (Harrington) 108*c*, 123
Oubre v. Entersy Operations 82
overmedication 54
OWL (Older Women's League) 209

Index

P

Palmore, Erdman 51, 125*b*
pandemics 8
Part A. *See* Medicare Part A
Part B. *See* Medicare Part B
Part C. *See* Medicare Advantage
Part D. *See* Medicare Prescription Drug benefit
participation, in retirement plans 40
part-time workers 32
Patient Self-Determination Act (1990) 55–56, **83**, 112*c*
pay-as-you-go system 13
payroll taxes 13, 14, 44, 52, 109*c*
PBGC. *See* Pension Benefit Guaranty Corporation
PBS (Public Broadcast Service) 36
pension. *See also* private pensions
  bibliography 168–181
  Cooper v. IBM 98–99
  defined 131*g*
  ERISA **35–37**, 80–81
  funding trends **37–41**
  Hazen Paper Company v. Biggins 92
  online research resources 140
  print research resources 143
  private pension rights **39–41**
  private pensions **33–40**
  recent trends in pension funding **37–41**

rights **33–44**
Social Security Act **72–74**
Social Security income **41–44**
for veterans 13, 105*c*
Pension Benefit Guaranty Corporation (PBGC) 204
  Bradley Belt and 121
  and Bethlehem Steel bankruptcy 36, 113*c*
  and corporate underfunding of pensions 37
  creation of 80–81
  deficits (2005–2006) 38, 115*c*
  defined-benefit pension protection 34
  ERISA and 35–36, 80–81, 109*c*
  Charles E. F. Millard and 124
  and Pension Protection Act 121
  and United Airlines bankruptcy 114*c*, 116*c*
  and US Airways pension liquidation 114*c*
pension insurance. *See* Pension Benefit Guaranty Corporation
Pension Protection Act (2006) **85**
  and benefit distribution to spouse 40
  George W. Bush and 117*c*, 121
  and *Cooper v. IBM* 99
  and defined-contribution pension plans 38–39
  online research resources 144

passage of 117*c*
and Retirement Protection Act 84
Pension Rights Center (PRC) 39, 40, 122, 210
Pepper, Claude 125*b*
perceptions, of elderly 5
Perry, Rick 115*c*
persons with disabilities. *See* disability
physical abuse 57
physical restraints 61, 82
physicians, ageism among 18
pilots 21, 79, 119*c*
plan fiduciary 34
police officers 22, 88–91, 95–97
poorhouse 9
population aging
  in 1900 106*c*
  in 20th/21st century 8–9
  and continued employment of elderly 32–33
  defined 131*g*
  and Medicare costs 49
  and Social Security 15
Posner, Richard 27, 31, 125*b*
poverty. *See also* low-income elderly
  in agricultural societies 7
  among elderly 10, 108*c*
  effects of government income programs on 41
  and Medicaid 14, 47–48, 109*c*
  and SSI 43
power of attorney 83
PPO. *See* Preferred Provider Organization
Pratt, Henry J. 15–16, 125*b*

PRC. *See* Pension Rights
Center
preferred drug list 85
Preferred Provider
Organization (PPO) 45,
50, 131*g*
preindustrial societies
5–7, 9, 11, 17, 20, 120
premiums
Medicare 46, 50
Medicare Act 78
Medicare Part B 115*c*
Medicare Prescription
Drug benefit 85,
115*c*–117*c*
Older Workers Benefit
Protection Act 83
and PBGC 35
Pension Protection
Act 86
prescription drug cover-
age 14, 46, 84–85,
114*c*–116*c*
pre-tax income 35
primary caregiver 100
privacy 47, 102, 103
private insurance
benefit denial to
Medicare recipients
118*c*–119*c*
Medicare Advantage
118*c*
Medicare Prescription
Drug Improvement
and Modernization
Act 84, 85, 115*c*
private pensions **33–40**
and ERISA 35, 80–81
and PBGC 124
and Pension Protection
Act 86
percentage of
population receiving
33
problems with corporate
funding of 36

and Retirement Equity
Act 81, 111*c*
and Retirement
Protection Act 84,
112*c*
rights **39–41**
and Social Security
13–14, 44
and Studebaker
bankruptcy 108*c*
and Welfare and
Pension Plans
Disclosure Act 74–
75, 108*c*
privatization 16, 44, 115*c*,
131*g*
productivity, effect of
mandatory retirement
on 21
programmers 25–26
Prudential Residential
Services 28
Public Broadcast Service
(PBS) 36
public health 8
public pensions 105*c*
public pensions, European
10

Q

Quality Improvement
Organization (QIO) 47
Quinn, Jane Bryant 39,
51, 125*b*–126*b*

R

Railroad Retirement Board
(RRB) 204–205
Rakowski, Erik 53, 126*b*
ration (term) 131*g*
rationing, of health care
52–54, 110*c*–111*c*, 121,
124, 126
Reagan, Ronald 81, 111*c*,
126*b*

recessions 37
reform
Medicaid asset
requirements 48,
111*c*
Medicare 49–52, 110*c*
Nursing Home Reform
Act 58–59, 81–82,
111*c*
nursing homes 124
Pension Protection
Act 39
Social Security 44,
115*c*, 123, 126
refusal of treatment **55–
56,** 83, 102, 112*c*
reimbursements 50, 85,
116*c*
release forms 55
Republican Party 44, 64
research materials/
resources, for elderly
rights issues 135–145
challenges to
researching elderly
rights 135–138
legal research 144–145
online resources
138–141
general sites 138–
139
organization sites
139
sites on specific
topics 139–141
print sources 141–144
restraints 61, 82
retirement 6, **9–11,** 64
retirement age 9, 44, 74,
110*c*, 123
Retirement Equity Act
(1984) **81,** 111*c*
Retirement Protection
Act (1994) 36, **84,** 112*c*,
121–122
Revolutionary War. *See*
American Revolution

reward, retirement as 10
right (term) 131*g*
Roosevelt, Franklin
  Delano 13, 73, 77, 106*c*,
  126*b*
Roosevelt, Theodore 77,
  106*c*
Rotter, John 23
RRB (Railroad Retirement
  Board) 204–205

S

safety net 79
salaries 26, 33
salespeople 63
Samuelson, Robert 11,
  126*b*
Scalia, Antonin 97
screenings, discrimination
  in 54, 114*c*
search engines, for
  research 138–139
Seligman, Dan 30–31,
  126*b*
Senate, U.S. 123, 124. *See
  also* Congress, U.S.
Senate Special Committee
  on Aging 114*c*, 205
Senior Care and
  Protection Act of 2003
  (Missouri) 57–58
Senior Citizens Freedom
  to Work Act (2000) 42,
  84, 113*c*
seniority 80, 92
Setting Limits (Callahan)
  53, 111*c*, 121
Seventh Circuit Court of
  Appeals 99
shelters. *See* emergency
  shelters, for abused elders
shortfalls. *See also* underfunded pension plans
  and PBGC 124
  and Pension Protection
    Act 86

and Retirement
  Protection Act 36,
  84, 112*c*
Sidley Austin Brown &
  Wood 115*c*–116*c*
Sienarecki, Patricia 102
*Sienarecki, Theresa v.
  Florida* **102–103**
single-payer health system
  16
slavery 7
small businesses 32, 87
*Smith, Azel P. v. City of
  Jackson, Mississippi* 29–
  30, 93, **95–97**, 116*c*
social effects, of aging 5
Social Security **13–14**
  AARP's lobbying
    efforts 16
  and Age Discrimination
    Act 110*c*
  and ageism 18
  and baby boomer
    retirement 3–4
  benefits 10, 41–43
  Ben Bernanke's
    warnings on deficits
    118*c*
  bibliography 168–181
  COLA adjustment to
    42, 74, 107*c*, 125,
    129*g*
  defined 131*g*
  differing viewpoints in
    research resources
    136
  early retirement
    provisions 108*c*
  eligibility age 4
  extension of benefits
    to dependents and
    survivors 107*c*
  and future of elderly
    rights 65
  Greenspan
    Commission 123,
    126

Michael Harrington's
  writings on 123
income from **41–44**
as largest federal
  program 15
long-term solvency of
  43–44
and mandatory
  retirement 10
and Medicare 45, 49,
  52, 78
online research
  resources 140
Claude Pepper's work
  on funding of 125
percentage of
  population receiving
  33
print research resources
  143
reform during Nixon
  administration
  124–125
rights/responsibilities
  of recipients **249–
  262**
Robert Samuelson's
  warnings of future
  funding problems
  126
and Senior Citizens
  Freedom to Work
  Act 84, 113*c*
spouse benefit 131*g*
and state laws 87
taxes 3–4
Frances Townsend and
  72–73, 106*c*
trust fund 132*g*
trust fund crisis report
  117*c*
social security (Europe)
  131*g*
Social Security Act (1935)
  13, **72–74**
  and Medicare Act 77,
  109*c*

Social Security Act
(*continued*)
and Medicare Act
amendments 14
and national health in-
surance proposals 77
online research
resources 144
Roosevelt's signing of
106*c*, 126
and Social Security
Protection Act 86
Social Security
Administration (SSA)
86, 120, 205–206
Social Security numbers 63
Social Security Protection
Act (2004) **85**
Society for Human Re-
source Management 25
solvency
of Medicare/Medicaid
49–54
of Social Security
43–44
South Carolina 88
Spanish flu epidemic
(1918–1919) 8
Sperino, Sandra 97
spouse
and Medicaid eligibility
48
and pension income 40
and Retirement Equity
Act 81
spouse benefit, Social
Security 42, 131*g*
SSA. *See* Social Security
Administration
SSI. *See* Supplemental
Security Income
standard of proof 30
state court decisions
100–103
state employees 22, 79,
93–95
state immunity from
federal lawsuits 93, 94

state laws/regulations
86–88
age discrimination laws
20, 22, 108*c*
elder abuse 57–58
Senior Care and
Protection Act 114*c*
State of the Union Address
(2004) 115*c*
steel industry 38, 124
stereotypes, of elderly
16–19. *See also* ageism
beliefs about older
workers **25–26**
changes in early 1900s
7
*Hazen Paper Company
v. Biggins* 92
inaccuracy of 5
and rationing 53
Stevens, John Paul 96
stewardesses 23
stock market 37
Streisand, Barbra 4
stress 12, 61
Studebaker 35, 108*c*
suicide 18, 56
Supplemental Security
Income (SSI) **43**
Michael J. Astrue's
administration of
program 120
creation of program
109*c*
defined 131*g*
description of program
43
effect on poverty rate
41
escalating costs of 14
and future of elderly
rights 65
and Medicaid 78
and Medicaid eligibility
87
percentage of popula-
tion receiving 33

and Social Security Act
amendments 74
and Social Security
Protection Act 86
and Social Security
reform 44
and state laws 86
Supplementary Medical
Insurance program. *See*
Medicare Part B
Supreme Court, California
100–102
Supreme Court, Florida
102–103
Supreme Court, New York
60, 118*c*
Supreme Court, U.S.
court decisions **88–97**
*Griggs v. Duke Power
Company* 95, 96
*Hazen Paper Company
v. Biggins* 91–93
IBM cash-balance plan
lawsuit 38, 118*c*
*Kimel v. Florida Board
of Regents* 22, 93–95
*Massachusetts Board of
Retirement v. Murgia*
88–91, 110*c*
*Oubre v. Entergy
Operations* 82
Smith v. City of Jackson
29–30, 93, 95–97,
116*c*
*United States v. Florida
Board of Regents* 93–95
survivor's benefit 35, 40,
131*g*
Survivors Insurance 41

T

taxation
and baby boomer
retirement 3
and future of elderly
rights 65

and long-term solvency
  of Social Security 44
and Medicare 3–4
and Medicare Act 77
and Medicare reform
  52
and Pension Protection
  Act 86
and Social Security
  3–4, 13, 15, 41
and Social Security Act
  73, 106*c*
on Social Security
  benefits 43
tax subsidies 86
telemarketing fraud 62–63
temporary workers 32
Tennessee 43, 87, 88
terminal illness 56
Texas 88, 115*c*
Texas Department of
  Health and Human
  Services 115*c*
Thane, Pat 9
Thomas, Clarence 97
Title VII (of Civil Rights
  Act of 1964) 95
Townsend, Frances 72–73,
  106*c*
Treasury Department,
  U.S. 73
treatment rights 51, 83,
  112*c. See also* refusal of
  treatment
Truman, Harry S. 77,
  107*c*, 126*b*
trust fund 15, 73, 117*c*,
  132*g*
Turnham, Hollis 82
two-tier system 44, 50

U

underfunded pension plans
  at Bethlehem Steel
  113*c*
  and ERISA 37

at Ford Motor
  Company 36–37,
  113*c*–114*c*
increase in percentage
  of (1992-2002) 36
and PBGC 124
and Pension Protection
  Act 38
and Retirement
  Protection Act 84,
  112*c*
unemployment 19, 23–24,
  89
unfunded pension
  liabilities 36
unintentional age
  discrimination. *See*
  disparate impact
United Airlines 36, 114*c*,
  116*c*
United Nations
  Programme on Ageing
  207
United Nations Second
  World Assembly
  (Madrid, 2002) 114*c*
*United States v. Florida
  Board of Regents* **93–95**
United Technologies 37
universal health coverage.
  See national health
  insurance
University of California,
  Berkeley 126
University of Chicago Law
  School 125
US Airways 36, 114*c*
U.S. Senate Special
  Committee on Aging
  124
Utah 87, 88, 123

V

vaccines 8
veneration 6
Vermont 87, 88

vesting
  defined 132*g*
  and defined-benefit
    pensions 34
  and ERISA 35, 80
  and firing of employees
    35
  and *Hazen Paper
    Company v. Biggins*
    35, 91
  and Retirement Equity
    Act 81
veterans' benefits 13, 71,
  105*c*, 106*c*
voluntary retirement 24

W

waiver 24, 83, 132*g*
Walker, David 65, 127*b*
Washington, George 7,
  123
waste disposal 8
water supply 8
Watson Wyatt pension
  plan study 36
wealthy elderly. *See* high-
  income elderly
Weems, Kelly M. 127*b*
Welfare and Pension Plans
  Disclosure Act (1958)
  74–75, 108*c*, 122
western Europe, medical
  care in 45
Westinghouse 36, 84
West Virginia 43, 87, 88
What You Need to
  Know When You
  Get Retirement of
  Survivors Benefits (SSA
  publication, 2007)
  249–262
WHO (World Health
  Organization) 207
*Why Survive: Being Old in
  America* (Butler) 121
Wick, James 25–26

widowers 42
widows
    in agricultural society
    7
    and Dependent
        Pension Act 105*c*
    and early veterans'
        benefits 72
    and Retirement Equity
        Act 81, 111*c*
    and Social Security
        benefits 42
    and veterans' pensions
        law 106*c*
Wikipedia 139
Wisconsin 87
WISER (Women's
    Institute for a Secure
    Retirement) 210
women
    age discrimination 26
    ageism 18
    elderly in workforce
        (2004) 11

life expectancy 9, 115*c*
medical treatment
    discrimination 54
and Pension Rights
    center 122
and persistence of
    stereotypes of elderly
    26
and Retirement Equity
    Act 81, 111*c*
retirement plan
    participation 40
workplace
    discrimination 26
Women's Institute for
    a Secure Retirement
    (WISER) 210
workplace issues/rights
    19–33. *See also* age
    discrimination
    beliefs about older
        workers **25–26**
    elderly in workforce
        (2004) 11

World Health Organization
    (WHO) 207
World War II 20
Wyoming 88

X
Xerox Corporation 114*c*

Y
youngest old 132*g*
Your Medicare Rights
    and Protections (2006)
    239–248
youth, worship of 17–18

OWENS COMMUNITY COLLEGE
P.O. Box 10,000
Toledo, OH 43699-1947